ALTERNATIVE TEACHER CERTIFICATION

A State-by-State Analysis 2003

C. EMILY FEISTRITZER

DAVID T. CHESTER

The National Center for Education Information (NCEI) is a private, non-partisan research organization in Washington, D. C. specializing in survey research and data analysis. Founded in 1980, NCEI has conducted several national and state studies which include: surveys of teachers, school administrators, school board presidents, state departments of education, local school districts and individuals interested in becoming teachers. NCEI has produced numerous data-based reports in the last decade, including: ALTERNATIVE TEACHER CERTIFICATION: A State by State Analysis, 2003, 2002, 2001, 2000, 1998-99, 1997, 1996, 1995, 1993-94, 1992-93, 1991 and 1990; THE MAKING OF A TEACHER; PROFILE OF TROOPS TO TEACHERS; WHO WANTS TO TEACH?; SURVEY OF ARMY PERSONNEL INTERESTED IN TEACHING; PROFILE OF TEACHERS IN THE U.S. (1996, 1990 AND 1986); PROFILE OF SCHOOL ADMINISTRATORS IN THE U.S.; PROFILE OF SCHOOL BOARD PRESIDENTS IN THE U.S.; TEACHER SUPPLY AND DEMAND SURVEYS; CHEATING OUR CHILDREN: WHY WE NEED SCHOOL REFORM; TEACHER CRISIS: MYTH OR REALITY?

Copies of ***ALTERNATIVE TEACHER CERTIFICATION: A State-by-State Analysis 2003*** *can be obtained for $110, plus $10 shipping and handling, from:*

NATIONAL CENTER FOR EDUCATION INFORMATION
4401A Connecticut Ave., N.W., PMB 212
Washington, D.C. 20008

Phone: 202-362-3444
Fax: 202-362-3493
Web site: www.ncei.com

Library of Congress

ISBN 1-928665-07-1

TABLE OF CONTENTS

STATE PROGRAM PROFILES:

** Program added in 2000*
*** Program added in 2001*
**** Program added in 2002*
***** Program added in 2003*

** Program added in 2000*
*** Program added in 2001*
**** Program added in 2002*
***** Program added in 2003*

** Program added in 2000*

*** Program added in 2001*

**** Program added in 2002*

***** Program added in 2003*

** Program added in 2000*
*** Program added in 2001*
**** Program added in 2002*
***** Program added in 2003*

INTRODUCTION

Alternative routes for certifying teachers are proliferating at a rapid rate in the United States. What began in the early 1980s as a way to ward off projected shortages of teachers and replace emergency certification has evolved into a sophisticated model for recruiting, training and certifying people who already have at least a bachelor's degree and want to become teachers.

Every state in the nation is now taking seriously the challenge to create alternatives to the traditional undergraduate college teacher education program route for certifying teachers.

The Federal government has entered the field by appropriating $41.65 million in the current 2003 fiscal year budget for a Transition to Teaching program to assist mid-career professionals to obtain certification as elementary and secondary teachers. This represents an increase of $6.65 million over last year's appropriation.

In addition, the Congress passed the Elementary and Secondary Education Act (ESEA) legislation in December 2001 that authorized $3.175 billion for fiscal year 2002 and "such sums as may be necessary for each of the 5 succeeding fiscal years" for "Title II -- Preparing, Training, and Recruiting High Quality Teachers and Principals." The provision includes "establishing programs that ... recruit qualified professionals from other fields ... and provide such professionals with alternative routes to teacher certification, including developing and implementing hiring policies that ensure comprehensive recruitment efforts as a way to expand the applicant pool, such as through identifying teachers certified through alternative routes, and using a system of intensive screening designed to hire the most qualified applicants."

We at the National Center for Education Information (NCEI) have been surveying the states since 1983 regarding alternative routes to the traditional undergraduate college approved program route for certifying teachers. The results of those efforts are published annually. This publication provides information and analyses to prospective teachers, as well as policy and decision-makers, about alternative routes to teacher certification, in the United States. This current edition, *ALTERNATIVE TEACHER CERTIFICATION: A State-by-State Analysis 2003*, is organized into six parts and includes:

I. Executive Summary

II. Overview of Alternative Teacher Certification

III. Results of 2003 NCEI State Survey of Alternative Teacher Certification

IV. State Contacts for Alternative Teacher Certification Routes

V. Summary of Entry and Program Requirements for Alternative Routes

VI. Profile and Classification of Each Alternative Teacher Certification Route in Each State

- Classification system developed by NCEI to characterize different programs states identify as "alternative routes."

- A detailed description of each of the alternative teacher certification programs in each of the states.

- Lists of colleges and universities in each state that have developed alternative teacher preparation programs.

- Lists of colleges and universities in each state that have any type of teacher preparation program.

- Numbers of types of teaching licenses issued in each state in the last decade.

- Numbers of teachers in each state and numbers of new hires in each state for each of the past 10 years.

- Contact people within each state for alternative teacher certification and for finding a teaching job.

I wish to thank the many people who made this project possible -- the people in every state agency of education who answered our questions, who put up with our numerous telephone calls, e-mails, faxes and mailings and came through with the information that makes this manual so valuable. They have enabled us to tell this current and complete story of alternative routes to teacher certification in the United States. Lastly, I wish to thank my colleague and friend of 15 years, David Chester, without whom this -- and all the projects NCEI undertakes -- would not be possible.

Emily Feistritzer
February 24, 2003

EXECUTIVE SUMMARY

Alternative routes for certifying non-traditional candidates for teaching are multiplying rapidly in the United States. Concerns about the quality of the teaching force, as well as fears of teacher shortages, have spawned the creation of new avenues whereby people from other careers, liberal arts graduates, military and other retirees, former teachers and people beginning a career later in life can be brought into teaching without having to go back to college and complete a campus-based teacher preparation program.

What were often called "scab programs" and "quick and dirty" ways to rush unprepared people into teaching in the early 1980s, when alternative routes first surfaced, are now models for the way all teachers are prepared.

The National Center for Education Information (NCEI) has been surveying the states regarding alternative routes for licensing teachers since the issue surfaced amid much controversy in New Jersey in 1983. At that time, there were only eight states that said they had *any* way for people who had not come through a regular college teacher education program to become certified to teach.

In 2003, 46 states and the District of Columbia report having some type of alternative route for certifying elementary and secondary teachers. The remaining four states say they are now considering or have proposed alternative routes.

An estimated 200,000 people have been certified to teach through alternative routes since 1985, with most of the growth occurring since the mid-1990s. Within the last five years, approximately 25,000 people, *per year*, have been certified to teach through alternative routes.

California, New Jersey and Texas have been developing and aggressively utilizing alternative routes for licensing teachers since the mid-1980s. Approximately 18 percent of new hires in California enter teaching through the state's alternative routes. In Texas, 24 percent of its new hires come through the state's 52 alternative routes, and in New Jersey, 24 percent of new teachers enter the profession through the state's alternative route.

States have designed *many* different alternative routes for certifying individuals who want to obtain a license to teach. Since the mid-1990s the number of these programs has risen rapidly. In 2003, states report a total of 144 routes other than the traditional approved college teacher education program route for certifying teachers. These routes range from requiring very little to requiring a lot.

However, there are emerging characteristics of all alternative routes that are being developed. Candidates who get licensed to teach through these routes:

- Have at least a bachelor's degree.
- Pass a screening process, such as passing tests, interviews, and demonstrated mastery of content to be taught.
- Begin teaching – usually full-time – early. They engage in on-the-job training.
- Complete any coursework or equivalent experiences in professional education studies occur while teaching.
- Work with mentor teachers.
- Meet high performance standards.

People coming into teaching through alternative routes tend to be older, people of color, include more men, have academic degrees other than education, and have experiences in other occupations.

Early data from several states indicate that individuals entering teaching through alternative routes have higher retention rates than those entering teaching from traditional college-based programs. Reasons given for this are:

- Teachers coming through alternative routes generally are older, more experienced and have a strong commitment to helping young people learn and develop. They are making a definitive decision to teach at this point in their lives.
- Their preparation programs have provided intense field-based, in-the-classroom training and instruction.
- They have received on-the-job training under the guidance of mentor or master teachers.
- They have had the support of college faculty, schoolteachers and their peers while actually teaching.

Good alternative teacher certification routes are market-driven. The programs are designed specifically to meet the demand for teachers in geographic areas and in subject areas where the demand for teachers is greatest. Prospective teachers are recruited to meet those specific demands.

Programs are job-specific. Rather than train people to teach who may or may not ever go into teaching, alternative route programs recruit individuals for specific teaching positions and place prospective teachers in those jobs early in their training.

Alternative teacher certification is an idea whose time has come. Every state in the nation is now taking seriously the challenge to create alternatives to the traditional undergraduate college teacher education program route for certifying teachers.

The Federal government has entered the field by appropriating $41.65 million in the current 2003 fiscal year budget for a Transition to Teaching program to assist mid-career professionals to obtain certification as elementary and secondary teachers. This represents an increase of $6.65 million over last year's appropriation.

In addition, the Congress passed the Elementary and Secondary Education Act (ESEA) legislation in December 2001 that authorized $3.175 billion for fiscal year 2002 and "such sums as may be necessary for each of the 5 succeeding fiscal years" for "Title II -- Preparing, Training, and Recruiting High Quality Teachers and Principals." The provision includes "establishing programs that ... recruit qualified professionals from other fields ... and provide such professionals with alternative routes to teacher certification, including developing and implementing hiring policies that ensure comprehensive recruitment efforts as a way to expand the applicant pool, such as through identifying teachers certified through alternative routes, and using a system of intensive screening designed to hire the most qualified applicants."

While criticisms of alternative teacher certification continue among a small band of educational researchers, the criticisms are based more on lack of definition, faulty data and biases than on actual facts.

The bottom line is there is a demand for high quality teachers in certain subject areas in select parts of the country. There is a huge population of non-traditional candidates – life-experienced adults from many walks of life – who want to meet that demand. Alternative routes to train and license this market for teaching are imperative.

ALTERNATIVE ROUTES TO TEACHER CERTIFICATION: AN OVERVIEW

Alternative routes to teacher certification are having a significant impact on the way all teachers are educated and brought into the profession. Few innovations in American education have spawned more controversy and debate than the alternative teacher certification movement, and few have ultimately resulted in more positive changes.

The term "alternative teacher certification" historically has been used to refer to every avenue to becoming licensed to teach, from emergency certification to very sophisticated and well-designed programs that address the professional preparation needs of the growing population of individuals who already have at least a bachelor's degree and considerable life experience and want to become teachers.

The National Center for Education Information (NCEI) has been polling the state departments of education annually since 1983 regarding alternatives to the traditional approved college of education program route for licensing teachers. We have found not only a rapid development of alternative routes at the state level, but also, an evolving consensus of the essential characteristics of an alternative teacher certification program.

In 2003, 46 states, plus the District of Columbia, report having some type of alternative teacher certification program. This compares with only eight states that said they had any kind of alternative route to teaching in 1983.

It is estimated that more than 200,000 persons have been licensed through these programs. Thousands more are being licensed to teach who are participating in college alternative teacher preparation programs.

Not only have more and more states instituted legislation for alternative teacher certification, but, also, more and more institutions of higher education have initiated their own alternative programs for the preparation of teachers leading to a license to teach.

In the last decade, alternative teacher certification has evolved as a respectable concept and has spawned many new programs that provide excellent preparation and training for a career in teaching.

The primary reason for this is that it is one of the few truly market-driven phenomena in American education.

The demand-for-teachers side of the teacher supply and demand issue has gotten considerable attention in the last several years. What has received much less "ink" is the supply side – the dramatic changes in who wants to teach.

Historically, the nation has relied almost exclusively on high school students who say they might major in education when they get to college as the pool of prospective teachers, both in terms of quantity and quality. In fact, in discussing the academic caliber of teachers, one still hears scare stories that use the SAT scores of high school students who say they might major in education when they get to college as the indicator of how smart people going into teaching are.

These concepts are archaic. There probably isn't any area of the teaching occupation that has changed more than the profile of individuals entering the profession.

The most dramatic change in the past few years has been a shift toward people beginning their preparation to teach later in life and later in their academic careers.

A 1999 survey of Institutions of Higher Education that have programs for the preparation of teachers conducted by our sister organization, the non-profit Center for Education Information (CEI), found that nearly three out of 10 (28 percent) prospective new teachers who completed teacher preparation in 1998 in college-based programs *began* their preparation to teach *after* they had already received at least a bachelor's degree.

Additional findings of the 1999 CEI study that point to significant changes in who is studying to be teachers are:

- Two-thirds (65 percent) of institutions surveyed by CEI indicated they have at least one program for the preparation of teachers in which candidates enter at the Post-baccalaureate level.
- Nearly eight out of 10 (79 percent) prospective secondary school teachers who had begun their preparation to teach at the Post-baccalaureate level had degrees in fields other than education. One-half (49 percent) of persons who completed an Undergraduate program prepared to teach at the secondary school level had a degree in a field other than education.
- Three out of four (75 percent) prospective elementary teachers who began their preparation to teach at the Post-baccalaureate level had a degree in a field other than education. One in three (29 percent) individuals who completed an Undergraduate program prepared to teach in elementary schools had a degree in a field other than education.
- At the middle school preparation level, 69 percent of the Post-baccalaureate candidates and one-third of the Undergraduates had degrees in fields other than education.
- More than half (55 percent) of the individuals who were admitted into Teacher Preparation Programs at the Post-baccalaureate level within the last year were transitioning into teaching from an occupation outside the field of education. More than one in 10 (11 percent) of those admitted into Teacher Preparation Programs at the Undergraduate level were transitioning into teaching from an occupation outside the field of education.
- More than one-third (36 percent) of persons admitted into Teacher Preparation Programs at the Post-baccalaureate level and 14 percent of those admitted as Undergraduates within the past year had prior teaching-related experience, such as substitute teacher, teacher's aide, or school paraprofessional.

The most significant variable in driving the alternative teacher certification movement forward is this changing market for teaching.

This population of non-traditional candidates wanting to become teachers is growing significantly. The quest for how best to prepare these people for the occupation of teaching has spawned the development of numerous alternative routes to teaching.

Not only has the supply of people interested in teaching grown and the profile of individuals interested in teaching changed dramatically, the demand for teachers is also different than in high-demand times of the past.

Post World War II, when the flood of baby-boomers hit the schools, there was a great demand for elementary school teachers throughout the nation. That is not true today. In fact, across the board, there is an oversupply of elementary school teachers. Today's demand for teachers is quite geographic and subject-matter specific. Demand for teachers is greatest in inner cities and outlying rural areas of the country and in mathematics, the sciences and special education and mostly at the high school level.

How to recruit, train, license, hire, place and keep teachers for these high-demand areas is the question. And alternative teacher certification is proving to be a big answer.

Why?

- Good alternative teacher certification programs are market-driven. The programs are designed specifically to meet the demand for teachers in geographic areas and in subject areas where the demand for teachers is greatest. Prospective teachers are recruited to meet those specific demands.
- Teacher preparation programs are tailor-made. Programs are specifically designed to meet the preparation needs of individuals who already have at least a bachelor's degree and, in many cases, experience in other occupations, to teach in specific areas and in specific subjects.
- Programs are job-specific. Rather than train people to teach who may or may not ever go into teaching, alternative route programs recruit individuals for specific teaching positions and place prospective teachers in those jobs early in their training programs.
- The teacher preparation program is field-based.
- Prospective teachers work with mentor teachers while teaching.
- Candidates usually go through their program in cohorts, not as isolated individuals.
- Most of these programs are collaborative efforts among state departments of education whose responsibility it is to license teachers, colleges and universities that historically have had the responsibility for educating and training teachers, and school districts that actually hire teachers.

Nearly all of the states now have some type of alternative to going back to college and majoring in education in order to become a teacher. Forty-six states, plus the District of Columbia, report that they are currently implementing alternatives to the approved college teacher education program route for certifying teachers. Two states say they have proposed alternatives and two say they are considering alternatives. (see Table 1).

The biggest change that has occurred in alternative teacher certification is not the sheer proliferation of programs, but the consensus of definition of what counts as an alternative route.

In just the last five years, states have passed new legislation and/or created 51 new alternative teacher certification routes that look amazingly similar. Ten such new programs were added four years ago, 12 more three years ago, 14 additional ones two years ago and 15 more this year. All of them include the following components:

- The program has been specifically designed to recruit, prepare and license talented individuals who already have at least a bachelor's degree for the teaching profession.
- Candidates for these programs pass a rigorous screening process, such as passing tests, interviews, and demonstrated mastery of content.

- The programs are field-based.
- The programs include coursework or equivalent experiences in professional education studies before and while teaching.
- Candidates for teaching work closely with mentor teachers.
- Candidates must meet high performance standards for completion of the programs.

California, New Jersey and Texas have been developing and aggressively utilizing alternative routes for licensing teachers since the mid-1980s. Approximately 18 percent of new hires in California enter teaching through the state's alternative routes. In Texas, 24 percent of its new hires come through the state's 52 Alternative Routes, and in New Jersey, 24 percent of new teachers enter the profession through the state's alternative route.

- People coming into teaching through alternative routes tend to be older, people of color, more men, have academic degrees other than education, and have experiences in other occupations.
- Early data from several states indicate that individuals entering teaching through alternative routes have higher retention rates than those entering teaching from traditional college-based programs. Reasons given for this are:
    - ♦ Teachers coming through alternative routes generally are older, more experienced and have a strong commitment to helping young people learn and develop. They are making a definitive decision to teach at this point in their lives.
    - ♦ Their preparation programs have provided intense field-based, in-the-classroom training and instruction.
    - ♦ They have received on-the-job training under the guidance of mentor or master teachers.
    - ♦ They have had the support of college faculty, schoolteachers and their peers while actually teaching.

One of the reasons given for the high attrition rate for new teachers in their first few years of teaching is that they receive very little support and professional development as beginning teachers. This issue is directly addressed in the very design of alternative preparation programs, which, if anything, err on the side of getting prospective teachers into classrooms too early.

History of Alternative Teacher Certification in the U.S.

To understand how alternative teacher certification evolved, it is necessary to understand the process by which individuals become licensed to teach in the United States.

The licensing (certification) of elementary and secondary teachers in the United States is a state responsibility. The regular route for licensing teachers is "the approved college teacher education program route." This process means that a college or university submits a plan for a teacher preparation program for each discipline and/or grade level(s), following state-established guidelines, which the state then "approves." A candidate for a teaching license applies directly to a college or university, takes the required courses and meets other specified requirements, such as student teaching, passage of tests and any other requirements specified by the college's "approved program". Upon completion of the "approved program", the candidate is then granted a license to teach.

The requirements for obtaining a license to teach through approved program routes vary enormously -- not only from state to state but from institution to institution.

Some states require passing different tests and differing lengths of time spent student teaching. Some require observation in schools before student teaching. Some institutions of higher education have added a "fifth year' to their teacher education programs. Others have added internships. Others have done away with undergraduate teacher preparation programs altogether -- and just have a postbaccalaureate program of teacher preparation.

Some states require only the initial certificate; other states require a second or third stage certificate -- sometimes with continuing education requirements and sometimes resulting in a life or permanent certificate.

The terminology used for various types of teaching licenses is terribly confusing. There are 30 different titles used for the initial teaching certificates, and more than 50 titles used for the second stage teaching certificates throughout the 50 states and the District of Columbia.

Emergency certificates have been the age-old means of bringing individuals quickly into teaching. Some states wanted to develop an alternative to such emergency routes.

New Jersey was the first state to garner a lot of publicity concerning alternative teacher certification when it enacted legislation for an alternative route for certifying teachers in 1984. The reason New Jersey initiated its program was to come up with a better solution to bringing non-traditional candidates into teaching other than issuing them emergency certificates until they fulfilled all the requirements for a regular teaching certification -- a process that usually involves teaching right away, with no orientation or instructional support, much less training, while taking education courses at night and during summers. New Jersey set out to design a new program that involved actively recruiting liberal arts graduates and putting them through a school-based program, in collaboration with universities, that entailed the candidate working with a mentor teacher, as well as formal instruction while teaching. New Jersey's alternative teacher certification program currently produces approximately one-fifth of all the new teachers hired.

The state of Texas first implemented a single alternative teacher certification program in 1985 in the Houston Independent School District, justifying the program on teacher shortage projections. Legislation passed in 1989 by Texas legislators eliminated the shortage requirement. Texas now has 52 alternative teacher certification programs throughout the state.

California has been struggling with finding ways to bring qualified individuals into teaching to meet its rapid and huge demand for teachers. Like other states across the United States, California has sought to cope with overall growth among the school-age population, as well as continuing, rapid expansion of minority student populations. And, most recently, California has faced the challenge of the statewide K-3 class size reduction initiative.

Almost half (48 percent) of the intern teachers were members of ethnic groups underrepresented in the state's teaching workforce. Twenty-nine percent were male. The retention for the first five years is 86 percent.

Most alternatively certified teachers are trained and teach in urban and rural areas. The greatest demands for new teachers across the nation are in large urban areas and outlying rural areas.

There has been an outpouring of interest in the teaching occupation from numerous sources -- people in other careers who wish to get into teaching; military personnel facing retirement or being relieved of their duties due to the projected down-sizing of the military in the next few years; former teachers trying to get back into teaching; people who trained to teach some years ago but never taught; and current students.

Growing numbers of governors, state legislators, state commissioners of education, deans of education and other political and educational leaders are stepping forward in favor of some type of alternative certification. Local school administrators, school board presidents, parents of school children, and the general public also recognize the value of alternate routes as a means of improving America's educational system. The 1996 NCEI survey of teachers showed that more than half (54 percent) of public school teachers agreed that recruiting adults who have experience in careers other than teaching would improve America's educational system.

Many in this nation have expressed concern about the declining numbers of minority teachers coming through traditional teacher education programs and, consequently, the declining proportion of the teaching force that is minority.

The use of alternate routes gives promise of increasing the representation of minorities in the nation's teaching force. Nationally, state education data show that nine percent of teachers and 26 percent of students are minorities. In New Jersey, where minorities comprise nine percent of the state's teachers and 33 percent of students, the state's use of an alternate route has been the biggest source of qualified, minority teachers. Since the program's inception, 20 percent of the teachers certified through the alternative route and hired by public and non-public schools in the state have been minority.

In Texas, while 91 percent of all public school teachers are white, 32 percent of teachers entering through the state's alternative programs are minority.

Nearly half (48 percent) of the interns entering teaching in California are members of ethnic groups underrepresented in the state's teaching workforce.

Twenty-nine percent of military people who have entered teaching through the Troops To Teachers Program are from a minority or ethnic group.

Other areas of concern regarding demand for teachers are: inner cities, math and science, bilingual education, and special education. Data support that the need to respond to those demands is being met. Surveys of individuals who had inquired about alternative teacher certification conducted by the National Center for Education Information in summer 1992 showed widespread interest in teaching in all parts of the country, all types of communities -- including inner cities, and in all subject areas.

A 1998 survey of Troops To Teachers shows that one in four (24 percent) TTT teachers is teaching in an inner city school. Thirty-nine percent of them said they were willing to teach in an inner city and 68 percent indicated they would be willing to teach in a rural community. This compares with 16 percent of public school teachers who currently teach in inner cities and 23 percent who teach in rural areas.

Alternative routes for preparing and licensing teachers are attracting large numbers of highly qualified, talented and enthusiastic individuals to the teaching profession. Applicants to these programs number in the thousands. Most are highly educated, life-experienced adults who want to teach and to improve America's educational system. They will do whatever is necessary in the way of preparation in order to accomplish those ends. Many of them think alternative routes not only make the most sense, but also provide the best preparation for the real world of teaching.

The Structure of Public Elementary and Secondary Education

Any discussion of supply and demand for qualified teachers in the United Sates must take into account the structure of public schooling. Public elementary and secondary education is primarily a state and local responsibility in the United States. States have the responsibility for certifying or licensing teachers. School districts have the responsibility for recruiting and hiring teachers.

There are approximately 90,000 public elementary and secondary schools in 15,000 school districts that employ 2.8 million teachers throughout the nation. School sizes and school district sizes range from very small to very large. Spending per student, as well as salaries for teachers, vary enormously. The racial/ethnic composition of the schools and the communities they are in are radically different in different parts of the country and in different regions of each state.

Some school districts, most notably those in wealthy suburbs, are not wanting for qualified teachers. Many of these districts receive hundreds of applicants for a single open position.

On the other hand, large inner cities have huge school districts that oversee many very large schools that enroll high proportions of students from many racial/ethnic groups and from high poverty areas. They have a much harder time recruiting and retaining qualified teachers.

- One-fourth on the students in this country is enrolled in inner city schools.
- Another fourth of the students are enrolled in rural areas where the other extreme prevails – very small schools where the likelihood of hiring a physics major to teach one physics class a day is remote.
- One in five (3,123) school districts enroll fewer than 300 students each. Nearly half of them (7,004) enroll fewer than 1,000 students each and account for just 6.3 percent of all the students enrolled.
- On the other hand, 216 out of the 14,883 (1.5 percent) school districts enroll 25,000 or more students each and account for nearly one-third of all the students.
- School size also varies enormously. Forty-one percent of schools enroll fewer than 400 students each but account for only 18 percent of all enrolled students.
- At the high school level, only three percent of all secondary schools enroll 1,500 students or more each, but they account for one-third (33.3 percent) of all high schools students.

It is terribly important to keep these facts about the structure of schooling in America in mind when considering teaching jobs. The demand for teachers is by no means uniform across the nation.

Teacher Supply and Demand

The demand for more teachers is based on enrollment increases, increased retirements of teachers, general attrition, and most recently, efforts to reduce class size.

The current projections call for 2.2 million new teachers in the next decade or 210,000 new teachers per year for the next 10 years.

But before millions -- or billions -- of additional dollars are spent to recruit, train and certify millions of new teachers, many of whom will never find a teaching job, we need to look beyond these numbers at some of the realities behind this "teacher crisis."

Changing definitions of "new teacher" muddle the issue. "New teacher" can refer to new to the nation, new to a particular state, new to a school district, new to a school building, new teacher graduate or brand new to teaching. Another complicating variable in the teacher shortage issue is how teachers are counted -- whether or not part-time teachers, substitutes, private school teachers are included in the counts.

When most people hear that we'll need 210,000 new teachers every year for the next decade, they think it means brand new teachers -- people who have never taught before. Well, that is not what it means. That projection means that 210,000 teachers may be "newly hired" in a given year. To illustrate, 210,000 people who are not currently teaching in the 2002-03 school year might be hired to teach in the 2003-2004 school year. They will be counted as "new" teachers, even though a large number of them will actually be former teachers coming back into the profession or people who trained to teach at some earlier time, but were not attending college the year immediately prior to being hired.

According to the National Center for Education Statistics Schools and Staffing Survey, 5.8 percent of the total teacher workforce of 2.39 million were "newly hired" in 1993-94. Of these 139,000 "newly hired" teachers, fewer than half (42 percent) were "newly minted" teachers, that is, teachers who had just finished a college program and had never taught before. Nearly one-fourth (24 percent) of them were "delayed entrants" -- people teaching for the first time, but who were doing something else other than going to college the year before teaching. The remaining third of "new" teachers were actually former teachers coming back into the profession.

These statistics are terribly important. The bottom line is the nation is hiring -- and is projected to need to hire -- approximately 45,000 newly minted teachers per year.

Most people who get a bachelor's degree in education are considered "qualified to teach." In fact, experts who are claiming that there are too many "unqualified" teachers teaching define "qualified to teach" as someone who has gone through a college education program approved by the state department of education which has the authority to then confer a license to teach.

There are a lot of people out there who, by this definition, are fully "qualified to teach' BUT who are not teaching. It's been known for a long time that only about a third of fully qualified teachers who graduate from the nation's 1,354 colleges that train teachers in any given year are actually teaching the following year.

Of note in this discussion is the fact that only about three out of four current teachers have a bachelor's degree in education. One fourth have a bachelor's degree in a field other than education.

Probably the biggest change that has occurred in this arena is the huge interest in teaching from older people -- life experienced people from other careers, early retirees from the military and other occupations, former teachers, people who have raised their own families and want to teach.

Alternative teacher preparation and certification routes have sprung up throughout the nation to respond specifically to the needs of this growing non-traditional market for teaching.

Research on Alternative Teacher Certification

There is a paucity of research on alternative teacher certification routes -- and with good reason. The biggest reason is that there is no clear-cut definition of alternative teacher certification. Another reason is that there are hundreds of different kinds of programs for the preparation of persons who already have at least a bachelor's degree and want to become teachers. Are they all "alternate routes"?

One needs to be very careful when looking at comparisons between "traditionally trained" and "alternatively trained" teachers. Who actually is being compared? Who decides who is a "traditionally trained" teacher and who is an "alternatively trained" teacher? Different states and different institutions answer those questions very differently.

These are not idle questions or evasive tactics to avoid potential criticism. They actually are at the heart of any research that attempts to make judgements about the effectiveness of alternative teacher certification programs.

While criticisms of alternative teacher certification continue among a small band of educational researchers, the criticisms are based more on lack of definition, faulty data and biases than on actual facts.

The bottom line is there is a demand for high quality teachers in certain subject areas in select parts of this country. There is a huge population of non-traditional candidates -- life experienced adults from many walks of life -- who want to meet that demand.

Since, by law, one cannot teach in public schools in this country without a teaching license, avenues need to exist to train and license this market for teaching. It doesn't matter what such routes are called. What does matter is that high quality programs be designed with the market in mind.

Table 1. Status of States Concerning Alternatives to Approved College Teacher Preparation Programs for Certifying Teachers: 2003

	Considering	Implementing alternatives	Proposed alternatives	Not even considering
Alabama		●		
Alaska		Not using		
Arizona		●		
Arkansas		●		
California		●		
Colorado		●		
Connecticut		●		
Delaware		●		
District of Columbia		●		
Florida		●		
Georgia		●		
Hawaii		●		
Idaho		●		
Illinois		●		
Indiana		●		
Iowa		●		
Kansas		●		
Kentucky		●		
Louisiana		●		
Maine		●		
Maryland		●		
Massachusetts		●		
Michigan		●		
Minnesota		●		
Mississippi		●		
Missouri		●		
Montana		●		
Nebraska		●		
Nevada			●	
New Hampshire		●		
New Jersey		●		
New Mexico		●		
New York		●		
North Carolina		●		
North Dakota	●			
Ohio		●		
Oklahoma		●		
Oregon		●		
Pennsylvania		●		
Rhode Island			●	
South Carolina		●		
South Dakota		●		
Tennessee		●		
Texas		●		
Utah		●		
Vermont	●			
Virginia		●		
Washington		●		
West Virginia		●		
Wisconsin		●		
Wyoming		●		

Table 2. Numbers of Teaching Certificates Issued, Numbers of Newly Hired Teachers, and Numbers of IHEs That Have Teacher Preparation Programs: 2003

STATE	To persons who completed an approved college teacher preparation program	Emergency	Temporary or Other	To teachers from out-of-state	To persons who completed an alternative route	# of Newly Hired Teachers	Total No. IHEs that have teacher preparation programs
Alabama	14,653	308		n/a	1,751	n/a	29
Alaska	587	37	37	n/a	0	n/a	5
Arizona	No data					n/a	9
Arkansas	1,350				164	n/a	18
California	20,055(99-00)	32,573		n/a	4,492	24,824	88
Colorado	2,196	937	1,196	n/a	475	2,700	15
Connecticut	7,184 initial certificates				213	3,836	14
DC	No data					302	7
Delaware	2,124	768	198	407	33	927	4
Florida	n/a				180 comp-based prog	12,317	28
Georgia	No data						35
Hawaii	542		257		158	1,008	5
Idaho	1,182	442		301	3	1,928	7
Illinois	10,611	0	919		274	13,090	57
Indiana	5,772 total initial licenses				0	1,049	38
Iowa	n/a	0	0		0	1,442	31
Kansas	3,104			1,087	new	1,769	22
Kentucky	2,248	1,812	99	n/a	282	n/a	29
Louisiana	2,936	5	5,950	240	612	n/a	20
Maine	600+					661	13
Maryland	2,332		2,163		15	7,385	23
Massachusetts					>600 since '99	n/a	59
Michigan	6,471	2,217	24	1,468	40	3422	32
Minnesota	5,841				9	2,000	27
Mississippi	1,448			676	354	2,010	15
Missouri	2,200				12	2,350	34
Montana	578			304	n/a	n/a	8
Nebraska	1,650		350	270	new	1,390	17
Nevada	No data					2,643	3
New Hampshire	1,224			470	470	n/a	13
New Jersey	4,412				1,826	7,527	25
New Mexico	1,296	1,356			60	~571	8
New York	18,619		15,347	2,154	951	10,287	110
North Carolina	No data						46
North Dakota	669	14			0	306	10
Ohio	7,050			4,080	35	n/a	50
Oklahoma	1,929	52	n/a		599	n/a	22
Oregon	~1579				271+	1,699	16
Pennsylvania	10,204	3,045			296	7,437	88
Rhode Island	963	269			0	n/a	8
South Carolina	3,341				434	n/a	30
South Dakota	930				76	436	12
Tennessee	3,219	1,603			1,478	n/a	39
Texas	9,290		3408 post bacc	3,009	4,628	19,631	71
Utah	2,330	96	998	n/a	120	1949	9
Vermont	No data					n/a	14
Virginia	3,822			n/a	2,746	6,800	37
Washington	3,785			1,593	new	1,667	20
West Virginia	1,167				0	415	19
Wisconsin	4,313		964	1,711	n/a	3,000	32
Wyoming	1,000	171	14	n/a	10	378	1

Table 3. Prior Activity Prior to Entering Alternative Teacher Certification Routes

Question: What do you estimate is the percent of individuals who enter your alternative teacher certification route(s) who were engaged in the following as their primary activity right before entering your teacher preparation program?

	No data	Professional	Other Occup.	Military	Retired Military	Other Retired	IHE in state	IHE out of state	Emer. Certif.	Teaching Occ	Non-teaching Ed.	Other
Alabama	x											
Alaska	x											
Arizona	x											
Arkansas		25	40	3	2	5	10	0	0	15	0	0
California		7.6	N/A	0.7	N/A	N/A	17.5	N/A	27.4	26.6	N/A	5
Colorado	x											
Connecticut		72	22	1	2	0	1	0	*	2	0	
DC												
Delaware		60	5	<1	<1	<10	N/A	~10	2	N/A		1
Florida	x											
Georgia												
Hawaii	x											
Idaho	x											
Illinois	x											
Indiana	x											
Iowa	x											
Kansas	x											
Kentucky		N/A	146	24	N/A	N/A	89	N/A			23	
Louisiana		0	30	5	10	10	0	0	40	5	N/A	N/A
Maine	x											
Maryland	x											
Massachusetts	x											
Michigan		1	1	1	1	1	1	5	0	70	20	1
Minnesota	x											
Mississippi		15	15	5	5	5	20	5	10	15	5	
Missouri	x											
Montana	x											
Nebraska	x											
Nevada												
New Hampshire	x	1	0	0	1	1	5	0	20	20	1	
New Jersey	x											
New Mexico	x											
New York	x											
North Carolina												
North Dakota		no program										
Ohio	x											
Oklahoma		50	30	5	10	0	5	0	0	0	0	
Oregon		25	25	0	0	0	0	0	0	50	0	
Pennsylvania	x											
Rhode Island		no program										
South Carolina		50	50	1	1	10	75	25	0	25	0	
South Dakota		15-20	60-75	15-20	10-15	0	60-75	20-30	0	20-30	0	
Tennessee	x											
Texas	x											
Utah		80	0	0	10	10	80	20	50	40-50	0	0
Vermont												
Virginia	x											
Washington	x									N/A	N/A	N/A
West Virginia	x									N/A	N/A	N/A
Wisconsin	x											
Wyoming		0	0	0	0	0	0	0	0	90	0	

Table 4. Status of Alternative Teacher Certification in the States, by Control: 2003

STATE	Question: Does your state currently have program(s) being implemented for the explicit purpose of recruiting, training and licensing individuals from careers other than education, the military, retirement, liberal arts graduates, etc. into the teaching profession?		Number of Alternate Route Programs Controlled by		
	Yes	No	School district	Institution of Higher Education	Collaborative
Alabama	x		2	1	0
Alaska		x			
Arizona	x		state, IHE and education cooperatives		
Arkansas	x				
California	x		8 (105 dists. involved)	71	71 (all IHE)
Colorado	x		38	2	All
Connecticut	x		0	0	0
DC	x				
Delaware	x		0	0	1
Florida	x		72	0	0
Georgia	x				
Hawaii	x				
Idaho		x			
Illinois	x		0	13	13
Indiana		x			
Iowa	x				
Kansas	x			2	
Kentucky	x		1	12	1
Louisiana	x		1	all others	1
Maine		x			
Maryland	x		4		1
Massachusetts	x				
Michigan	x		0	5	4
Minnesota		x			
Mississippi	x		0	1	2
Missouri		x			
Montana		x			
Nebraska		x	0	1	0
Nevada	x				
New Hampshire	x		1	0	0
New Jersey	x				
New Mexico	x		0	2	0
New York	x				17
North Carolina	x				
North Dakota		x			
Ohio	x		1	0	1
Oklahoma	x		0	0	0
Oregon	x		5		5
Pennsylvania	x		0	37	3
Rhode Island		x			
South Carolina	x		1	1	2
South Dakota	x		0	all	0
Tennessee	x		0	2	0
Texas	x		4	28	20
Utah	x		1	0	3
Vermont	x				
Virginia	x		1	1	2
Washington	x		0	0	3
West Virginia		x			
Wisconsin	x				5
Wyoming	x		0	1	1

Table 5. Race/ethnicity and Gender of Alternative Teacher Certification Candidates

	Question: What percent of your alternative teacher certification candidates are represented by each of the following ethnic/racial groups?							Question: What percent of your alternative teacher certification candidates are represented by each of the following gender groups?	
	Ethnicity/race							Gender	
	State does not have data	Asian	American Indian/ Alaskan Native	Black	White	Hispanic	Other	Male	Female
Alabama	x								
Alaska	x								
Arizona									
Arkansas		0	0	25	70	5	0	35	65
California		5	0.7	7	52.5	24.9	4	29	71
Colorado [1]	x								
Connecticut		1	1	9	79	10	0	40	60
DC									
Delaware		2		19	73	6		52	48
Florida	x								
Georgia									
Hawaii	x								
Idaho	no program								
Illinois	x								
Indiana	no program								
Iowa	x								
Kansas	new program								
Kentucky		0.23	0.23	3.9	49	2.1	0.9	43	50
Louisiana	x								
Maine	x								
Maryland	x								
Massachusetts	x								
Michigan		5	0	75	10	10	0	30	70
Minnesota	x								
Mississippi		5	4	40	31	20	0	45	55
Missouri	x								
Montana	no program								
Nebraska	x							30	70
Nevada									
New Hampshire		0	0	0.5	98.5	0	0	50	50
New Jersey	x								
New Mexico	x								
New York		6	0.4	6	54	17	16	31	68
North Carolina									
North Dakota	no program								
Ohio	x								
Oklahoma	x							45	55
Oregon		4	0.4	2	79	11	3.6	32	68
Pennsylvania	x							n/a	n/a
Rhode Island	no program								
South Carolina		1	0	32	66	1		30	70
South Dakota		5	25	5-10	50-85	0	0	50	50
Tennessee	x								
Texas		1.8	0.7	10.5	62.2	24.8	0	75	25
Utah	x								
Vermont									
Virginia	x								
Washington	x								
West Virginia	x								
Wisconsin	x								
Wyoming		0	0	0	100	0	0	50	50

Table 6. Age of Alternative Teacher Certification Candidates

	Question: What do you estimate is the average age of students currently enrolled in your state's alternative teacher certification program (s) in 1998-99?		Question; What percent of your alternative teacher certification candidates are represented by the following age groups?					
	State does not have data	Average age	18-24 years	25-29 years	30-39 years	40-49 years	50 years or more	Not sure
		In years	%	%	%	%	%	%
Alabama	x							
Alaska	x							
Arizona								
Arkansas		35	20	40	25	10	5	
California		34	48		30.8	14.4	6.8	
Colorado	x							
Connecticut		39	1	7	55	32	5	0
DC								
Delaware		35	0	36	43	15	8	
Florida	x							
Georgia								
Hawaii	x							
Idaho	no program							
Illinois	x							
Indiana	no program							
Iowa	x							
Kansas	new							
Kentucky		38	5	21	29	29	15	0.48
Louisiana	x							
Maine	no program							
Maryland	x							
Massachusetts	x							
Michigan		39	0	35	30	25	10	
Minnesota	x							
Mississippi		26	10	35	35	15	5	
Missouri	x							
Montana	x							
Nebraska	x							
Nevada								
New Hampshire		30			most in this range			
New Jersey	x							
New Mexico	x							
New York		32	24	29	24	13	10	
North Carolina								
North Dakota	no program							
Ohio	new							
Oklahoma		25-55						x
Oregon	x							
Pennsylvania		n/a	18.2	26.3	30.2	19.5	5.8	
Rhode Island	no program							
South Carolina		32	20	23	25	20	10	
South Dakota		35-45						x
Tennessee	x							
Texas		33 or more	6.4	33.9	30.9	20.1	8	0.7
Utah		30+	5	50	40	5		
Vermont								
Virginia	x							
Washington	x			5		95		
West Virginia	no program							
Wisconsin	x							
Wyoming		45		20	40	30	10	

Table 7. Types of Communities Alternative Teacher Certification Participants Teach In

State	Question: What percent of participants in your alternative route programs teach in the following types of communities?				
		Types of communities			
State	State does not have data	Inner-city	Small town	Suburban	Rural
		%	%	%	%
Alabama	x				
Alaska	x				
Arizona					
Arkansas		20	40	10	30
California		67	6	6	21
Colorado	x				
Connecticut		45	25	25	5
DC					
Delaware		30	10	30	30
Florida	x				
Georgia					
Hawaii	x				
Idaho	no program				
Illinois	x				
Indiana	no program				
Iowa	x				
Kansas	x				
Kentucky	x				
Louisiana	x				
Maine	x				
Maryland		100 (1 district)		100 (3 districts)	
Massachusetts					
Michigan		100			
Minnesota	x				
Mississippi		30	25	30	15
Missouri	x				
Montana	no program				
Nebraska	x				
Nevada					
New Hampshire	x				
New Jersey	x				
New Mexico	x				
New York		97	2		1
North Carolina					
North Dakota	no program				
Ohio	x				
Oklahoma		27.3	30	28.7	14
Oregon		20	30	40	10
Pennsylvania	x				
Rhode Island	no program				
South Carolina	x				
South Dakota		0	30	30	35-40
Tennessee	x				
Texas		24.5	30.3	30.7	14.2
Utah		50	10	30	10
Vermont					
Virginia	x				
Washington	x				
West Virginia	x				
Wisconsin	x				
Wyoming	x				

Table 8. Employment and Cost of Alternative Teacher Certification Programs

State	Question: What percent of those who enter alternative teacher certification routes in your state complete the program and get certified to teach?	Question: Are individuals in your alternative route program employed by a school district while participating in your program?		Question: If "Yes", are they employed full-time or part-time?		Question: How much does it cost to participate in your state's alternative teacher certification program?	Question: Who pays?
	%	Yes	No	Full-time	Part-time	Cost	Source
Alabama	n/a	x		x			
Alaska	program not used	x		x		$1,000 and transportation/lodging, etc.	Applicant
Arizona							
Arkansas	75	x		x		$1,000	State $500; Individual $500
California	98.2	x		x	x	Varies from $0 to $17,000	Intern (all are eligible for grants, loans)
Colorado	85	x		x		$2,000-$5,000	Candidates
Connecticut	90	x		x		$3,000 plus $500 books and supplies	Candidates
DC							
Delaware	80-85	x		x		about $2,500 tuition	Candidates. Reimbursement and scholarship aid are available for qualififed candidates.
Florida	n/a	x		x		Varies from district to district -- from 0 to $2,000	Some districts absorb cost; others share with the participant
Georgia							
Hawaii	n/a	x		x	x	n/a	State and Candidate
Idaho	no program						
Illinois	n/a	x		n/a		Varies by institution	Varies by program
Indiana	no program						
Iowa	n/a	n/a		n/a		n/a	n/a
Kansas	new	x		x		Varies by institution	Candidates
Kentucky	57% of ARTC receive full certification	x [via intern-ship]	x	x	x	Varies per program	Candidate (with limited district support)
Louisiana	85	usually		x	x	Varies by provider	Candidate
Maine	n/a	n/a		n/a		n/a	Individual
Maryland	n/a	x		x		Varies from $700/candidate to $600/candidate	District/candidate share, varies
Massachusetts	n/a	n/a		n/a		n/a	n/a
Michigan	97	x		x	x	$9,000 - $12,000	Both the district and the candidate
Minnesota	n/a	n/a		n/a		n/a	n/a
Mississippi	80	x		x		Varies by institution	Candidate
Missouri	n/a	n/a		n/a		n/a	n/a
Montana	no program						
Nebraska	n/a	x		x		Varies	Candidate usually
Nevada							
New Hampshire	80	x		x		Alt. 3- $100; Alt. 4 - $105; Alt. 5 - $105	
New Jersey	n/a	x		x		varies by program	Candidate unless subsidized by district or state
New Mexico	n/a	Most	n/a	most		Tuition costs	The candidate, and in some instances, the district
New York	74	x		x		Varies by institution	Varies
North Carolina							
North Dakota	no program						
Ohio	new						
Oklahoma	n/a	x		x	x	$140 ($40 for application; $100 for Teacher Competency Review Panel; $435+ for testing)	Applicant
Oregon	new	x		x		Tuition rates of institutions	Candidate or district; some federal funds
Pennsylvania	n/a	x		x		Tuition fees	Candidate
Rhode Island	no program						
South Carolina	n/a	x		x	x	State awarded funds to 2 IHEs to administer Critical Needs Program	Cost of lodging and graduate courses paid by individual. Loan forgiveness for teaching critical subjects or in critical districts.
South Dakota	25	x		x		Tuition plus expenses	Alternative certification teacher
Tennessee	n/a	x		x		Varies by institution	Candidate
Texas	n/a	x		x		$2,000-6,000	Student
Utah	95	x		x	x	Tuition varies with each program. All pay $60 for background check and license fee of $15 for Temporary License	Candidate
Vermont							
Virginia	97	x		x		~$4,000 for career switchers; for standard program, $500-700 per course needed	Candidate
Washington	new	x		x		Varies	State, district and intern share cost
West Virginia	no program						
Wisconsin[1]	n/a	Some		Varies		Varies by program	Varies
Wyoming	n/a	not required				fee upon presenting portfolio - $645	Candidate

[1] Wisconsin -- The state is piloting a variety of programs.

STATE CONTACTS FOR ALTERNATIVE TEACHER CERTIFICATION

Alabama Dept. of Education
5201 Gordon Persons Bldg.,50 N. Ripley St.
P.O. Box 302101
Montgomery, AL 36130-2101
Attn.: June H. Mabry
(334) 242-9977
Fax: (334) 242-0498
e-mail: tcert@alsde.edu

Alaska Dept. of Education and Early Dev.
Teacher Ed & Certification
Attn: Assessment Center
801 West Tenth St., Suite 200
Juneau, AK 99801-1984
Attn: Julie Orsborn
(907) 465-2026
e-mail: julie_orsborn@educ.state.ak.us

Arizona Dept. of Education
Teacher Certification Unit
1535 West Jefferson
Phoenix, AZ 85007
Attn: Lanny Standridge
(602) 542-4367

Arkansas Dept. of Education
Non-Traditional Licensure Program
623 Woodlane
Little Rock, AR 72201
Attn: Jim Chism, Program Manager
Norene Drinkwater, Program Advisor
(501) 371-1580

California Commission on
Teacher Credentialing
1900 Capitol Avenue
Sacramento, CA 95814-4213
Attn: Michael McKibbin
(916) 445-4438
e-mail: mmckibbin@ctc.ca.gov
Web site: http://www.cde.ca.gov

Colorado Dept. of Education
Office of Professional Services
& Educator Licensing
201 E. Colfax Avenue, Room 105
Denver, CO 80203
Attn: Dorothy Gotlieb
(303) 866-6932
e-mail: gotlieb_d@cde.state.co.us

Connecticut Bureau of Certification
& Professional Development
P.O. Box 150471
Hartford, CT 06115-0471
Attn: Peter Behuniak, Acting Chief
(860) 713-6708
e-mail: teacher.cert@po.state.ct.us

Delaware Department of Education
P.O. Box 1402
Townsend Building
Dover, DE 19903
Critical Areas Program (math, science, & speech pathology) -- Contact: (302) 739-4686
Web site: www.doe.state.de.us.

Delaware Alternative Routes to Certification/
Secondary Program --
Contact: Linda Hughes, Ph.D.
University of Delaware
Delaware Center for Teacher Education
Willard Hall
Newark, DE 19711
(302) 831-4598 or 831-1100
e-mail: artc-de@udel.edu
Web site: www.udel.edu/artc/

Special Institute for Teacher Certification
Contact: Barbara Van Dornick
University of Delaware,
DCTE, Willard Hall
Newark, DE 19711
(302) 831-3000
Web site: www.udel.edu/teachered/

Master's in Primary/K-4 or
Middle Level/5-8 Education
Contact: Richard Gochenauer, Ed.D.
Wilmington College
30 DuPont Highway
New Castle, DE 19720
(302) 328-9407

Master's in Secondary Education With Initial
Certification
Contact: Thomas Sturgis, Ed.D.
Wesley College
306 DuPont College Center
Dover, DE 19901
(301) 736-2352

District of Columbia Dept. of Education
Educational Credentialing and Standards Branch
825 North Capitol Street, N.E., Sixth Floor
Washington, DC 20002-4232
Attn: Ken Bungert
Phone: (202) 442-5377
Fax: (202) 442-5311

Florida Dept. of Education
Bureau of Educator Certification
325 W. Gaines Street
Tallahassee, FL 32399
Attn: Karen B. Wilde
(850) 488-2137
e-mail: wildek@mail.doe.state.fl.us

STATE CONTACTS FOR ALTERNATIVE TEACHER CERTIFICATION

Georgia Professional Standards Commission
2 Peachtree Street, Suite 6000
Atlanta, GA 30303
Attn: Cynthia Stephens
(404) 657-9014
Web site: www.teachforgeorgia.org

Hawaii Department of Education
Office of Personnel Services
P.O. Box 2360
Honolulu, HI 96804
Attn: Clara Burrows
(808) 586-3276
e-mail: clara_burrows@notes.k12.hi.us

Idaho Dept. of Instruction
Teacher Education/Professional Standards
P.O. Box 83720
Boise, ID 83720-0027
Attn: Michael P. Stefanic
(208) 332-6800

Illinois State Board of Education
Div. of Professional Preparation & Recruitment
100 North First Street
Springfield, IL 62777-0001
Attn: Martha A (Marti) Woelfle
(217) 782-4330
Fax: (217) 782-3687
e-mail: mwoelfe@isbe.net
Web site: http//www.isbe.net/profdevelopment

Indiana Professional Standards Board
251 E. Ohio St., Suite 201
Indianapolis, IN 46204
(317) 232-9010

Iowa Board of Educational Examiners
Grimes State Office Bldg.
East 14th and Grand
Des Moines, IA 50319
Attn: Anne E. Kruse
(515) 281-3611

Kansas Dept. of Education
Division of Certification
120 East Tenth Street
Topeka, KS 66612
Attn: Dr. Martha Gage
Director of Cert. and Teacher Education
(785) 296-8012
e-mail: mgage@ksde.org

Kentucky Education Professional Standards Board
1024 Capital Center Dr.
Frankfort, KY 40601
Attn: Dr. Susan Leib or Mary Ellen Wiederwohl
Phone: (502) 573-4606
Fax: (502) 573-1610
e-mail: mwiederw@kde.state.ky.us

Louisiana Department of Education
Teacher Certification & Higher Education
P.O. Box 44064
Baton Rouge, LA 70804
Attn: Mary Helen S. McCoy, Ph.D.
(504) 342-3490
e-mail: mhmccoy@doe.state.la.us

Maine Dept. of Education
Certification Office
23 State House Station
Augusta, ME 04333-0023
Attn: Nancy Ibarguen
(207) 624-6603
email: nancy.ibarguen@state.me.us

Maryland Dept. of Education
Teacher Education/Certification
200 W. Baltimore Street
Baltimore, MD 21201
Attn: Norma Allen / Virginia Pilato
Phone: (410) 767-0391
Fax: (410) 767-0390
e-mail: nallen@msde.state.md.us

Massachusetts Dept. of Education
Bureau of Educator Certification
350 Main Street
Malden, MA 02148
Attn: Dennis DiCarlo
Phone: (781) 338-8000
Fax: (781) 388-3475
Web site: www.doe.mass.edu/educators

Michigan Dept. of Education
Office of Professional Preparation Services
P.O. Box 30008
Lansing, MI 48909
Attn: Frank Ciloski
Phone: (517) 373-6791
Fax: (517) 373-0542
e-mail: ciloski@michigan.gov

STATE CONTACTS FOR ALTERNATIVE TEACHER CERTIFICATION

Minnesota Board of Teaching
1500 Highway 36 West
Roseville, MN 55113
Attn: Dr. George Maurer
(651) 582-8833

Mississippi Dept. of Education
Office of Educator Licensure
P. O. Box 771
Jackson, MS 39205
Attn: Regina Ginn, Director
(601) 359-3483
email: rginn@mde.k12.ms.us

Missouri Dept. of Education
Teacher Ed./Certification
Dept. of Elementary/Secondary Educ.
P.O. Box 480
Jefferson City, MO 65102
Attn: John Miller
(573) 751-0051

Teacher Education/Certification
Office of Public Instruction
P.O. Box 202501
Helena, MT 59601-2501
Attn: Marilyn Roberts
Phone: (406) 444-3150
Fax: (406) 444-2893
e-mail: marilynr@state.mt.us

Nebraska Dept. of Education
Teacher Education/Certification
P. O. Box 94987
301 Centennial Mall Square
Lincoln, NE 68509
Attn: Robert Crosier
(402) 471-2496 or (402) 471-0739
Fax: (402) 471-9735

Nevada Dept. of Education
State Mail Room
1820 E. Sahara #205
Las Vegas, NV 89104-3746
Attn: Chopin Kiang
(702) 486-6458

New Hampshire Dept. of Education
Bureau of Credentialing
101 Pleasant Street
Concord, NH 03301
Attn: Kathleen M. Moulis
(603) 271-2407
e-mail: kmoulis@ed.state.nh.us

New Jersey Dept. of Education
Office of Licensure and Credentials
P.O. Box 500
Trenton, NJ 08625-0500
Attn: Joan E. Brady
(609) 292-2045

New Mexico Dept. of Education
Asst. Director, Professional Licensure
300 Don Gasper
Santa Fe, NM 87501-2786
Attn: James Ball
Phone: (505) 827-1200
Fax: (505) 827-4148
e-mail: jball@sde.state.nm.us

New York Education Dept.
Office of College and University Evaluation
5 N Mezzanine, Education Building
Albany, NY 12234
Attn: Ruth I. Pagerey
(518) 474-1914
rpagerey@mail.nysed.gov

North Carolina Dept. of Public Instruction
Div. of Teacher Education Services
114 West Edenton Street
Raleigh, NC 27611
Attn: Van Brock Murray
(919) 733-4125

North Dakota Education Standards
and Practices Board
600 East Boulevard Ave.
Bismarck, ND 58505-0540
Attn: Janet Placek Welk, Exec. Director
Deb Jensen, Asst. Director
Phone: (701) 328-1659
Fax: (701) 328-2815
e-mail: jwelk@state.nd.us

STATE CONTACTS FOR ALTERNATIVE TEACHER CERTIFICATION

Ohio Dept. of Education
Center for the Teaching Profession
Office of Certification/Licensure
25 S. Front St., Mail Stop 105
Columbus, OH 43215
Attn: Leonard Crawford
(614) 466-3593
e-mail: leonard.crawford@ode.oh.us

Oklahoma Dept. of Education
Professional Standards Section
Teacher Education/Certification
2500 N. Lincoln Blvd., Rm. 211
Oklahoma City, OK 73105
Attn: Cindy Marose
Phone: (405) 521-3337
Fax: (405) 522-1520
e-mail: cindy_Marose@sde.okla.ok.us

Oregon Teacher Standards/Practices
255 Capitol St., N.E.
Public Service Bldg., Suite 105
Salem, OR 97310-1332
Attn: Linda Samek
(503) 378-3757
e-mail: linda.samek@state.or.us

Pennsylvania Dept. of Education
Bureau of Certification
333 Market Street
Harrisburg, PA 17108
Attn: Ronald Simanovich
Phone: (717) 783-9252
Fax: (717) 783-6736
e-mail: rsimanovic@state.pa.us

Rhode Island Dept. of Education
Ofc. of Teacher Preparation, Certification
and Professional Development
255 Westminster Street
Providence, RI 02903
Attn: Joseph Gaudiosi
(401) 277-4600, ext. 2254
e-mail: ride1512@ride.ri.net

South Carolina Dept. of Education
Teacher Education/Certification
1600 Gervais Street
Columbia, SC 29201
Attn: Sandra Rowe
(803) 734-8466

South Dakota Dept. of Education
and Cultural Affairs
Div. of Elementary/Secondary Educ.
Kneip Building
Pierre, SD 57501
Attn: Dean Buchanan
Phone: (605) 773-4771
Fax: (605) 773-6139
e-mail: dean.buchanan@state.sd.us

Tennessee Dept. of Education
Teacher Licensing
5th Floor, Andrew Johnson Tower
710 James Robertson Parkway
Nashville, TN 37243-0377
Attn: Vance Rugaard
(615) 532-4880

Texas State Board for Educator Certification
4616 W. Howard Lane, Suite 120
Austin, TX 78728
Attn: Dr. William Wale
Dr. Ed Fuller
(512) 238-3200

Utah State Office of Education
Division of Teacher Certification
250 East Fifth South
Salt Lake City, UT 84111
Attn: Ronald Stanfield / Diane DeMan
Phone: (801) 538-7741
Fax: (801) 538-7973
e-mail: rstanfie@usoe.k12.ut.us

Vermont Dept. of Education
Educational Resources Unit
State Dept. of Education
Montpelier, VT 05602
Attn: Patricia Pallas
(802) 828-2445

Virginia Dept. of Education
Div. of Teacher Education and Licensure
P.O. Box 2120
Richmond, VA 23218-2120
Attn: Paul F. Joseph
(804) 371-2472
e-mail: pjoseph@mail.vak12ed.edu or
pjoseph@pen.k12.va.us

STATE CONTACTS FOR ALTERNATIVE TEACHER CERTIFICATION

Professional Educator Standards Board
Old Capitol Building
P.O. Box 47236
Olympia, WA 98504-7200
Attn: Jennifer Wallace
(360) 725-6275
e-mail: jwallace@ospi.wednet.edu

West Virginia Dept. of Education
Capitol Complex
Building #6, Room 337
Charleston, WV 25305-0330
Attn: Barbara Brazeau
(304) 558-7010 or (800) 982-2378

Wisconsin Dept. of Public Instruction
Bureau of Teacher Education
Licensing and Placement
P.O. Box 7841
Madison, WI 53707-7841
Attn: Peter Burke
(608) 266-1027

Wyoming Professional
Teaching Standards Board
2300 Capitol Ave.
Hathaway Building, 2nd Floor
Cheyenne, WY 82002-0190
Attn: Linda Stowers
(307) 777-6261
email: lstowe@state.wy.us

If you wish to purchase this report, which details all of the states' requirements and program descriptions for alternative routes toward certification, send $110, plus $10 for shipping and handling. If you are interested in only certain states, send $13.00 for the first state and $6.00 for each additional state to: NCEI, 4401-A Connecticut Ave., N.W., PMB 212, Washington, DC 20008. For credit card orders (VISA and MasterCard), telephone (202) 362-3444 or FAX (202) 362-3493 or order directly from our Web site: http://www.ncei.com.

Reciprocity and Acceptance of Teaching Certificates Across State Lines

NASDTEC Interstate Contract --- Most states have signed the Interstate Contract, in order to make it easier and more efficient for licensed educators from one state to become credentialed to work in another state where they move and establish residence. Forty-one states, the District of Columbia, Guam, and Puerto Rico have currently signed the Interstate Contract for teacher certification.

According to the National Association of State Directors of Teacher Education and Certification (NASDTEC), which administers the reciprocity agreement: "The NASDTEC Interstate Contract is an agreement which facilitates the movement of educators among the various states and other jurisdictions which have signed the contract. Although there are conditions applicable for each jurisdiction, the Contract allows an educator certificate or license in one state or jurisdiction to be accepted for certification in another state or jurisdiction. For example, a professionally certified Alabama teacher generally will be given a certificate in Georgia, with certain special state conditions imposed by Georgia, the receiving state. Of course those conditions imposed by the receiving jurisdiction vary. If you are certified in one state and seek reciprocal certification under the terms of the NASDTEC Interstate Contract, contact the certification office in the intended receiving jurisdiction."

The following jurisdictions have signed the NASDTEC Interstate Contract for teacher certification:

Alabama
Arizona
Arkansas
California
Colorado
Connecticut
Delaware
District of Columbia
Florida
Georgia
Guam
Hawaii
Idaho
Illinois
Indiana
Kentucky
Louisiana
Maine
Maryland
Massachusetts
Michigan
Mississippi
Montana
Nevada
New Hampshire
New Jersey
New Mexico
New York
North Carolina
Ohio
Oklahoma
Oregon
Pennsylvania
Puerto Rico
Rhode Island
South Carolina
Tennessee
Texas
Utah
Vermont
Virginia
Washington
West Virginia
Wyoming

NCATE -- National Council for Accreditation of Teacher Education --- Some states accept individuals who completed teacher preparation in another state at an institution of higher education whose teacher preparation program has been accredited by NCATE.

NERC -- Northeast Regional Credential --- New York and the six New England states -- Connecticut, Maine, Massachusetts, New Hampshire, Rhode Island, Vermont -- have joined together in the Northeast Compact, and they have agreed to recognize the NERC. A person who is awarded a teaching certificate in any of the seven states may apply for and be awarded the Regional Credential, which (with some limitations as to the subject areas for which the NERC will be accepted in some of the states) will be recognized in any of the other participating states.

MOINKSA (Missouri, Oklahoma, Iowa, Nebraska, Kansas, South Dakota, and Arkansas) Agreement --- In the Midwest, seven states have joined to cooperate in this regional exchange agreement. Through the agreement, each state's respective minimum standards are protected, but the teacher applicant is guaranteed an initial two-year license in the receiving state.

CLASSIFICATION OF ALTERNATIVE ROUTES

NCEI, for the sake of consistency in reporting and analyzing what is going on in the field of alternative teacher certification, has developed the following classification system for categorizing the "alternative routes" to the approved college teacher education program route for certifying teachers submitted by the states.

CLASS A is the category reserved for those programs that meet the following criteria:

- The program has been designed for the explicit purpose of attracting talented individuals who already have at least a bachelor's degree in a field other than education into elementary and secondary school teaching.
- The program is not restricted to shortages, secondary grade levels or subject areas.
- The alternative teacher certification programs in these states involve teaching with a trained mentor, and formal instruction that deals with the theory and practice of teaching during the school year -- and sometimes in the summer before and/or after.

CLASS B: Teacher certification routes that have been designed specifically to bring talented individuals who already have at least a bachelor's degree into teaching. These programs involve specially designed mentoring and formal instruction. However, these states either restrict the program to shortages and/or secondary grade levels and/or subject areas.

CLASS C: These routes entail review of academic and professional background, transcript analysis. They involve specially (individually) designed inservice and course-taking necessary to reach competencies required for certification, if applicable. The state and/or local school district have major responsibility for program design.

CLASS D: These routes entail review of academic and professional background, transcript analysis. They involve specially (individually) designed inservice and course-taking necessary to reach competencies required for certification, if applicable. An institution of higher education has major responsibility for program design.

CLASS E: These post-baccalaureate programs are based at an institution of higher education.

CLASS F: These programs are basically emergency routes. The prospective teacher is issued some type of emergency certificate or waiver which allows the individual to teach, usually without any on-site support or supervision, while taking the traditional teacher education courses requisite for full certification.

CLASS G: Programs in this class are for persons who have few requirements left to fulfill before becoming certified through the traditional approved college teacher education program route, e. g., persons certified in one state moving to another; persons certified in one endorsement area seeking to become certified in another.

CLASS H: This class includes those routes that enable a person who has some "special" qualifications, such as a well-known author or Nobel prize winner, to teach certain subjects.

CLASS I: These states reported in 1999 that they were not implementing alternatives to the approved college teacher education program route for licensing teachers.

CLASS J: These programs are designed to eliminate emergency routes. They prepare individuals who do not meet basic requirements to become qualified to enter an alternate route or a traditional route for teacher licensing.

SUMMARY OF ALTERNATIVE TEACHER CERTIFICATION ROUTES FOR NON-TRADITIONAL CANDIDATES

While states accurately report 144 alternatives to the traditional undergraduate teacher education program route for becoming certified to teach, not all of them meet the criteria of having been established to provide an avenue for persons who already have at least a bachelor's degree -- many of whom have experience in other careers -- who want to teach.

We at NCEI have identified 59 routes to certification that have been designed by the states for the explicit purpose of attracting and certifying individuals who meet these criteria. Nearly all of these 59 routes have been created since 1983; 48 have been created since 1990, and more than half (31) have been created in just the last five years.

A summary of each of these routes follows on pages 30-53.

For the sake of clarity, a glossary of terms and abbreviations used follow:

A.A.	Associate of Arts degree
B.A.	Bachelor of Arts degree
education service center	a state-operated regional facility that may provide technical assistance to several local school districts
field experience	a real-world experience in a school
GPA	grade point average
GRE	Graduate Record Examination, an entrance exam for graduate school
IHE	institution of higher education, a college or university
in-service	training conducted for working teachers
LEA	local education agency, a local school district
MAT	Miller Analogies Test, an entrance exam for graduate school
M.A.T.	Master of Arts in Teaching degree
mentor	an experienced, licensed teacher assigned to support a beginning or intern teacher
NTE	National Teachers Examinations, general knowledge or specialty area tests
portfolio	a collection of a teacher's work, to demonstrate knowledge and skills
practicum	a field-based experience in a school
Praxis	The Praxis Series: Professional Assessments for Beginning Teachers, including Praxis I: Academic Skills Assessments, and Praxis II: Subject Assessments (specialty area tests), Principles of Learning and Teaching (PLT), and Pre-Professional Skills Tests (PPST) in reading, writing, and math
pre-service	training before prospective teachers begin teaching
professional development	classes, training, or other opportunities for school staff to improve their knowledge and skills

ENTRY REQUIREMENTS INTO ALTERNATIVE CERTIFICATION ROUTES, State-by-State: 2003

State	Name of Program	Year Began	Degree	Grade Point Average	Tests	Prior Experience	Courses	Other
Alabama	**Alternative Fifth-Year Program**	1986	B.A.	2.5	GRE or MAT		Prerequisite coursework in general studies and the chosen teaching field	
	Alternative Baccalaureate-Level Approach	1992	B.A.			24 months professional and/or work experience in field or related fields in which certification if sought	Minimum 48 semester hours of academic credit or equivalent nonacademic credit in field or related field	Candidate must be candidate for employment by local board or nonpublic accredited school
	Preliminary Certificate Approach	1997	B.A.					Local superintendent applies for Preliminary Certificate in speech and language impaired and other teaching fields
Alaska	**No Program. Alaska had an Alternate Route Program which was discontinued. In 1994-95, four apprentice teachers were placed from the program. Two were hired in 1995-96 as full-time teachers. There have been no teachers since then in the Alternate Route Program.**							
Arizona	**No Program. In 1998, as a result of changes in Arizona State Board of Education certification rules, the Alternative Secondary Certification Program, initiated in 1988, was discontinued.**							
Arkansas	**Non-Traditional Licenusre Program**	1988	B.A.	cumulative 2.75 or 3.0 in last 60 hours of degree work	Praxis I and II	Summary of work history or resume	For secondary, a non-education major in content area, or meet coursework requirements in content area	Three letters of reference. Demonstration of good communication skills through interview by selection committee and written work history
California	**District Intern Certificate**	1983	B.A.		Pass CBEST basic skills test. Pass subject area portions of state-approved exam		Complete approved program of study (or pass subject area portions of state-approved exam).	Bilingual teachers must pass oral language component of state exam. Knowledge of U.S. Constitution
	University Intern Credential	1967	B.A.		Pass CBEST basic skills test. Pass subject area portions of state-approved exam		Complete approved program of study (or pass subject area portions of state-approved exam).	The teachers union for the hiring LEA must sign off on application. The Commission on Teacher Credentialing must approve the applicant. Knowledge of U.S. Constitution
	S.B. 57: Intern -- Early Completion Option	2001	B.A.		Show subject matter content proficiency by passing exam (or completing coursework). Complete written assessment of teaching knowledge and subject matter pedagogy.		Show subject matter content proficiency by completing coursework (or passing exam).	Character fitness (fingerprints)
	Pre-Internship Teaching Certificate	1998	B.A.		Pass CBEST basic skills test		Complete specified number of subject matter units.	No eligibility or participation in an internship or other teacher preparation program.

ENTRY REQUIREMENTS INTO ALTERNATIVE CERTIFICATION ROUTES, State-by-State: 2003

State	Name of Program	Year Began	Degree	Grade Point Average	Tests	Prior Experience	Courses	Other
Colorado	**Teacher in Residence**	1999	B.A.				30 semester hours in the content area	Pass background check, including fingerprinting
	Alternative Teacher Program	1991	B.A.		Pass state's required assessments in content (endorsement) area		Demonstrate subject matter knowledge necessary for teaching in an endorsement area through transcript review (30 semester hours), standardized assessment, or portfolio review	Pass background/security check
Connecticut	**Alternate Route to Teacher Certification**	1988	B.A.	3.0	Passing score on PRAXIS I or on an approved substitute exam; passing score on subject area test, PRAXIS II or ACTEL	Experience in an educational environment with children of age group one wishes to teach	Major in or closely related to field to be taught.	
DC	**D. C. Teaching Fellows**	2001	B.A.					Application, cover letter and resume
	Provisional Teacher Program	1992	B.A.				24-30 credit major in the appropriate subject field through applicable coursework and/or life experiences	Completed application. Interview
Delaware	**Delaware Alternative Route To Certification / Secondary Education**	1997	B.A.		Pass state's basic skills tests. When approved by the State Board of Education, pass subject matter tests in teaching field.		Major in teaching subject	Satisfactory health and criminal background checks. Employment by LEA or charter school to teach secondary subject designated by state as critical need area.
Florida	**Alternative Certification Program**	2002	B.A.	2.5	Meet specialized requirements in subject			Obtain employment in a FL public or private school with a state-approved system for demonstration of professional education competencies
Georgia	**Georgia Teacher Alternative Preparation Program**	2001	B.A.	2.5 on 4.0 scale	Praxis I			Criminal background check. Teaching job offer from LEA.

ENTRY REQUIREMENTS INTO ALTERNATIVE CERTIFICATION ROUTES, State-by-State: 2003

State	Name of Program	Year Began	Degree	Grade Point Average	Tests	Prior Experience	Courses	Other
Georgia (contd)	**Post-Baccalaureate Non-Degree Preparation Programs for Transitioning Military Personnel**	1993	B.A.	2.5 on 4.0 scale			Other requirements determined by the IHE.	
Hawaii	**Alternative Licensing Program in Special Education**	1991	B.A.	2.75				Special ed full-time contracted teaching position with State Dept. of Ed. Complete admissions file at IHE.
Idaho	**Secondary Field Centered Teacher Training Program**	1990	B.A.	2.0			Hold academic credits comparable with current major and minor requirements for secondary endorsement(s)	Fingerprinting and background check
Illinois	**Alternative Route to Teacher Certification**	1999	B.A.		Pass the Illinois Basic Skills Test	Employed at least 5 years in area requiring application of the participant's education		
Indiana	**No Program. Teacher preparation programs in the state offer alternative routes to full licensing. State legislators are considering other alternative teacher certification.**							
Iowa	**Teacher Intern License**	2002	B.A.	2.5		Minimum 3 years post-baccalaureate work experience		Be admitted to a teacher intern program; meet requirements of at least one of the board's secondary endorsement areas; meet all non-academic requirements, including fingerprinting and criminal background checks.
Kansas	**Restricted Teaching License**	2003	B.A. or graduate degree in content area in which license is sought	2.5				Offer of employment from local school district. District must document they have exhausted attempts to fill position with a licensed person
Kentucky	**Alternative Route -- Local District Certification Option**	1990	B.A.	2.5 or 2.0 with "exceptional life experience" related to teaching	Pass written tests of knowledge in specific teaching field (must have completed a 30-hour major/minor, or have 5 years' experience in the field)			Candidate must have been offered employment in a district which has an alternative certification program approved by the state's Education Professional Standards Board

ENTRY REQUIREMENTS INTO ALTERNATIVE CERTIFICATION ROUTES, State-by-State: 2003

State	Name of Program	Year Began	Degree	Grade Point Average	Tests	Prior Experience	Courses	Other
Kentucky (contd)	**Alternative Route -- Exceptional Work Experience Certification Option**	1998	B.A.	2.5		10 years' exceptional work experience in area for which certification is sought		
Louisiana	**Practitioner Teacher Program**	2002	B.A.	2.5	pass content-specific exams for the PRAXIS			
Maine	**No Program**							
Maryland	**Resident Teacher Certificate**	1991	B.A.	3.0	Praxis I and II tests			
Massachusetts	**Massachusetts Institute for New Teachers (MINT)**	1999	B.A.	3.0 in major subject or overall 3.0 or top 10th percentile on a national recognized exam (mid-career professional exempt from above)	Pass both sections (communication/literacy skills and a subject area)of the Massachusetts Test for Educator Licensure (MTEL)			
Michigan	**Michigan's Alternative Routes to Teacher Certification**	1993	B.A.	2.5	Pass basic skills exam and comprehensive elementary exam or subject area exam for secondary.	Except for foreign language teachers, have not less than 2 years of work experience in the last 5 years in the subject to be taught. For elementary, have documented relevant work experience (voluntary or paid), or experience with children of elementary school age.	Must have a major or graduate degree in the subject to be taught.	Pass a criminal history check. Be employed by a qualified LEA.

ENTRY REQUIREMENTS INTO ALTERNATIVE CERTIFICATION ROUTES, State-by-State: 2003

State	Name of Program	Year Began	Degree	Grade Point Average	Tests	Prior Experience	Courses	Other
Michigan (contd)	**Limited License to Instruct (Mid-career Model)**		B.A.			Except for foreign language teachers, have not less than 2 years of work experience in the last 5 years in the subject to be taught	Must have a major or graduate degree in the subject to be taught -- OR -- Have completed at least 120 semester hours in an approved teacher preparation program, including a major and a minor or the equivalent and at least 15 semester hours in professional education.	
	Limited License to Instruct (General Model)		B.A.	2.5 overall and 2.5 in major and/or minor or equivalent or 2.0-2.5 and pass state subject area test by 2nd request for renewal		Major and/or minor or graduate degree in field of specialization or 1 year of work experience in that field.		Pass a criminal history check.
Minnesota	**Alternative Preparation To Teacher Licensure Program**	1991	B.A.		Pass Pre-Professional Skills Tests in reading, writing, and math	Experience in field related to subject to be taught; document successful experiences working with children		Candidate must be hired by a school district
Mississippi	**Teach Mississippi Program**	2003	B.A.					
	Mississippi Alternate Path to Quality Teachers	2003	B.A.	2.5 for individuals graduated less than 7 years; 2.0 if graduated from college 7 years or more	Praxis I and Praxis II			
	Alternate Route License	1997	B.A.		Praxis I and subject area exam of Praxis II			

ENTRY REQUIREMENTS INTO ALTERNATIVE CERTIFICATION ROUTES, State-by-State: 2003

State	Name of Program	Year Began	Degree	Grade Point Average	Tests	Prior Experience	Courses	Other
Missouri	**An Alternative Certification Program**	1989	B.A.	2.5		Minimum of 5 years of successful employment, during which the content of the B.A. major was significantly applied. Documentation shall be defined and required by the IHE.	Verify completion of a general education background satisfactory to the IHE with an approved teacher ed program. Enroll in the IHE and complete coursework (in: Adolescent Development; Psychology of Learning; and Teaching Methodology in the Content Area) prior to certification and employment.	Be employed by an LEA. Participate in a structured interview selected by the teacher ed IHE, to assess the candidate's beliefs regarding the nature of teaching, the nature of students, and the goals and mission of education as a profession. The interview may be utilized for screening purposes or for diagnostic and counseling purposes. Enter into a 4-party contract with the IHE, LEA, and SEA, allowing IHE enrollment.
Montana	**No Program**							
Nebraska	**No Program**							
Nevada	**No Program**							
New Hampshire	**Alternative 5: Site-Based Certification Plan**	1990	B.A.	2.5 or the equivalent.		A person who fails to meet the GPA may still qualify if: all other requirements are met; college graduation was more than 5 years ago; and he or she has 5 years of work experience directly related to the area to be taught.	Secondary -- the equivalent of a 30 credit major in the subject to be taught. Elementary -- a 4-year arts and sciences background, including a major.	A person who fails to meet the GPA may still qualify if: all other requirements are met; college graduation was more than 5 years ago; and he or she has 5 years of directed related work experience.
	Alternative 4: Individual Professional Development Plan (Restricted)	1989	B.A.	2.5			Major compatible with prospective teaching assignment.	
New Jersey	**Provisional Teacher Program**	1984	B.A.	2.5, 2.75 after 9/1/2004	Praxis II Subject Assessment for subject area; for elementary Ed, NTE General Knowledge			Applicant must be offered employment.

ENTRY REQUIREMENTS INTO ALTERNATIVE CERTIFICATION ROUTES, State-by-State: 2003

State	Name of Program	Year Began	Degree	Grade Point Average	Tests	Prior Experience	Courses	Other
New Mexico	**Alternative Licensure**	2000	B.A. with 30 semester hours of grad or undergrad credit in field to be taught OR Master's with minimum of 12 hours in field to be taught					
New York	**Alternative Teacher Certification - Transitional B**	2000	B.A. with major in field to be taught for secondary; in liberal arts and sciences for elementary teachers	3.0 or written recommendation from college				
North Carolina	**Lateral Entry Provisional License**	1985	B.A.	2.5 -- Or, for person who has passed Praxis I: 3.0 in major, or on all work relevant to teaching area completed in senior year, or on minimum of 15 semester hours of courses (relative to licensure) completed in past 5 years.			Major in the teaching subject area	
North Dakota	**No Program**							
Ohio	**Alternative Educator License**	2000	B.A.	2.5	Praxis II	Major in a secondary teaching subject, OR 5 years of recent, related work experience in the teaching subject. Have completed 6 semester hours of		
Oklahoma	**Alternative Placement Program**	1991	B.A.		Pass competency test in area of specialization and pass general education test	2 years work experience related to subject area of specialization (may be waived if person has no postbaccalaureate work experience)		
Oregon	**Restricted Transitional License**	1999	B.A.					Evidence of content expertise in area
	Teaching Associate License	1999			Pass test of knowledge of civil rights laws at conclusion of approved course or workshop	1 year as full-time intern and 3 years full-time experience as teaching assistant	Enrollment in and completion of 75% of undergraduate teacher preparation program	Furnish fingerprints

ENTRY REQUIREMENTS INTO ALTERNATIVE CERTIFICATION ROUTES, State-by-State: 2003

State	Name of Program	Year Began	Degree	Grade Point Average	Tests	Prior Experience	Courses	Other
Oregon (contd)	**Limited Teaching License**	1999	A.A.		Demonstrate knowledge of applicable civil rights laws			Furnish fingerprints
Pennsylvania	**Alternative Candidate Certification**	1998	B.A., or an advanced degree in the subject to be taught, or a minimum of 10 years of exceptional service in a career compatible with the subject to be taught	3.0	Pass Praxis I and appropriate Praxis II specialty area test. Pass Elementary Education Content Knowledge test.	10 years of exceptional service in a career compatible with the subject to be taught (or a B.A. or an advanced degree in the subject to be taught)		
Rhode Island	**No Program. Rhode Island is currently developing an alternative route to certification program. The program is aimed at the secondary and special subjects**							
South Carolina	**Program of Alternative Certification for Educators**	1984	B.A.		PRAXIS II	2 years of post-baccalaureate experience	Major in an initial certification subject	Employment by an LEA
South Dakota	**Alternative Certification**	1985	B.A.				Major in a certifiable subject	Must not have had student teaching experience. Must be employed by LEA willing to cooperate in alternative route program
Tennessee	**Interim License Type C -- Alternative Preparation for Licensure**	1990	B.A.		Testing requirements for admission to a teacher education program			Screening by IHE and K-12 practitioners
	Interim License Type D -- Alternative Preparation for Licensure	1990	B.A.		Testing requirements for admission to a teacher education program			Screening by IHE and K-12 practitioners
Texas	**Alternative Teacher Certification**	1985	B.A.		Demonstrate acceptable college level skills in reading, oral and written communication, critical thinking and math			Complete screening activities to determine appropriateness for certification sought

ENTRY REQUIREMENTS INTO ALTERNATIVE CERTIFICATION ROUTES, State-by-State: 2003

State	Name of Program	Year Began	Degree	Grade Point Average	Tests	Prior Experience	Courses	Other
Utah	Alternative Routes to Licensure	2002	B.A.			Must be employed by district/school		
	LAUNCH (1 LEA)	2001	B.A.			Obtain LEA employment		Background clearance check
	Northern Utah Alternative Routes to Licensure (6 LEAs)	2002	B.A. in high-need area					Background clearance check
Vermont	No Program							
Virginia	Alternate Route to Licensure	1998	B.A.				Satisfy one or more specific endorsement areas (teaching areas)	
	Career Switcher Alternative Route to Licensure Pilot Programs for Career professions	2000	B.A.		Praxis I and II	5 years full-time employment in a profession	Meet teaching area requirements or equivalent	
Washington	Alternative Route Three under Partnership Grants Program	2001	B.A.	GPA may be considered as a selection factor	Pass state content test and basic skills exam, when available.	5 years' experience in the work force		Priority for teachers in subject matter or geographic shortage areas. Also nonshortage secondary teachers. Experience with students or children (demonstrated by reference letters, letters of support from previous employers). Meet age, good moral character, and personal fitness requirements.
West Virginia	No Program. The Alternative Program for the Education of Teachers (APET) was mandated by the state legislature to be in place by July 1, 1991, but the program has never been used.							
Wisconsin	Alternative Programs Leading to Initial Educator Licensing	2001	Requirements defined by programs; vary from program to program					
Wyoming	No Program							

SUMMARY OF PROGRAM REQUIREMENTS FOR ALTERNATIVE TEACHER CERTIFICATION ROUTES

Pages 40-53 following are summary tables for requirements for completion of the alternative route in each of the 59 states, plus information about providers for the program, who controls it, how long it takes and other.

PROGRAM REQUIREMENTS FOR ALTERNATIVE CERTIFICATION ROUTES, State-by-State: 2003

State	Name of Program	Pre-service	Field-Based	Courses in education	Content Courses	Mentor	Providers	Who Controls	Length	Other
Alabama	**Alternative Fifth-Year Program**	M.A.T. program	Full-time internship as teacher in teaching field for at least 12 weeks and at least 300 clock hours	curriculum and teaching; professional studies; special education; evaluation of teaching and learning; technology; reading	One-third of graduate hours in the M.A.T. program	No	IHE	IHE	Determined by participant and IHE	Program does not require that participant be employed as a teacher
	Alternative Baccalaureate-Level Approach		Participant employed with same local board or nonpublic school for three consecutive years, and much teach a majority of the time in the area and at grade level of certificate	12 semester or 18 quarter hours		Mentor for years one and two	LEA or nonpublic school	LEA or nonpublic school	3 years	
	Preliminary Certificate Approach		Holder is eligible for the Professional educator Certificate upon completion of two years of successful teaching while holding the Preliminary Certificate				LEA or nonpublic school	LEA or nonpublic school	2 years	Preliminary Certificate valid for two years and may be re-issued one time for one year
Alaska	**No Program**									
Arizona	**No Program**									
Arkansas	**Non-Traditional Licensure Program**	2 weeks of intensive summer training	1 year of teaching, under a mentor; additional training; and another 1-year period of teaching -- a total of 2 years training	7 monthly training sessions during first school year. 2 weeks of tailored training sessions during summer following first year of teaching. 7 additional monthly sessions during second year of teaching		Qualified mentor assigned by school district	SEA, Prof. Quality Enhance-ment, Non-Traditional Licensure Program	LEA	2 years	Passing score on PRAXIS II specialty area test and PRAXIS II P.L.T. and PPST.
California	**District Intern Certificate**	120 clock hours or equivalent component in child dev. and methods of teaching and ongoing teacher preparation over two years	2-year professional development program (approx. additional 360 clock hours), including training, support and assistance, and annual evaluation. For special ed, an additional 120 clock hours.			Each intern must be supported by at least one mentor or designated support person.	LEA	LEA	2 years; may be extended. Special ed 3 years.	

PROGRAM REQUIREMENTS FOR ALTERNATIVE CERTIFICATION ROUTES, State-by-State: 2003

State	Name of Program	Pre-service	Field-Based	Courses in education	Content Courses	Mentor	Providers	Who Controls	Length	Other
California (contd)	**University Intern Credential**	Training to ensure minimum level of knowledge in 10 performance compe-tencies.	Professional ed courses in methods completed while individual is employed as an intern teacher	Professional education courses in methods. Completion of an approved teacher ed program. IHE may require courses it deems necessary to achieve competencies, but less than one year of full-time study (approx. 36 semester units).		LEA must designate someone to provide support and evaluation for the intern and the university must provide systematic ongoing supervision.	IHE	IHE	2 years; may be extended. Special ed 3 years.	
	S.B. 57: Intern -- Early Completion Option		Candidate demonstrates performance in the classroom.				LEA	LEA	No limit. As little as 1 semester	Complete California Teaching Performance Assessment (or other authorized assessment of classroom performance), and other LEA requirements. Candidates for multi-subject credential must also pass Reading Instruction Competency Assessment.
	Pre-Internship Teaching Certificate	In pre-service or early service, candidate completes a minimum 40 hours of courses in classroom management, instructional strategies, and student discipline. Candidate participates in LEA's approved program. Subject matter advising and preparation in collaboration with an IHE.				Regular support through a permanently employed experienced educator or certificated retiree of an LEA throughout the school year.	LEA	LEA	1 year; renewable for 2nd year.	Take required subject matter competence exam at least once.

PROGRAM REQUIREMENTS FOR ALTERNATIVE CERTIFICATION ROUTES, State-by-State: 2003

State	Name of Program	Pre-service	Field-Based	Courses in education	Content Courses	Mentor	Providers	Who Controls	Length	Other
Colorado	**Teacher in Residence**		Teachers in residence hired by district serve as non-licensed teachers for 2 years	District collaborates with an IHE in design and delivery of a teacher Ed program based on same performance-based standards used in collegiate teacher Ed programs		Mentor and supervisor. Must be observed and supervised for a minimum of 100 hours each year	LEA and IHE	LEA and IHE	2 years	Must pass state's content test prior to April 15 of first year
	Alternative Teacher Program		One year of teaching, training and supervision	225 clock hours of professional education based on same performance based standards used in collegiate teacher Ed programs		Supervision and guidance by members of support team, including mentor teacher, principal and rep of an IHE	LEA and IHE	LEA and IHE	1 year	CO Dept. of Ed. Evaluates for eligibility to initially participate in the program. Performance evaluations conducted consistent with the district's adopted evaluation system.
Connecticut	**Alternate Route to Teacher Certification**	8-week summer term of full-time study, including 3-week student teaching experience OR weekend program that runs from Oct. to May, and includes 4 weeks of student teaching	Employed Alternate Route teachers participate in the Beginning Educators Support and Training (BEST) Program of the State Dept. of Ed			Mentor	CT public school teachers, IHEs and professional from diverse public and non-public agencies	SEA	8 weeks followed by BEST or weekends Oct.-May	Non-credit program
District of Columbia	**D.C. Teaching Fellows**	Comprehensive instructional summer institute		18 semester hours		Extensive support network	D.C. Teacher Education and Certification Branch and local school administrators		2 year commitment to teach in a D.C. public school	D.C. Mayor and Public Schools Supt. Calling on 100 of nation's most outstanding professionals to become Fellows and commit two years to teaching in D.C. public schools.

PROGRAM REQUIREMENTS FOR ALTERNATIVE CERTIFICATION ROUTES, State-by-State: 2003

State	Name of Program	Pre-service	Field-Based	Courses in education	Content Courses	Mentor	Providers	Who Controls	Length	Other
District of Columbia (contd)	**Provisional Teacher Program**		One successful year of teaching in lieu of student teaching	18 semester hours of Professional Education		Support from local school, IHE personnel	D.C. Teacher Education and Certification Branch and local school administrators, local school administrators, IHE personnel		18 months	Program consists on 3 basic components: professional education, field experience, and a support structure.
Delaware	**Delaware Alternative Route To Certification / Secondary Education**	Summer institute (approx. 120 clock hours) covering instruction strategies, assess-ment, classroom and behavioral manage-ment, and adolescent develop-ment. Orientation to LEA policies, organization, curriculum.	1st year is full-time practicum experience, with intensive on-the-job coaching by a trained mentor and supervision by a school administrator.	Equivalent of 15 credit hours of professional education courses, completed in 1 calendar year. Seminars on teaching (approx. 120 clock hours) on cultural diversity, teaching reading in content area, methods of teaching (content specific), and teaching exceptional students. Learning experiences co-taught by IHE faculty and experienced content area practitioners.	Candidates who need additional courses in subject area may take longer to complete certification requirements.	Intensive on-the-job coaching by trained mentor.	LEA, IHE	Consor-tium of state, LEAs, IHEs, General Assembly and other stake-holders.	1 year	
Florida	**Alternative Certification Program**		Two years to complete requirements for the professional Certificate, which are to: satisfy professional ed courses and practical experience requirements; satisfy recency of credit requirements; demonstrate professional ed competencies. Attain passing score on Professional Education Subtest; passing score on General Knowledge Test; Passing score on subject area exam				Local school district works with candidate to achieve the required competencies set by the state. Each school district must offer a competency-based alternative certification program.		up to 3 years	

PROGRAM REQUIREMENTS FOR ALTERNATIVE CERTIFICATION ROUTES, State-by-State: 2003

State	Name of Program	Pre-service	Field-Based	Courses in education	Content Courses	Mentor	Providers	Who Controls	Length	Other
Georgia	**Georgia Teacher Alternative Preparation Program**	Intensive 4-week summer preparation program; introduction to teaching.	2-year classroom based induction training period while teaching. Intensive monitoring, supervision, and mentoring during this period.				Collaborative unit made up of IHE, LEA, and Regional Education Service Agency (RESA)	IHE, LEA, RESA	2 years	Pass Praxis II content exam during 1st year. For hires after school year begins, shorter pre-service training, with classes held after school hours.
	Post-Baccalaureate Non-Degree Preparation Programs for Transitioning Military Personnel			Complete individualized program of study developed by IHE in subject area, based upon candidate's education and experience. Some preparation may be completed in LEA staff development. Minimum 2.5 GPA required.						
Hawaii	**Alternative Licensing Program in Special Education**		2-year on-the-job program, based on special education competencies	24 semester hours of special education			SEA and IHE	SEA and IHE	2 years	
Idaho	**Secondary Field Centered Teacher Training Program**	9 semester hours from an IHE. Complete 30 contact hour pre-service orientation by the LEA prior to employ-ment	Internship of 2 academic years.	6 to 9 semester hour program during the second summer from an IHE. Consortium composed of the mentor teacher, rep from the school district, rep from Office of Teacher Ed and Cert, and rep from participating IHE will determine the content required for the trainee, which may include both pedagogical and subject area coursework. Pre-service and second summer total 15-18 semester hours		Each trainee must be assisted by and guided throughout the 2-year training program by a mentor -- a certified employee of the district	SEA, LEA and IHE	Consor-tium	2 years	
Illinois	**Alternative Route to Teacher Certification**	Successful completion of intensive course of study in ed theory, instructional methods and practice teaching. Pass IL Subject Matter Knowledge Test	Full-time teaching for one year with advice and assistance of mentor teacher			Mentor	IHE, LEA	IHE	1 to 3 years	Assessment of teaching performance by school officials and program participants and recommendation for certification by the IHE

PROGRAM REQUIREMENTS FOR ALTERNATIVE CERTIFICATION ROUTES, State-by-State: 2003

State	Name of Program	Pre-service	Field-Based	Courses in education	Content Courses	Mentor	Providers	Who Controls	Length	Other
Indiana	**No Program**									
Iowa	**Teacher Intern License**	12 semester hours of the teacher intern program prior to fall employment	Integrated field experience	4 semester hours of a teacher intern seminar during internship year designed to provide continued support and extension of coursework taken during prior summer. 12 additional semester hours during the summer after the teacher intern year		Mentor	Local district and college or university offering an approved teacher intern program	State Board of Education		After completing these requirements, Teacher Intern may apply for issuance of an Initial License
Kansas	**Restricted Teaching License**		Individual contacts a Kansas teacher Ed institution to develop an approved teacher Ed program of study to be completed in not more than 3 years	Determined by IHE		Mentor provided by district. IHE provides on-site support	Teacher Ed institution in cooperation with a school district		3 years	Program completers will be required to complete a content and pedagogy assessment to qualify for an initial conditional license. During conditional license period, candidate will complete a performance assessment to move to a professional license
Kentucky	**Alternative Route -- Local District Certification Option**	full-time seminar and practicum of no less than 8 weeks	18 week period of supervision while teaching full-time	250 hours of formal instruction		Four-member support team (school principal, experienced teacher, instructional supervisor, college/university faculty member)		Professional support team	44 weeks	
	Alternative Route -- Exceptional Work Experience Certification Option		State's Internship Program required of all candidates	No additional credit hours				EPSB	1 year internship	Documentation that state's New Teacher Standards have been addressed and professional recommendations

PROGRAM REQUIREMENTS FOR ALTERNATIVE CERTIFICATION ROUTES, State-by-State: 2003

State	Name of Program	Pre-service	Field-Based	Courses in education	Content Courses	Mentor	Providers	Who Controls	Length	Other
Kentucky (contd)	**Alternative Route -- Exceptional Work Experience Certification Option**		State's Internship Program required of all candidates	No additional credit hours					1 year internship	Internship committee assesses first-year performance
Louisiana	**Practitioner Teacher Program**	9 credit hours or 135 contact hours during summer	Teaching internship as full-time teacher	2 seminars during year to address immediate needs of participants		Mentor teachers provided by the LA Teacher Assistance and Assessment Program and principals	Receive one-on-one supervision through an internship program by the program providers	Private providers and colleges or universities	2 years	Program providers, principals, mentors and practitioner teachers form teams to review and evaluate performance and recommend types of instruction needed
Maine	**No Program**									
Maryland	**Resident Teacher Certificate**	135 clock hours of Ed courses	1 year of successful teaching	135 additional hours for elementary teachers and 45 additional hours for secondary teachers		Certified teacher serves as mentor	Local School System or cooperatively with an IHE, or other approved educational course provider	Local School System	1 year. After an additional year of successful teaching, Resident Teacher may be issued the Standard Professional Certificate	
Massachusetts	**Massachusetts Institute for New Teachers (MINT)**	200 clock hours of professional development during summer	teach full-time	18 clock hours of support seminars				Educator Quality Enhancement cluster of State Dept. of Education	7-week summer program followed by one year of full-time teaching	MINT participants compile a portfolio that reflects how they meet the Department of Education's Professional Standards for Teachers. Final portfolio assessment evaluated by the Dept. of Ed's Portfolio Advisory Team, which is comprised of master teachers

PROGRAM REQUIREMENTS FOR ALTERNATIVE CERTIFICATION ROUTES, State-by-State: 2003

State	Name of Program	Pre-service	Field-Based	Courses in education	Content Courses	Mentor	Providers	Who Controls	Length	Other
Michigan	**Michigan's Alternative Routes to Teacher Certification**									
	Limited License to Instruct (Mid-career Model)	Complete a 4-8 week SEA approved orientation								
	Limited License to Instruct (General Model)	Orientation to teaching offered by LEA with IHE					Collaborative among SEA, LEA, and IHE	SEA, LEA, IHE	1 year; renewable up to 4 years total	Take basic skills exam, including reading, writing, and math, and pass 1 of 3 in 1st year. For 2nd renewal, pass 2 of 3. For 3rd renewal, pass 3 of 3. 3. Pass teacher certification exam for field of specialization by 2nd renewal request. Pass Annual Performance Evaluation, based on at least 2 observations of classroom teaching. Be admitted to partner IHE. Have approved plan of work for earning a Michigan Provisional Certificate.
Minnesota	**Alternative Preparation To Teacher Licensure Program**	Instruction phase involving intensive preparation before candidate assumes responsibility for a classroom	Formal instruction and peer coaching during school year. Assessment, supervision and evaluation to determine candidate's specific needs			Staff development conducted by a Resident Mentorship Team made up of administrators, teachers, and postsecondary faculty members		Resident Mentorship Team	1 year	Research-based and results-oriented approach, focused on skills teachers need to be effective

PROGRAM REQUIREMENTS FOR ALTERNATIVE CERTIFICATION ROUTES, State-by-State: 2003

State	Name of Program	Pre-service	Field-Based	Courses in education	Content Courses	Mentor	Providers	Who Controls	Length	Other
Mississippi	**Teach Mississippi Program**	8 week, 9 semester hour program	1 semester, 3 semester hour, supervised internship, to be completed while the teacher is employed as a full-time teacher intern in a school district					Mississippi State Dept. of Education		
	Mississippi Alternate Path to Quality Teachers	2-3 week Teach Mississippi Training Institute	Complete new teacher practicums, new teacher training models, and a local district evaluation during first year of employment			Mentor and intensive induction program		Mississippi State Dept. of Education	3 years	Pass Praxis II Specialty Area Test at end of 3rd year - issued Standard 5-Year License
	Alternate Route License			9 semester hours of pedagogy courses				Mississippi State Dept. of Education	3 years	
Missouri	**An Alternative Certification Program**			Enroll in 8-9 semester hours of professional education courses no later than the summer following award of provisional certificate. Follow-up assistance from IHE. Participate in LEA's professional development.		Mentor assigned by LEA.	IHE, LEA	IHE, LEA	2 years	Complete LEA's Performance Based Teacher Evaluation. Prior to 2nd year, pass appropriate exit test required of all pre-service teacher candidates.
Montana	No Program									
Nebraska	No Program									
Nevada	No Program									
New Hampshire	**Alternative 5: Site-Based Certification Plan**	Study of: human growth, development, learning, including characteristics of age group; techniques to determine students' learning needs; techniques for using available resources to meet those needs; techniques for orderly classroom routines. Assessment of candidate's background may show some or all of this study has already been completed. Pre-service includes performance evaluations.		In-service training, completed during the 1st year of service, addresses requirements deemed necessary by an assessment of the candidate's previous training and experience, and includes performance evaluations.		A mentor teacher or mentoring team works with the candidate for at least 1 school year. The SEA provides the mentor a minimum of 12 hours training in the mentoring process.	SEA, LEA	SEA, LEA	1 year	The LEA may request an extension of time (for no longer than 1 year) for completing pre-service and in-service training.

PROGRAM REQUIREMENTS FOR ALTERNATIVE CERTIFICATION ROUTES, State-by-State: 2003										
State	**Name of Program**	**Pre-service**	**Field-Based**	**Courses in education**	**Content Courses**	**Mentor**	**Providers**	**Who Controls**	**Length**	**Other**
New Hampshire (contd)	**Alternative 4: Individual Professional Development Plan (Restricted)**				The teacher may be required to complete additional preparation at an IHE.		The LEA assigns a mentor certified in the content area. The mentor develops a Professional Development Plan, which the teacher has 3 years to complete. The teacher is also given assessments on the basis of competencies.	SEA, LEA, IHE	SEA	3 years
New Jersey	**Provisional Teacher Program**		34 weeks of full-time classroom competency development	200 hours of essential professional knowledge and skills presented after school and/or on Saturdays at a district-operated or state-operated training center		Experienced mentor teacher	LEA, IHE, SEA	State Board of Examiners	1 year	Evaluations conducted by school principal or administrative designee. At least 3 evaluations
New Mexico	**Alternative Licensure**		Student teaching or field-based program	12-18 semester hours at a college or university		1-3 year mentorship	IHE with district	State Board of Education	1 to 3 years	

PROGRAM REQUIREMENTS FOR ALTERNATIVE CERTIFICATION ROUTES, State-by-State: 2003

State	Name of Program	· Pre-service	Field-Based	Courses in education	Content Courses	Mentor	Providers	Who Controls	Length	Other
New York	**Alternative Teacher Certification - Transitional B**	200 clock hours of pedagogy, including 40 hours of field experiences	Part-time collegiate study in pedagogy while teaching				IHE with district		valid for 3 years	To begin mentored teaching with a Transitional B Certificate, candidate must pass the New York Liberal Arts and Sciences test and the Content Specialty Test. Also, complete an approved 2 clock hour course in the identification and reporting of suspected child abuse or maltreatment and a 2-hour course on school violence prevention and intervention
North Carolina	**Lateral Entry Provisional License**		Successful teaching experience in the program will be accepted for the student teaching requirement.	Complete professional education and/or other requirements for clear licensure through an approved teacher ed program at a participating IHE. Initial 2-year license can be extended on a yearly basis for up to 3 years, if the holder earns a minimum of 6 semester hours of appropriate coursework per year.					2 years; can be extended on yearly basis up to 3 years	Pass Praxis II by end of initial 2-year lateral license.
North Dakota	**No Program**									
Ohio	**Alternative Educator License**	6 semester hours of pre-service coursework	2 years full-time classroom teaching in subject area	12 semester hours of professional education coursework, with 2.5 GPA, from teacher ed IHE in principles and practices of teaching, student development and learning, pupil assessment procedures, curriculum development, classroom management, and teaching methodology.			IHE, LEA	SEA, LEA	2 years	

PROGRAM REQUIREMENTS FOR ALTERNATIVE CERTIFICATION ROUTES, State-by-State: 2003

State	Name of Program	Pre-service	Field-Based	Courses in education	Content Courses	Mentor	Providers	Who Controls	Length	Other
Oklahoma	**Alternative Placement Program**			270 clock hours or 18 semester hours				Profession-al Standards Section of State Department of Education	3 years maximum	Meet all state's regular certification requirements while teaching
Oregon	**Restricted Transitional License**		Pass basic skills and content tests; complete two teacher work samples; demonstrate competencies	Complete approved teacher preparation program		School district mentor	LEA, IHE	LEA, IHE	3 years maximum	
	Teaching Associate License		Pass basic skills and content tests; complete two teacher work samples; demonstrate competencies	Complete approved teacher preparation program and all degree requirements		Mentor	IHE, LEA	IHE, LEA	2 years	
	Limited Teaching License		Pass basic skills test; pass test of knowledge of civil rights laws at conclusion of approved course or workshop			Mentor provided by LEA during first year	LEA	State	3 years; renewable	
Pennsylvania	**Alternative Candidate Certification**	2-week intensive seminar	The candidate develops a portfolio in the 1st semester of teaching (6 credit hours), and completes up to an additional 180 clock hours or 6 credit hours of instruction (any combination of credit hours, in-service credit, continuing education credits relative to the candidate's teaching area, or SEA-approved instructional clock hours). Professional development includes instructional program competencies: Planning of instruction; Managing the instructional environment; Selecting, analyzing, and modifying instructional materials, to meet the learning needs and reading levels of diverse learners; Monitoring student understanding of content, providing feedback to assist learning, and adjusting instructional strategies; Developing a knowledge of professional organizations, state and federal laws, regulations, and ethical practices; Developing the ability to foster professional relationships with school colleagues to improve student learning; Developing the ability to communicate effectively with parents/guardians, other agencies, and the community at large, to support learning by all students.			Supervised and mentored by IHE and LEA, in conjunction with any other participating education entities.	A collaborative unit of education entities for the purpose of developing alternative teacher certification programs, recognized by the SEA.	Collaborative unit	15 months	A professional development team (representatives from each entity in the collaborative unit) provides the candidate's educational program plan. After the 15-month experience, pass Praxis II Principles of Learning and Teaching 7-12.

PROGRAM REQUIREMENTS FOR ALTERNATIVE CERTIFICATION ROUTES, State-by-State: 2003

State	Name of Program	Pre-service	Field-Based	Courses in education	Content Courses	Mentor	Providers	Who Controls	Length	Other
South Carolina	**Program of Alternative Certification for Educators**	Pre-service institute to prepare teacher for the opening of school (with training during 1st year, a total of 15 days).	Complete 3 years of full-time teaching. Training -- 1st year: sessions totaling 15 days, including pre-service institute; 2nd year: sessions totaling 12 days, including an institute during 2nd summer.	Over 3 years, complete 3 graduate-level professional education courses as prescribed in the teacher's professional development plan.			LEA and IHE	LEA, IHE	3 years	Pass Principles of Learning and Teaching exam.
South Dakota	**Alternative Certification**	Pre-school orientation by LEA.		Complete a teacher ed program. IHE evaluates transcript; outlines courses. Plan approved by SEA. Courses taken through IHE in no more than 2 years.		LEA provides supervision and mentoring.	IHE, LEA	SEA, IHE	2 years	
Tennessee	**Interim License Type C -- Alternative Preparation for Licensure**	The alternative certification	Employed as teacher	Participate in additional preparation activities planned by IHE and LEA collaboratively		The alternative certification	IHE, LEA	IHE	1 year; renewable once	
	Interim License Type D -- Alternative Preparation for Licensure		Teaches as intern for 1 year	Coursework specified by IHE		Closely supervised mentoring program	IHE, LEA	IHE	1 year; renewable twice	
Texas	**Alternative Teacher Certification**		Teaches as intern for 1 year	Curricula covers same State standards included in undergraduate programs. Instruction delivered by partners most suited to the task		Mentor	LEA, IHE, education service center	LEA, IHE, education service center	1 year, renewable for one year	All programs jointly created through collaborative process involving LEA, IHE and education service center.

PROGRAM REQUIREMENTS FOR ALTERNATIVE CERTIFICATION ROUTES, State-by-State: 2003

State	Name of Program	Pre-service	Field-Based	Courses in education	Content Courses	Mentor	Providers	Who Controls	Length	Other
Utah	**Alternative Routes to Licensure**		LEA observations of classroom performance	Show competencies through 15 semester hours of IHE courses, LEA professional development, or content tests		Trained mentor	LEA, IHE	LEA	4 years	
	LAUNCH		Teach full-time	21 semester hours teacher prep at night			LEA, IHE	LEA	1-1/2 years	
	Northern Utah Alternative Routes to Licensure		Teach as intern for 1 year	15 semester hours professional education, complete portfolio, pass Praxis I		Trained mentor for 3 years	LEA, IHE	LEA	1 year	Tuition scholarships: teach 3 years in high-need school or repay
Vermont	**No Program**									
Virginia	**Alternate Route to Licensure**		1 year full-time teaching in endorsement area	Early/primary, elementary, middle, special Ed -- 18 semester hours; Adult, PreK-12, secondary 6-12 -- 15 semester hours		Mentor available in school building to assist	LEA, IHE	LEA	1 year	
	Career Switcher Alternative Route to Licensure Pilot Programs for Career professions	160 clock hours of intensive induction program	20 clock hours of field experiences	15 semester hours professional coursework or complete a program integrating content			IHE	IHE	1 year	
Washington	**Alternative Route Three under Partnership Grants Program**	Cohorts of candidates attend intensive summer teacher academy.	1year internship employed by LEA, followed, if necessary, by a 2nd summer teacher academy.			Mentor provided b LEA.	LEA, IHE	LEA, IHE	1 year	
West Virginia	**No Program.**									
Wisconsin	**Alternative Programs Leading to Initial Educator Licensing**	Vary by program; must assure proficiency in state standards					Not limited	Program provider	Varies	
Wyoming	**No Program**									

STATE ALTERNATIVE ROUTE PROFILES

ALABAMA — Class E

TITLE: Alternative Fifth-Year Program

HISTORY: Approved by the Alabama State Board of Education in 1986; implemented the same year; IHEs set up proposed programs.

MOTIVATION: To create a quality-controlled alternative route to teacher certification.

GRADE LEVELS AND/OR SUBJECT AREA(S) COVERED: All

WHO OPERATES: IHE

REQUIREMENTS TO ENTER PROGRAM:

The individual must have an earned bachelor's degree from a regionally accredited college or university.

The participant must have a 2.5 grade point average (on a 4-point scale), submit a score on the GRE or MAT, and meet prerequisite coursework in general studies and the chosen teaching field.

PROGRAM DESCRIPTION:

The master's degree program requires:

A teaching field of at least one-third of the total number of graduate hours in the program.

Study in each of the following areas: curriculum and teaching; professional studies; special education; evaluation of teaching and learning; technology; and reading.

and

A full-time internship as a teacher in the teaching field for at least 12 weeks and at least 300 clock hours. The college may request a waiver of the internship if the individual has 1-year full-time teaching experience in the same area as the alternative program being completed.

Upon completion of the program, the individual receives a regular certificate at a higher level than that issued to a graduate of a four-year teacher education program.

The program does not require the participant to be employed as a teacher. If employed as a teacher, a one-year Special Alternative Certificate may be requested a maximum of three times by the local superintendent or headmaster of a nonpublic school (the nonpublic school must be accredited, State-approved and/or State-registered).

NUMBER OF CREDIT HOURS TO COMPLETE:

Determined by the institution.

LENGTH OF TIME: Determined by the participant and IHE regulations.

ALABAMA — Class C

TITLE: Alternative Baccalaureate-Level Approach

HISTORY: Created by the Alabama Legislature as part of the Alabama Education Improvement Act of 1991. The Act authorized the program for grades 9-12 subject areas and for grades K-8 in the subject areas of the fine arts and foreign languages. Approved by the Alabama State Board of Education in Feb. 1992; implemented in the 1992-93 school year; expanded by the State Board in 1993 to include special education for grades 9-12, and in 1997, to include grades 6-8 for special education, and in 2000, to include dance and theatre.

MOTIVATION: To increase the pool of applicants from which LEA superintendents and headmasters may select persons who appear qualified to fill vacancies.

GRADE LEVELS AND/OR SUBJECT AREA(S) COVERED:

K-8 -- art, music, foreign languages, physical education, dance and theatre.

6-8 and 9-12 -- art, music, foreign languages, sciences, social sciences, English language arts, career/technical education, mathematics, health, driver education, physical education, dance, theatre, English as a second language, and all areas of special education except early childhood.

WHO OPERATES: LEA

REQUIREMENTS TO ENTER PROGRAM:

The participant must hold an earned baccalaureate degree from a regionally accredited college or university.

The participant must provide evidence of one of the following to the local superintendent or headmaster of a nonpublic school for his/her review and approval (the nonpublic school must be accredited, State-approved and/or State-registered):

> At least 24 months of professional and/or other work experience in the field or related fields for which certification is sought.

A minimum of 48 semester hours or 72 quarter hours of academic credit or the equivalent nonacademic credit in the field or related fields for which certification is sought.

The participant must be a candidate for employment by a local board of education or a nonpublic school.

PROGRAM DESCRIPTION:

The participant must be employed with the same local board of education or nonpublic school for three consecutive scholastic years, and must teach a majority of the time in the area and at the grade level of the certificate.

The participant has a mentor for years one and two.

The certificate issued is valid for one-year periods.

Prior to the end of the third year of employment, the participant must have earned a grade of "C" or above in each course of the specified 12 semester hours/18 quarter hours.

At the end of year three, the participant applies for the Class B (baccalaureate level) professional teacher's certificate (the initial regular certificate in Alabama).

NUMBER OF CREDIT HOURS TO COMPLETE:

12 semester hours or 18 quarter hours in specified coursework.

WHO EVALUATES CANDIDATES:

The local superintendent (or headmaster of nonpublic school).

LENGTH OF TIME: Three scholastic years.

TITLE: Preliminary Certificate Approach

HISTORY: Approved by the Alabama State Board of Education in 1997; implemented in 1997.

MOTIVATION: To increase the pool of applicants from which LEA superintendents and headmasters may select persons who appear qualified to fill vacancies.

GRADE LEVELS AND/OR SUBJECT AREA(S) COVERED:

Speech and language impaired and any teaching field requested by a local superintendent.

WHO OPERATES: LEA

REQUIREMENTS TO ENTER PROGRAM:

A local superintendent may apply for a Preliminary Certificate in speech and language impaired and other teaching fields. A headmaster of a nonpublic school may apply for a Preliminary Certificate in speech and language impaired only (the nonpublic school must be accredited, state-approved and/or state-registered).

The individual must have at least an earned bachelor's degree from a regionally accredited college or university.

PROGRAM DESCRIPTION:

The holder of a Preliminary Certificate must teach a majority of the time in the teaching field endorsed on the certificate.

The holder is eligible for the professional educator certificate upon completion of two years of successful teaching while holding the Preliminary Certificate.

NUMBER OF CREDIT HOURS TO COMPLETE:

None.

LENGTH OF TIME: The Preliminary Certificate is valid for two years and may be reissued one time with a one-year valid period.

ALABAMA

Number of Teaching Licenses Issued

	2000-01	1999-00	1998-99	1997-98	1996-97	1995-96	1994-95	1993-94	1992-93	1991-9
Persons who completed an approved college teacher preparation program	14,653	15,839	~8,000	~6,000	~7,000	~7,000	~6,000	~5,600	5,541	4,828
Emergency	308	384	300							
Temporary				N/A	N/A	N/A	N/A	N/A	N/A	N/A
Alternative Baccalaureate-Level Approach	784	584	259	180	85	54	54	22	17	
Alternative Fifth Year Program	967	1,012	~900	~700	800	800	555	~500	542	460

Number of Teachers Employed

	2000-01	1999-00	1998-99	1997-98	1996-97	1995-96	1994-95	1993-94	1992-93	1991-92
Total Teachers Employed in the State	48,163	55,439	~ 47,000	~ 43,000	~ 43,000	~ 43,000	42,307	41,700	est. 41,000	39,100
Newly Hired Teachers in Each Year	N/A	N/A	N/A	N/A	N/A	N/A	N/A	N/A	est. 2,250	N/A

Alabama Dept. of Education
5201 Gordon Persons Bldg.
50 N. Ripley St.
P.O. Box 302101
Montgomery, AL 36130-2101
Attn: June H. Mabry
Phone: (334) 242-9977
Fax: (334) 242-0498
tcert@alsde.edu

ALABAMA

Institutions of higher education that have developed alternative teacher preparation programs leading to a teaching license:

Alabama A&M University
Alabama State University
Auburn University
Auburn University Montgomery
Jacksonville State University
Samford University
Spring Hill College
Troy State University, Troy
Troy State University Dothan
Tuskegee University
University of Alabama, Tuscaloosa
University of Alabama at Birmingham
University of Alabama in Huntsville
University of Mobile
University of Montevallo
University of North Alabama
University of South Alabama
University of West Alabama

States with which the state has reciprocity of teacher licenses:

NASDTEC Interstate Contract with all states, except Iowa, Minnesota, Missouri, South Dakota and Wisconsin ("but we can usually certify their teachers")

Institutions of higher education that have *any* teacher preparation programs leading to a license to teach.

Alabama A&M University
Alabama State University
Athens State University
Auburn University
Auburn University Montgomery
Birmingham-Southern College
Concordia College
Faulkner University
Huntington College
Jacksonville State University
Judson College
Miles College
Oakwood College
Samford University
Spring Hill College
Stillman College
Talladega College
Troy State University
Troy State University Dothan
Troy State University in Montgomery
Tuskegee University

University of Alabama
University of Alabama at Birmingham
University of Alabama in Huntsville
University of Mobile
University of Montevallo
University of North Alabama
University of South Alabama
University of West Alabama

Contact for persons interested in finding a teaching position in the state:

Barbara G. Fennell
State Department of Education
50 North Ripley Street
P.O. Box 302101
Montgomery, AL 36130-2101
Phone: (334) 242-9935

ALASKA

Alaska had an alternate route program which was discontinued. In 1994-95, the state had four apprentice teachers placed from the Alternate Route Program. Two were hired in 1995-96 as full-time teachers. There have been no teachers since then in the Alternate Route Program.

Number of Teaching Licenses Issued

	1999-2000	1998-99	1997-98	1996-97	1995-96	1994-95	1993-94	1992-93	1991-92	1990-
Persons who completed an approved college teacher preparation program	587	N/A	N/A	N/A	N/A	N/A	N/A	N/A	N/A	8,59
Emergency	75	N/A	N/A	6	10	2	N/A	N/A	20	23
Temporary	37	N/A	N/A	120	50	50	N/A	N/A	5	23
Alternative Route	N/A	N/A	N/A	0	0	2				

Number of Teachers Employed

	1999-2000	1998-99	1997-98	1996-97	1994-95	1993-94	1992-93	1991-92	1990-91	1989-
Total Teachers Employed in the State *	7,945**	9,438	N/A	9,365	8,725	8,792	8,599	7,672	7,818	6,319
Newly Hired Teachers in Each Year	N/A	N/A	N/A	N/A	N/A	N/A	N/A	N/A	N/A	N/A

* *All certified staff*

** *Calculated differently than in previous years.*

Alaska Dept. of Education and Early Development
Teacher Education and Certification
Attn: Assessment Center
801 West Tenth St., Suite 200
Juneau, AK 99801-1984
Attn: Julie Orsborn
(907) 465-2026
email: julie_orsborn@educ.state.ak.us

ALASKA

Institutions of higher education that have developed alternative teacher preparation programs leading to a teaching license:

States with which the state has reciprocity of teacher licenses:

Alaska has signed the NASDTEC Interstate Contract with states that are NCATE Partnership States.

Institutions of higher education that have any teacher preparation programs leading to a license to teach:

Alaska Pacific University
Sheldon Jackson College
University of Alaska, Anchorage
University of Alaska, Fairbanks
University of Alaska Southeast, Juneau

Contact for persons interested in finding a teaching position in the state:

Jackie Fennoor Individual School Districts
Alaska Teacher Placement
University of Alaska, Fairbanks
Fairbanks, AK 99775
Phone: (907) 474-6644

TITLE: Alternative Secondary Certificate

HISTORY: Effective April 25, 1988. On June 1, 1998, the State Department of Education wrote: "As a result of recent changes in Arizona State Board of Education certification rules, the Alternative Secondary Certification Program initiated in 1988 has been discontinued." The recently approved certification rules can be reviewed by accessing the Department's Web site (on the Internet) at: http://www.ade.state.az.us.

MOTIVATION: To increase the pool of qualified secondary teachers through an individualized certification program.

GRADE LEVELS AND/OR SUBJECT AREA(S) COVERED: Grades 7-12

WHO OPERATES: State/LEA

REQUIREMENTS TO ENTER:

Verification of a State Board approved District Alternative Secondary Teacher Training Program. Must be verified in writing by appropriate Arizona Department of Education designee.

Bachelor's degree from a regionally accredited institution.

Arizona Teacher Proficiency Examination (ATPE), Basic Skills Component.

Major in each subject to be taught from a regionally accredited institution as verified by that institution OR a minimum of 30 semester hours in each subject to be taught, from a regionally accredited institution, and a passing score on a State Board approved examination in each subject area to be taught.

The local school district proposes the program in conjunction with a college and/or the state.

ARIZONA

Class B

PROGRAM DESCRIPTION:

A training program is developed with training to be conducted in a college or in the local school district with assistance from the state staff.

The individual completes a three-phase program with an evaluation conducted at the end of each period, to determine whether he or she should proceed:

Phase 1 -- four weeks of training, with actual classroom observation and academic instruction;

Phase 2 -- 10 weeks of actual teaching in a classroom, under the

direction of a supervising team; the teacher must be observed a minimum of one period per week;

Phase 3 -- 12 weeks, during which the teacher has full control of the classroom; the teacher must be observed a minimum of one period per month.

After completing the program, the individual can be recommended to the state for a regular certificate. If he/she holds a bachelor's degree, a Standard Secondary Certificate is issued. It is valid for six years, and is renewable.

During the initial year of certification, the following deficiencies must be satisfied:

-- Arizona Constitution (a college course or the approximate examination).

-- U.S. Constitution (college course or appropriate examination).

NUMBER OF CREDIT HOURS TO COMPLETE: Not specified

WHO EVALUATES: LEA and IHE when involved.

LENGTH OF TIME: Initial 26-week period.

ARIZONA

Class F

TITLE: Emergency Certificate

HISTORY: In use for many years.

MOTIVATION: Shortage

GRADE LEVELS AND/OR SUBJECT AREA(S) COVERED:

Grades K-12, Elementary, Secondary or Special Education

REQUIREMENTS TO ENTER:

A bachelor's degree.

The local school district and county superintendent certifies that no qualified teacher can be found.

PROGRAM DESCRIPTION:

State officials said emergency certification is seldom issued in metropolitan areas. It is usually used in isolated, remote areas.

The certificate is valid only for the specific school district and specific assignment for which it was issued.

NUMBER OF CREDIT HOURS TO COMPLETE: Six semester hours each year.

WHO OPERATES: LEA

LENGTH OF TIME: Valid for one year.

May be renewed if the local school district shows that the shortage still exists and the individual completes six semester hours of coursework per year toward completion of regular teacher education requirements.

ARIZONA

Number of Teaching Licenses Issued

	1992-93	1991-92	1990-91	1989-90	1988-89
Persons who completed an approved college teacher preparation program	N/A	N/A	N/A		Data Not Available
Internship program					
Emergency					
Temporary					
Alternative Route	32	5	11	3	
Other -- Probationary					

Number of Teachers Hired

	1992-93	1991-92	1990-91	1989-90	1988-89
Total Teachers Employed in the State	N/A	N/A	N/A	N/A	39,911
Newly Hired Teachers in Each Year	N/A	N/A	N/A	N/A	N/A

Arizona Dept. of Education
Teacher Certification Unit
1535 West Jefferson
Phoenix, AZ 85007
Attn: Lanny Standridge
(602) 542-4367

ARIZONA

Institutions of higher education that have developed alternative teacher preparation programs leading to a teaching license:

States with which the state has reciprocity of teacher licenses:

NASDTEC Interstate Contract.

Institutions of higher education that have *any* teacher preparation programs leading to a license to teach.

Arizona State University
Chapman University
Grand Canyon College
Northern Arizona University
Prescott College
Southwest Conservative Baptist College
Ottawa University
University of Arizona
University of Phoenix

Contact information for persons interested in finding a teaching position in the state:

Districts do all their own hiring

TITLE: Non-Traditional Licensure Program

HISTORY: In 1987 the Arkansas Department of Education realizing that a rich pool of experienced people exists who may wish to enter the teaching profession developed the Non-Traditional Licensure Program (NTLP) to attract and train well-qualified individuals to stem the growing teacher shortage in Arkansas. The NTLP is a developmentally appropriate teacher-training program for persons who have a four-year degree or higher that includes 288 hours of intensive specialized training and two years of support from a site-based trained mentor to assist with the guidance of professional growth for the new teacher during the first two years of teaching employment.

MOTIVATION: "The program is intended to attract and train qualified individuals to fill teaching assignments in districts which have a history of difficulty in recruiting certified teachers. The Department is committed to assisting local school district efforts to identify, recruit and employ teachers; we encourage nominations of minority candidates in all certifiable areas."

GRADE LEVELS AND/OR SUBJECT AREA(S) COVERED:

P-4 grades Pre-school – 4th, Middle Childhood grades 4th - 8th, Secondary Education grade 9th –12th .

WHO OPERATES: State Department of Education, Professional Quality Enhancement, Non-Traditional Licensure Program

ARKANSAS — Class B

REQUIREMENTS TO ENTER PROGRAM:

First Year

- Official Transcripts (showing a four year or higher degree awarded)
- Praxis I passing scores
- Praxis II passing tests scores in content.
- Summary of work history or resume
- Three letters of reference
- NTLP application
- The NTLP Writing Assignment must be completed in longhand.
- Arkansas and FBI Background Check

REQUIREMENTS TO RECEIVE TWO-YEAR LICENSE:

- Verification of employment by an Arkansas School (public or private)
- Payment of the $750 NTLP fee
- Mandatory Attendance of all training sessions.
- The office of Professional Quality Enhancement will conduct a review of the admission documents and arrange for an admission interview for qualified candidates.

Second Year

- Verification of employment by an Arkansas School (public or private)
- Payment of the $750 NTLP fee
- Mandatory Attendance of all training sessions
- Praxis II Principals of Learning and Teaching passing scores
- Praxis II Content Area Pedagogical passing scores

SELECTION OF SCHOOL DISTRICTS:

All districts in Arkansas are eligible to participate.

PROGRAM DESCRIPTION:

The Non-Traditional Licensure Program strives for best practice instructional delivery to the NTLP candidates in the following areas:

- Pathwise
- Arkansas current practices and issues
- Classroom management
- Positive classroom discipline
- Legal responsibilities of teachers
- IDEA, 504, ESL
- Instructional delivery strategies
- Diverse needs of learners, multiple intelligences, and learning styles
- Thinking skills strategies
- Writing across the curriculum

- Technology integration in instruction
- Organizing content knowledge for student learning
- Assessments/performance tasks/rubric development instruction
- Managing the learning environment for diverse learners
- Arkansas content standards and curriculum frameworks

To complete the program the participant must have

- Successfully taught as teacher of record for 120 days for two years
- Pass the Praxis II Principles of Learning and Teaching
- Pass the Praxis II pedagogical portion of the participant s content area.

The program starts with two weeks of summer training. This is followed by two-years of teaching under a Pathwise trained mentor.

Time Line Recommendations

January – June 13, 2003	*ALL* required paperwork and tests scores to the Non-Traditional Licensure Program Office.
	Criminal Background Check Completed.
March - June 13, 2003	Interview and Orientation
	Return Eligibility Letter signed by superintendent to Non-Traditional Licensure Program Office as soon as you are hired.
July 2003	Two weeks of NTLP Trainings
August 2003	Begin Teaching classes with two-year provisional license; *Mentor Assigned and documentation to NTLP Office*
September 2003	First of seven monthly trainings
April 2004	Apply for second year of program with renewal application, re-hire letter from district office and program fee
July – August 2004	Two weeks of NTLP Trainings
September 2004	First of seven monthly trainings
November – March 2004	Praxis II – Principles of Learning and Teaching Scores and the application to Convert Provisional License to Standard
August – October 2004	Three year license issued
May 2005 - May 2007	Praxis III Performance Based Assessment (may be taken in last semester of NTLP)

Apply for standard five-year license with renewal application and passing Praxis III Assessment Score.

It is the intention of the initial summer training to provide participants with the skills required to be effective in the classroom. Follow-up training, along with mentor guidance, will take place throughout the program.

Once the initial summer training is completed, a qualified mentor is assigned by the school district where employed.

Apprentice teachers will participate in seven Saturday training sessions during the first school year.

A passing score on the Praxis II Principles of Learning and Teaching or Content Pedagogy tests along with completion of all workshop training is required for Initial Licensure.

NUMBER OF CREDIT HOURS TO COMPLETE:

Three areas of licensure require additional coursework.

Early Childhood	Teaching Reading -3 hours and Arkansas History - 3 hours
Middle Childhood	Arkansas History -3 hours
Secondary Social Studies	Arkansas History -3 hours

WHO EVALUATES: Performance evaluation is conducted by the local school district where participates are employed. The Department of Education Non-Traditional Licensure Program monitors evaluations of the Non-Traditional Licensure Program requirements.

LENGTH OF TIME: Two years.

OTHER: Each participant will be required to pay $750 upon selection to the program. The remaining $750 will be paid prior to the second summer session.

ADE-Non-Traditional Licensure Program
623 Woodlane, Little Rock, AR 72201
Attn: Jim Chism, Program Manager
Norene Drinkwater, Program Advisor
(501) 371-1580

ARKANSAS

Number of Teaching Licenses Issued

	1998-99	1997-98	1994-95	1992-93	1991-92	1990-91	1989-90
Persons who completed an approved college teacher preparation program	2,500	N/A		N/A	N/A	N/A	N/A
Alternative Route	400		100	50	6	10	11
Applied	250	260		N/A	131	42	
Accepted *	100	150		N/A	70	33	
Trained	80	116		N/A	48	29	
Placed	250**	100		N/A	30	20	
Other -- Probationary	N/A	N/A		N/A	N/A	N/A	40

Number of Teachers Employed

	1997-98	1994-95	1992-93	1991-92	1990-91	1989-90
Total Teachers Employed in the State	23,500	N/A	N/A	N/A	N/A	N/A
Newly Hired Teachers in Each Year	N/A	N/A	N/A	N/A	N/A	N/A

* *According to state officials, the primary reasons applicants are not accepted are: they failed to meet testing requirements*

** *Total currently enrolled.*

ADE-Non-Traditional Licensure Program
623 Woodlane, Little Rock, AR 72201
Attn: Jim Chism, Program Manager
Norene Drinkwater, Program Advisor
(501) 371-1580

ARKANSAS

Institutions of higher education that have developed alternative teacher preparation programs leading to a teaching license:

University of Arkansas at Monticello
University of Arkansas at Little Rock
Henderson State University

States with which the state has reciprocity of teacher licenses:

Most. NASDTEC Interstate Contract.

Institutions of higher education that have *any* teacher preparation program(s) leading to a license to teach.

Arkansas Baptist College
Arkansas State University
Arkansas Tech University
Harding University
Henderson State University
Hendrix College
John Brown University
Lyon College
Ouachita Baptist University
Philander Smith College
Southern Arkansas University
University of Arkansas at Fayetteville
University of Arkansas at Little Rock
University of Arkansas at Monticello
University of Arkansas at Pine Bluff
University of Central Arkansas
University of the Ozarks
Williams Baptist College

Contact information for persons interested in finding a teaching position in the state:

ADE Non-Traditional Licensure Program
623 Woodlane
Little Rock, AR 72201
Jim Chism, Program Manager
Norene Drinkwater, Program Advisor
Phone: (501) 371-1580

TITLE: District Intern Certificate

HISTORY: Legislation passed in 1983 originally authorized the program for secondary school teachers only; the first interns were in place in 1984. The law was changed in 1987 to expand the program to include bilingual and elementary teachers and again in 2002 to include special education teachers.

MOTIVATION: Teacher supply and demand, but available in all grades and subject areas.

GRADE LEVELS AND/OR SUBJECT AREA(S) COVERED:

Originally for secondary only; later expanded to include bilingual and elementary and then special education teachers. One district pilot project in Special Education -- Mild-Moderate Disabilities -- in 2002.

WHO OPERATES: LEA

REQUIREMENTS TO ENTER:

A bachelor's degree.

Major or minor in subject to be taught.

A passing score on the CBEST basic skills test

Subject matter competence demonstrated by completing an approved program of study, or passing appropriate subject area portions of the state-approved subject matter exam.

Bilingual classroom teachers must pass oral language component of state exam. ed note (There are special course requirements in the program but not for entry).

Knowledge of U.S. Constitution.

PROGRAM DESCRIPTION:

The school district must employ persons to provide guidance and assistance. Each intern must be supported by at least one mentor or other designated support person.

The school district must develop a professional development plan for intern -- including training (120 clock hours or equivalent pre-service component in child development and methods of teaching), and ongoing teacher preparation over two years, support and assistance, and annual evaluation.

The intern will be eligible for a preliminary credential with the school district's recommendation and two years of successful teaching.

NUMBER OF CREDIT HOURS TO COMPLETE:

120 clock hours of professional development training and a two-year professional development program (approximately 360 additional clock hours). Special education has an additional 120 clock hour requirement.

WHO EVALUATES: LEA evaluates candidates; state evaluates LEA programs.

LENGTH OF TIME: The Intern Credential is valid for two years of teaching and may be extended.

OTHER: Less than 12 percent of the state's Intern teachers are teaching as district interns.

Of these, about 85 percent are in Los Angeles Unified School District.

Smaller districts often lack the personnel or financial resources to do so. Most smaller school districts have dropped their programs. Three county offices of education have developed consortium programs for 20, 30 and 50 districts in their respective service areas. $38 million has been allocated in the state's budget act for alternative certification (both University and District Intern and Pre-intern programs). More than 8,500 interns (both University and District) are teaching in 730 districts through 80 funded programs. Approximately 20 percent are district interns.

Sacramento County has a program, which involves 30 districts in a teacher preparation consortium. San Joaquin County has a consortium with 50 participating districts and Orange County has a consortium with 20 participating districts.

Large districts with staff development resources can successfully manage the training, support, and evaluation components.

Currently there are 8 District Intern programs with 105 participating districts.

The retention rate of participating District Interns is approximately 91 percent (after 3 years in the classroom).

Interns receive full beginning teacher's salary and benefits.

The total number of District Interns in classrooms in 2000-01 was 1,600.

CALIFORNIA

Class D

TITLE: University Intern Credential

HISTORY: Authorized by legislation in 1967, but issuance of the first such credentials dates back to the early 1950s.

MOTIVATION: In practice, its use is targeted at subject area shortages, although this is not required by law.

GRADE LEVELS AND/OR SUBJECT AREA(S) COVERED:

The state's fastest-growing route, especially in special education, but available for all types of credentials.

WHO OPERATES: IHE and LEA (must be collaborative programs)

REQUIREMENTS TO ENTER:

A bachelor's degree.

A passing score on the CBEST basic skills test.

Subject matter competence demonstrated by completing an approved program of study, or passing appropriate subject area portions of the state-approved subject matter exam.

Knowledge of U.S. Constitution.

The teacher's union for the local school district hiring the intern must sign-off on the application.

PROGRAM DESCRIPTION:

Professional education courses in methods must be completed while the individual is employed as an intern teacher.

The individual must demonstrate subject matter competencies through an approved teacher education program. For elementary teachers, this means competencies in the seven subjects taught in elementary schools; for secondary teachers, this means competency in the subject area to be taught, at the level equivalent to a major. The college may require completion of courses it deems necessary to achieve these competencies.

Admission requirements must take into account the accelerated responsibilities of interns. Applicants should have a high degree of maturity and previous experience with children.

Pre-service training must be provided to ensure a minimum level of knowledge in 10 performance competencies. Programs emphasize blending theory and practice and frequently include professors and experienced teachers on the program's faculty.

The local school district must designate someone to provide support and evaluation for the intern.

NUMBER OF CREDIT HOURS TO COMPLETE:

Coursework as required by the IHE to meet competencies (approximately 36 semester units usually spread over two years).

WHO EVALUATES: Individuals are evaluated by the IHE.

IHE programs are subject to periodic review by the state.

LENGTH OF TIME: The intern may teach two years with the credential, which may be extended.

OTHER: University Internships are offered in elementary, secondary, administrative, pupil personnel, special education and bilingual credential programs. There are more than 180 intern programs available at California colleges and universities.

This program is operated on 21 campuses of the California State University System, 7 campuses of the University of California System, and 28 campuses of independent colleges and universities. A new program operated by the California State University system will provide a program throughout the state using distance learning, internet technology, and on-site support and assessment.

Interns receive full beginning teacher's salary and benefits.

$38 million has been allocated in 2000-01 in the state's budget act for alternative certification. Approximately, 5,400 interns are in university internships.

CALIFORNIA

Class K

TITLE: SB 57: Intern -- Early Completion Option

HISTORY: Legislation passed and signed by the governor in 2001.

MOTIVATION: Provides fast-track options for:

a) Private school teachers who want to become public school teachers;

b) Well-qualified individuals who can demonstrate that pedagogical preparation or supervised field experience is unnecessary for them through passage of the Foundations in Teaching exam.

GRADE LEVELS AND/OR SUBJECT AREA(S) COVERED:

Multiple and Single Subject (K-12) teachers, all content areas.

WHO OPERATES: California Commission on Teacher Credentialing, in cooperation with internships and school districts.

REQUIREMENTS TO ENTER:

Early Completion Internship

1. Baccalaureate degree

2. Subject matter content proficiency (exam or coursework)

3. Character fitness (fingerprints)

4. Written assessment of teaching knowledge and subject matter pedagogy in the areas of:

   a. Special needs students and learning differences

   b. English learners

   c. Classroom management

   d. Subject matter pedagogy

   e. Assessment of pupil progress

PROGRAM DESCRIPTION:

Individuals who complete the prerequisites -- including the Foundations in Teaching exam -- may enter the Early Completion Option if they are offered a teaching position and are accepted into the internship program.

Once admitted into the Early Completion Internship Option, a candidate completes the California Teaching Performance Assessment or other authorized assessment of classroom performance. The candidate's performance is demonstrated with his or her students in the classroom. If the candidate passes all sections or elements of the performance assessment and other district requirements, he or she is eligible for a preliminary credential.

If the candidate does not pass all sections of the performance assessment, he or she continues in the intern program and receives an individualized program of study, based on the assessment results and any district or intern program requirements. Early Completion Option interns, as well as all interns, must pass the Teaching Performance Assessment at the end of the internship to be recommended for a preliminary credential. Candidates for a multiple-subject credential must also pass the Reading Instruction Competency Assessment for credential recommendation.

NUMBER OF CREDIT HOURS TO COMPLETE:

No set number of credit hours. Completion is determined by the candidate successfully passing the exam and assessment.

WHO EVALUATES: California Commission on Teacher Credentialing and participating internship program and districts.

LENGTH OF TIME: No time limit, but could be completed in as little as one semester.

OTHER: In addition to the Early Completion Option, the statute also allows private school teachers to achieve California credentials, and has an option for challenging the induction portion of teacher preparation.

The private school option allows teachers with six years of full-time teaching experience in a regionally accredited private school and two years of rigorous performance evaluations to seek a preliminary credential. The evaluations must address the effectiveness areas in the California Standards for Teacher Profession.

Private school teachers with three years of successful teaching and two years of successful evaluations under the same conditions as above may waive teacher preparation fieldwork.

Private school applicants also must demonstrate knowledge of basic skills, reading, the U.S. Constitution, and subject matter, and have fingerprint clearance.

The statute also requires development of a fast track method to complete the formative assessment of teaching performance portion of the professional clear teaching credential.

TITLE: Pre-Internship Teaching Certificate

HISTORY: Instituted in 1998.

MOTIVATION: Under-trained teachers.

GRADE LEVELS AND/OR SUBJECT AREA(S) COVERED:

All grades, all subjects.

WHO OPERATES: LEA.

REQUIREMENTS TO ENTER:

A bachelor's degree.

Successfully complete the CBEST basic skills test.

Have completed specified number of subject matter units in the areas assigned to teach.

No eligibility or participation in an internship or other teacher preparation program.

PROGRAM DESCRIPTION:

The employing agency must provide:

Subject matter advising and preparation in collaboration with a college or university.

Preliminary teacher preparation when an individual obtains a Pre-Intern Certificate as prescribed by an approved pre-internship program. Pre-service or early service preparation should include a minimum of 40 hours of instruction in: (a) classroom management; (b) instructional strategies; and (c) student discipline. Subsequent preparation shall continue throughout the year.

Regular support for each pre-intern through a permanently employed experienced educator or a certificated retiree of a

California school district or county office of education throughout the school year.

The pre-intern must:

Take the required subject matter competence examination(s) for their subject area at least once during each certificate issue.

Participate in the employer's approved program.

WHO EVALUATES: LEA.

LENGTH OF TIME: Valid for one year. May be renewed for a second year if the school district verifies that the individual is participating in the pre-internship program designed to prepare the individual to become a fully credentialed teacher and continues to need assistance in meeting prerequisites for entry into an internship program. Certificates are restricted to the employing school district.

OTHER: **The legislation for the Pre-Internship Program would eventually eliminate emergency permits and replace them with Pre-Internship Certificates. Until the transition is complete, emergency permits will continue to be available to qualified individuals.**

Only multiple subject (elementary) pre-internships were offered in the first year. The program has since expanded to serve single subject (secondary) and special education teachers.

$11.8 million was allocated for pre-internship programs in 2001-02, with additional funding potentially available through internship program funding. More than 8,200 pre-interns were supported and prepared with these funds.

The programs are sponsored by county offices of education and school districts, in collaboration with colleges and universities.

TITLE: Emergency Teaching Permit

HISTORY: Available for more than 50 years.

MOTIVATION: Shortage

GRADE LEVELS AND/OR SUBJECT AREA(S) COVERED: All

WHO OPERATES: LEA

REQUIREMENTS TO ENTER:

A bachelor's degree.

Successfully complete the CBEST basic skills test.

Have completed specified number of subject matter units in the areas assigned to teach and have passed assessment administered by the district.

A request from the local school district, with approval of local school board, that declares it has been unable to find a fully credentialed teacher to fill the vacancy.

A teachers' union may agree or disagree with the school district's justification.

The school district must first consider other alternative certification routes (such as district or university internships or pre-intern programs), and must show cause why those routes have not been used.

PROGRAM DESCRIPTION:

The individual must:

Attend an orientation to curriculum and to techniques of instruction and classroom management;

Take six semester units toward a credential preparation to renew emergency.

The individual will be eligible for a credential with completion of the teacher preparation program.

The state legislature expressed its preference for the use of internships over the emergency route, but emergency permits continue to be used in great numbers, especially in special education and, due to initiative that reduced K-3 classes to a 20:1 ratio and in mathematics and English in secondary schools.

Currently, the state issues three types of Emergency Teaching Permits:

Long-term -- the vast majority fall into this group; renewed annually for individuals who complete required coursework toward a full credential;

Limited assignments available only to credentialed teachers to allow them to teach in a subject area not authorized by their credential. Renewed annually for teachers who make progress toward adding an authorization in the new subject area.

30-day -- for substitutes -- authorizes substituting for one year, but for a maximum of 30 days for any particular teacher. Renewal requires only application and fee.

One-year, non-renewable -- Available only to individuals who are certified to teach in another state and who have not had an opportunity to pass the CBEST. Upon passing the CBEST, teachers credentialed in other states obtain a preliminary teaching credential. These teachers are evaluated individually to identify any California requirements for which comparable requirements were not met in previous preparation activities.

NO. OF CREDIT HOURS TO COMPLETE:

6 semester units per year to qualify for renewal.

WHO EVALUATES: LEA

LENGTH OF TIME: Valid for one year. May be renewed if the school district verifies that the individual is participating in on-going training or seminars designed to prepare the individual to become a fully credentialed teacher, and has completed 6 semester units toward teacher preparation course requirements.

OTHER: Emergency permit usage has been reduced by eight percent in each of the last two years.

CALIFORNIA Class H

TITLE: Eminence Credential

HISTORY: First available in the early 1950s.

MOTIVATION: To enable a local school district to employ an individual from another profession who possesses unique abilities.

GRADE LEVELS AND/OR SUBJECT AREA(S) COVERED: All

WHO OPERATES: LEA

REQUIREMENTS TO ENTER:

The local school district must nominate the individual for a specific teaching assignment.

PROGRAM DESCRIPTION:

The individual must pass the CBEST basic skills test during the first year of teaching.

The individual is eligible for a clear credential upon completion of five years of successful teaching.

NUMBER OF CREDIT HOURS TO COMPLETE: Not applicable.

WHO EVALUATES: LEA

LENGTH OF TIME: The credential is valid for two years and may be renewed one time for a three-year period.

After five years of successful service, the individual is eligible to apply for a professional clear teaching credential.

OTHER: Fewer than 5 such credentials are issued each year. During the 2000-01 school year, only three Eminence Credentials were issued, compared to 25,000 other first-time teaching credentials issued.

TITLE: Sojourn Credential

HISTORY: Available for at least 20 years.

MOTIVATION: Currently used to provide native speakers of Spanish to teach secondary Spanish courses or bilingual classes.

GRADE LEVELS AND/OR SUBJECT AREA(S) COVERED:

Currently, Spanish and bilingual.

WHO OPERATES: LEA

REQUIREMENTS TO ENTER:

LEA must nominate the individual.

PROGRAM DESCRIPTION:

The individual is allowed to teach without having earned a bachelor's degree -- the only such program still in effect in California.

The individual must have completed 90 semester units of college study.

Holders of this credential are currently used to teach high school Spanish and bilingual classes.

The individual must pass the CBEST basic skills tests within the first year, in order to qualify for renewal.

The credential may be renewed if the individual completes an additional 6 semester units of coursework each year toward completion of an approved college teacher education program and a bachelor's degree (if the individual has no degree).

NUMBER OF CREDIT HOURS TO COMPLETE:

6 semester units per year toward completion of an approved teacher education program and bachelor's degree.

WHO EVALUATES: LEA

LENGTH OF TIME: One year; renewable if the individual passes the CBEST and completes 6 semester units of coursework in an approved teacher education program.

OTHER: A state official said these individuals are largely recruited in Spain and Mexico, many teach for one year, do not complete the basic skills test or the required college coursework, and return to their home countries.

CALIFORNIA

Number of Teaching Licenses Issued

	2000-01	1999-00	1998-99	1996-97	1995-96	1994-95	1993-94	1992-93	1991-92	1990-91
Persons who completed an approved college teacher preparation program		20,055	19,451	19,200	16,718	15,155	12,130	15,873	a/ 16,191	a/ 18,000
Alternative Routes										
Internship program -- District Enrolled	1,603	1,693	1,745	1,322	1,053	691	720	379	558	588
Graduated from program	805	791	731	409	390	345	240	221	279	331
Internship program -- Univ. Enrolled	5,462	3,134	2,828	2,449	1,218	758	b/ 1,849	1,310	1,272	704
Have achieved a teaching credential	3,650	1,712	1,311	785	620	390	c/ 961	918	d/ 909	631
Other -- Eminence Credential	3	3	2	3	2	0	0	0	1	1
Sojourn Credential	18	44	96	53	30	37	55	48	67	64
Exchange	16	13	25	21	18	18	25	30	34	
Emergency Teaching Permits	32,573	30,607	28,617	13,230	9,678	4,950	e/ 4,586	2,751	3,125	3,100
Pre-Internship Teaching Certificate	8,092	3,185	955							

Number of Teachers Employed

	2000-01	1999-00	1998-99	1997-98	1995-96	1992-93	1991-92	1990-91	1989-90	1988-89
Total Teachers Employed in the State	301,361	292,055	284,030	250,527	232,559	220,000	220,000	210,000	N/A	198,521
Newly Hired Teachers in Each Year	24,824	23,260	24,849	20,442	15,000	10-15,000	16-20,000	20,000	N/A	N/A

a/ Figures include all types of first-time credentials issued.

b/ Includes 471 in Special Education.

c/ Includes 278 in Special Education.

d/ Includes 289 in Special Education.

e/ Emergency Teaching Permit total includes only new long-term permits, not 30-day permits for substitutes or one-year non-renewable permits. The one-year permits are issued to persons certified to teach in another state. They have two years to successfully complete California's basic skills test and pass the Praxia or obtain certification from an IHE that they have achieved equivalency in subject matter competency.

Commission on Teacher Credentialing
1900 Capitol Avenue
Sacramento, CA 95814-4213
Attn: Michael McKibbin
(916) 445-4438
e-mail: mmckibbin@ctc.ca.gov
Web site: http://www.cde.ca.gov

CALIFORNIA

Institutions of higher education that have developed alternative teacher preparation programs leading to a teaching license:

Alliant University
Azusa Pacific University
Concordia University
California Lutheran University
California Polytechnic State Univ., San Luis Obispo
Cal State Teach (CSU Systemwide)
California State Polytechnic Univ., Pomona
California State University, Bakersfield
California State University, Chico
California State University, Dominguez Hills
California State University, Fresno
California State University, Fullerton
California State University, Hayward
California State University, Long Beach
California State University, Los Angeles
California State University, Northridge
California State University, Sacramento
California State University, San Bernardino
California State University, San Marcos
Chapman College-Orange
Claremont Graduate School
College of Notre Dame
Fresno Pacific College
John F. Kennedy University
Loyola Marymount University
La Sierra University
Mills College
National University
Pepperdine University-Malibu
Point Loma Nazarine College
San Diego State University
San Francisco State University
San Jose State University
Santa Clara University
Sonoma State University

University of California, Berkeley
University of California, Davis
University of California, Irvine
University of California, Los Angeles
University of California, Riverside
University of California, San Diego
University of California, Santa Barbara
University of LaVerne
University of Redlands
University of San Francisco
University of the Pacific
Whittier College

School-District Based Alternative Programs

Project Pipeline
San Joaquin County Office of Education
Compton School District
Los Angeles Unified School district
Long Beach Unified School District
Orange County Office of Education
Ontario Montclair Unified School district
San Diego Unified School district

CALIFORNIA

Institutions of higher education that have *any* teacher preparation programs leading to a license to teach.

Antioch University of Southern California
Azusa Pacific University
Bethany Bible College
Biola University
California Baptist College
California Lutheran College
California Polytechnic State Univ., San Luis Obispo
California State Polytechnic Univ., Pomona
Cal State Teach
California State University, Bakersfield
California State University, Chico
California State University, Dominguez Hills
California State University, Fresno
California State University, Fullerton
California State University, Hayward
California State University, Long Beach
California State University, Los Angeles
California State University, Monterey Bay
California State University, Northridge
California State University, Sacramento
California State University, San Bernardino
California State University, San Marcos
California State University, Stanislaus
Chapman College-Fort Ord
Chapman College-Orange
Christian Heritage College
City University, Los Angeles
Claremont Graduate School
College of Notre Dame
Concordia University
Dominican College of San Rafael
Fresno Pacific College
Holy Names College
Humboldt State University
John F. Kennedy University
La Sierra University

Loma Linda University
Loyola Marymount University
Masters College
Mills College
Mount St. Mary's College
National Hispanic University

National University
New College of California
Nova Southeastern University

Occidental College
Pacific Christian College
Pacific Oaks College
Pacific Union College

Patten College
Pepperdine University

Point Loma Nazarine College
Saint Mary's College
San Diego State University-Imperial Valley
San Diego State University-San Diego
San Francisco State University
San Jose State University
Santa Clara University
Simpson College
Sonoma State University
Southern California College
Stanford University
United States International University
University of California, Berkeley

University of California, Davis
University of California, Irvine
University of California, Los Angeles
University of California, Riverside
University of California, San Diego
University of California, Santa Barbara
University of California, Santa Cruz
University of LaVerne
University of Phoenix
University of Redlands
University of San Diego
University of San Francisco
University of Southern California
University of the Pacific
Westmont College
Whittier College

Contact information for persons interested in obtaining information on Teacher Preparation Programs in the state:

Michael McKibbin, California Commission on Teacher Credentialing, 1900 Capitol Avenue, Sacramento, CA 95814-4213, Phone: (916) 445-4438

TITLE: Teacher in Residence

HISTORY: The program was created in legislation in 1999 (SB 99-154).

MOTIVATION: The program was created to address teacher shortages and school districts' inability to find qualified and fully-licensed individuals for teaching positions. The legislation recognized that school districts have increased the use of emergency authorizations to employ individuals who do not have licenses and may not have received any former teacher preparation. The new policy further recognized that persons with experience in areas other than teaching can help alleviate teacher shortages faced by many school districts, provided these persons receive adequate supervision and education in teaching.

GRADE LEVELS AND/OR SUBJECT AREA(S) COVERED:

All elementary and secondary teaching areas for which the State Board of Education has established teacher standards.

WHO OPERATES: Programs are the primary responsibility of school districts or Board of Cooperative Education Services (BOCES), but must be planned and operated with an institution of higher education that has an approved teacher education program..

REQUIREMENTS TO ENTER:

Candidates interested in employment as an alternative teacher must:

Hold a bachelor's degree from a regionally accredited college or university.

Have completed the necessary subject knowledge required for teaching in the endorsement/content area (30 semester hours in the content area).

Pass a background check conducted by the employing school district including fingerprinting.

PROGRAM DESCRIPTION:

School districts that choose to implement a teacher in residence program may do so without obtaining prior approval from the State Board of Education. However, the district must submit a proposal for approval by the Board during the first year of implementation. If the Board approves the proposal, the district may continue the program for the second year.

School districts may employ a teacher in residence without consulting the Department of Education.

Within 30 days of employment, the district must report the hiring of a teacher in residence to the Department.

Teachers in residence serve as non-licensed teachers for two years.

Districts are required to collaborate with an approved teacher education institution in the design and delivery of a teacher education program based on performance-based standards adopted by the State Board of Education. These performance-based teacher education standards are the same standards used in the preparation of teachers in collegiate teacher education programs.

Teachers in residence must have an assigned teacher mentor and supervisor.

Candidates must be observed and supervised for a minimum of 100 hours each year for the duration of the two-year program.

Candidates must also pass the state's adopted content (endorsement) test prior to April 15 of the first year of employment or be discontinued from the program at the end of the first year.

NUMBER OF CREDIT HOURS TO COMPLETE:

Credit hours or clock hours of training are not specified. Candidates must complete the teacher education program provided by the school district and/or institution of higher education. The program is performance based and districts must continually assess each teacher in residence's progress in meeting performance-based standards.

WHO EVALUATES: The local school district makes the recommendation for licensure in consultation with the cooperating institution of higher education upon completion of the program.

LENGTH OF TIME: Two years.

OTHER: During the 2000-01 school year, 208 teachers in residence were enrolled in the first year of the two-year program.

During the 2002-03 school year, 264 teachers in residence were enrolled in the first year of the program and 251 in the second year. Participants for the 2002-03 school year totaled 515.

TITLE: Alternative Teacher Program

HISTORY: Began Sept. 1, 1991.

MOTIVATION: Programs are intended to attract talented individuals into public education who are recent liberal arts graduates, non-public school teachers, college professors, successful individuals seeking career changes, and minorities.

GRADE LEVELS AND/OR SUBJECT AREA(S) COVERED:

Available in endorsement areas which require completion of undergraduate level programs. Does not include special education, special services or administration/principal endorsements.

WHO OPERATES: School districts, independent schools, boards of cooperative educational services (BOCES), and/or institutions of higher education.

REQUIREMENTS TO ENTER:

Candidates interested in employment as an alternative teacher must:

Hold a bachelor's degree from a regionally accredited institution.

Pass the state's required assessments in the content (endorsement) area.

Demonstrate subject matter knowledge necessary for teaching in an endorsement area through transcript review (30 semester hours), standardized assessment, or portfolio review.

Pass a background/security check.

Agree to participate in an alternative teacher program.

COLORADO — Class A

PROGRAM DESCRIPTION:

Approved alternative teacher program sites provide a one-year program of teaching, training, and supervision for the alternative teacher. The program includes: 225 clock hours of professional education, based on performance-based standards adopted by the State Board of Education. These performance-based teacher education standards are the same standards used in preparation of teachers in collegiate teacher education programs.

Training may be modified by the support team, based on assessment of the alternative teacher's knowledge, skills, and ability.

Supervision and guidance by members of a support team, including a mentor teacher, principal, and representative of a higher education institution.

Performance evaluations conducted consistent with the district's adopted evaluation system.

After successfully completing an approved alternative teacher program, the candidate is recommended by the approved agency for a Colorado Provisional Teaching License.

NUMBER OF CREDIT HOURS TO COMPLETE:

225 clock hours of professional education (unless modified).

WHO EVALUATES: Evaluation for eligibility to participate in the program is done by the Colorado Department of Education; evaluation for employment is conducted by a designated agency.

LENGTH OF TIME: One year.

COLORADO

Number of Teaching Licenses Issued

	2002-03	2001-02	2000-01	1999-00	1998-99	1997-98	1996-97	1995-96	1994-95	1993-94	1992-93
Persons who completed an approved Colorado college teacher preparation program				2,336	2,991	N/A	N/A	2,205	2,258	2,686	2,389
Emergency				937	809	1,175	714	343	626	429	424
Temporary				1,196	2,500	2,336	2,219	2,996	883	400	407
Alternative Route	475	359	268	236	187	88	60	48	65	44	41

Number of Teachers Employed

	1999-00	1998-99	1997-98	1996-97	1995-96	1994-95	1993-94	1992-93	1991-92	1990-91	1989-90
Total Teachers Employed in the State	42,000*	39,439	37,840	36,398	35,388	34,571	33,661	33,419	33,093	32,341	31954
Newly Hired Teachers in Each Year	2,700*	2,535	2,315	1,832	1,611	3,063	2,619	N/A	N/A	N/A	N/A

** Approximate Numbers*

Colorado Dept. of Education
Office of Professional Services and Educator Licensing
201 E. Colfax, Room 105
Denver, CO 80203
Attn: Dorothy Gotlieb
(303) 866-6932

COLORADO

Institutions of higher education that have developed alternative teacher preparation programs leading to a teaching license:

States with which the state has reciprocity of teacher licenses:

NASDTEC Interstate Contract.

Institutions of higher education that have *any* teacher preparation programs leading to a license to teach.

Adams State College
Colorado Christian University
Colorado College
Colorado State University
Fort Lewis College
Mesa State College
Metropolitan State College
Regis University
University of Colorado-Boulder
University of Colorado-Colorado Springs
University of Colorado-Denver
University of Denver
University of Northern Colorado
University of Southern Colorado
Western State College

Contact information for persons interested in finding a teaching position in the state:

Positions are handled through each local school district

CONNECTICUT Class A

TITLE: Alternate Route to Teacher Certification

HISTORY: Created in 1986 as part of the Connecticut Education Enhancement Act. The first class (106 candidates) began the program June 20, 1988.

MOTIVATION: The state describes it as: "An innovative and exciting program to attract talented individuals from fields outside of education into teaching. . . . The program is intended for professionals from diverse fields such as industry, government, and the military or human services that wish to change careers. Individuals who have substituted, who have taught part-time, or who have experience as teachers in independent schools are also encouraged to apply."

SUBJECT AREAS/GRADE LEVELS COVERED:

Middle school grades 4 - 8 to prepare candidates to teach in middle schools in specific subjects. A teacher endorsed in middle grades will only be able to teach in the subjects endorsed on the certificate.

Secondary grades 7 - 12 to teach specific subject areas. The subject areas include English, history/social studies, mathematics, and sciences (biology, chemistry, earth science, physics, and general science).

Pre-K-12 certification to teach art, music, world languages, bilingual education, family and consumer science, and technology education.

WHO OPERATES: The Connecticut Department of Higher Education conducts two Alternate Route to certification programs. Monitoring during the first two years of teaching is under the auspices of the Connecticut Department of Education.

REQUIREMENTS TO ENTER:

Minimum of a bachelor's degree from an accredited institution with a major in or closely related to, the intended teaching field. Prospective middle school teachers, secondary school teachers and special area (art and music) teachers must have the subject-area semester hours required for certification.

A minimum grade point average of "B" (3.00 on a 4.00 scale) in undergraduate studies or the same average in at least 24 semester hours of graduate study.

A passing score on Praxis I (PPST) or a passing score on an approved substitute exam.

A passing score on a subject area test, Praxis II or ACTEL.

Experience in an educational environment with children of the age group the individual wishes to teach.

PROGRAM DESCRIPTION:

The Summer Alternate Route to Certification Program is an intensive eight-week summer term of full-time study. A three-week student teaching experience in a summer school setting is included in the eight-week program. The faculty consists of Connecticut public school teachers, teacher-educators from the state's public and private higher education institutions, and professionals from diverse public and non-public agencies. The curriculum is innovative and interdisciplinary, based on the Connecticut Teaching Competencies and utilizing teaching methods of demonstrated effectiveness.

The other Alternate Route to Certification Program is a weekend program which runs from October to May, and includes four weeks of student teaching. This program focuses on shortage areas: bilingual education, mathematics, science, world languages, family and consumer science, and technology education.

Employed Alternate Route teachers participate in the Beginning Educators Support and Training (BEST) Program of the State Department of Education. BEST includes a mentoring component and subject specific portfolio assessment.

Additionally, employing school districts must provide Alternate Route teachers with a special plan of supervision that may exceed that provided to other novice teachers.

NUMBER OF CREDIT HOURS TO COMPLETE:

The Alternate Route is a non-credit program.

WHO EVALUATES:	State Department of Higher Education screens for eligibility and admission to the program. Admissions are competitive. Final decisions are made in conjunction with review of certification eligibility by the State Department of Education. Continued state certification of applicants is determined based upon their successful completion of the state's induction program. The Alternate Route to Certification Program (ARC) is evaluated on a five-year cycle, as are all teacher preparation programs in the state. Program approval is granted by the State Board of Education for a specified period of time.
LENGTH OF TIME:	ARC I: Summer sessions: 8 weeks. ARC II: Weekends October - May.

CONNECTICUT **Class E**

TITLE: Post Baccalaureate Certification

HISTORY:

MOTIVATION: Students with a bachelor's degree may apply to a college or university and, upon acceptance, take the courses designed to meet certification or program requirements. Many institutions combine the certification/program courses with a master's degree.

SUBJECT AREAS/GRADE LEVELS COVERED:

Early childhood, elementary, middle grades areas, secondary academic areas, art, music, physical education, technology education, and special education.

WHO OPERATES: The following Institutions of Higher Education in the state:

Central Connecticut State University
Connecticut College
Eastern Connecticut State University
Fairfield University
Quinnipiac University
Sacred Heart University
Saint Joseph College
Southern Connecticut State University
University of Bridgeport
University of Connecticut
University of Hartford
University of New Haven
Yale University

REQUIREMENTS TO ENTER:

Bachelor's degree from an accredited institution.

B-grade point average.

Subject area major as required by Connecticut regulations.

Passing score on Praxis I PPST, or a passing score on an approved substitute exam.

CONNECTICUT Class E

PROGRAM DESCRIPTION:

Students complete a post baccalaureate level planned program, which includes, at a minimum, professional education courses in: foundations of education, educational psychology, curriculum and methods of teaching, student teaching, and special education.

NUMBER OF CREDIT HOURS TO COMPLETE:

The number of credits required to complete these post baccalaureate programs varies, depending upon whether or not the higher education institution requires that a master's degree also is completed.

WHO EVALUATES: All post baccalaureate planned programs have been approved by the Connecticut State Board of Education.

LENGTH OF TIME: The length of time required to complete these programs varies, depending upon whether or not the higher education institution requires that a master's degree also is completed.

CONNECTICUT

Class G

TITLE: Cross Endorsement

HISTORY:

MOTIVATION: Teachers who have Connecticut certification may become certified in another endorsement area by taking the required cross endorsement courses and achieving a passing score on the required Praxis II or ACTFL assessment. Individual courses may be taken at any higher education institution. Connecticut State Department of Education certification consultants review transcripts, to ensure that required courses have been taken.

SUBJECT AREAS/GRADE LEVELS COVERED:

Early childhood (requires completion of a planned program)
Elementary
Middle grades academic areas
Secondary academic areas
Art
Music
Physical education
Technology education
Special education
Health
Bilingual education
Teaching English as a second language
Remedial reading and remedial language arts (require completion of a planned program)
School library media specialist

WHO OPERATES: The following IHEs in the state:

Central Connecticut State University
Connecticut College
Eastern Connecticut State University
Fairfield University
Mitchell College
Quinnipiac University
Sacred Heart University
Saint Joseph College
Southern Connecticut State University
University of Bridgeport
University of Connecticut
University of Hartford
University of New Haven
Western Connecticut State University
Yale University

CONNECTICUT — Class G

REQUIREMENTS TO ENTER:

Connecticut certification.

Relevant academic or subject area major.

PROGRAM DESCRIPTION:

Students complete the required courses for a cross endorsement. The courses may be taken at any of the higher education institutions in the state, which offer them.

NUMBER OF CREDIT HOURS TO COMPLETE:

The number of credits required to complete cross endorsement requirements varies, depending on the specific endorsement area.

WHO EVALUATES: The college/university transcript(s) are evaluated by certification consultants in the Bureau of Certification and professional development.

LENGTH OF TIME: The length of time required to complete these programs varies, depending upon the number of credits required, and how many courses a student wishes to take at one time.

CONNECTICUT

Number of Teaching Licenses Issued

	2001-02	2000-01	1999-00	1998-99	1997-98	1996-97	1995-96	1994-95	1993-94	1992-93	1991-92
Persons who completed an approved college teacher preparation program	N/A	N/A	N/A	N/A	N/A	N/A	N/A	N/A	N/A	N/A	a/ 817
Initial certificates issued b/	7,184	5,502	7,912	6,459	4,169	7,467	6,975	3,981	3,981	N/A	N/A
TOTAL CERTIFICATES ISSUED c/	23,180	17,798	22,947	19,660	14,376	17,012	15,640	14,745	14,578	N/A	12,428
Emergency	N/A	N/A	N/A	N/A	N/A	N/A	N/A	N/A	N/A	N/A	32
Temporary	N/A	N/A	N/A	38	N/A	54	42	N/A	N/A	N/A	N/A
Alternative Route d/	213	199	219	159	N/A	108	90	70	N/A	59	38

Number of Teachers Employed

	2001-02	2000-01	99-2000	1998-99	1997-98	1996-97	1995-96	1994-95	1993-94	1992-93	1991-92
Total Teachers Employed in the State e/	45307	50,261	47,800	46,478	45,326	47,307	43,261	42,457	41,324	41,197	41,733
Newly Hired Teachers in Each Year f/	3,836	4,486	4,526	3,771	3,364	3,542	2,687	3,141	2,200	2,384	1,526

a/ Persons who received bachelor's degrees from Connecticut IHEs in all education fields. In addition, about 3,000 received master's degrees in all education fields annually. For persons earning degrees in various education specialties, such as mathematics, it is not possible to determine which graduates were preparing to teach in grades K-12.
b/ Numbers include teachers and a small number of administrators from out of state.
c/ In 1989, Connecticut also issued 35,000 new Professional Educator Certificates -- all holders of old standard and permanent certificates were required to apply for the new credential.
d/ Approximately 100 candidates complete the program each summer. The figures show the numbers which were issued certificates.
e/ The count includes full-time and part-time teachers and administrators in public schools.
f/ Numbers include full-time and part-time teachers and administrators who were not employed in Connecticut in the previous year. The percentage of returning experienced teachers has ranged from 56.8% in 1991 to 28.4% in 1999.

Connecticut Bureau of Certification
and Professional Development
P.O. Box 150471
Hartford, CT 06115-0471
Attn: Peter Behuniak, Acting Chief
(860) 713-6708
e-mail: teacher.cert@po.state.ct.us

CONNECTICUT

Institutions of higher education that have developed alternative teacher preparation programs leading to a teaching license:

See "Post baccalaureate certification" program.

States with which the state has reciprocity of teacher licenses:

NASDTEC Interstate Contract.

Institutions of higher education that have *any* teacher preparation programs leading to a license to teach.

Central Connecticut State University
Connecticut College
Eastern Connecticut State University
Fairfield University
Mitchell College
Quinnipiac University
Sacred Heart College
Saint Joseph College
Southern Connecticut State University
University of Bridgeport
University of Connecticut
University of Hartford
University of New Haven
Western Connecticut State University
Yale University

Contact information for persons interested in finding a teaching position in the state:

Connecticut Bureau of Certification
& Professional Development
P.O. Box 150471
Hartford, CT 06115-0471
Attn: Peter Behuniak, Acting Chief
Phone: (860) 713-6708

DELAWARE

Class B

TITLE: Delaware Alternative Route To Certification/Secondary Education

HISTORY: Program developed by Alternative Routes to Certification Consortium under the direction of the Delaware Professional Standards Council, 1995-96. Legislation was approved in 1996. Program was approved by the State Board of Education to operate in 1997.

MOTIVATION: The program developed out of the Professional Standards Council's "Educational Plan for Certification and Career Development." The desire was to develop a less traditional route (that meets the same standards as traditional routes) for talented individuals to enter the teaching profession more quickly while being trained as teachers.

GRADE LEVELS AND/OR SUBJECT AREA(S) COVERED:

Secondary content areas.

WHO OPERATES: A Consortium with members representing the Professional Standards Council, the Department of Education, Chief School Officers, the University of Delaware, Delaware State University, the General Assembly, and other stakeholders. A Program Coordinator is housed at the University of Delaware. An Associate Coordinator is housed at Delaware State University.

REQUIREMENTS TO ENTER:

A Bachelor's Degree or equivalent from an accredited college with a major in the field to be taught/certified.

Passing scores on the state's basic skills tests and, when approved by the State Board of Education, on subject matter tests in the field(s) of specialization.

Satisfactory health and criminal background checks.

Employment by a Delaware public school district or charter school in a position that requires instructional certification in a secondary content area.

As of 2001, candidates must be employed in a subject area designated by the state as "critical needs" because of a shortage of certified teachers.

DELAWARE — Class B

PROGRAM DESCRIPTION:

The program is offered in three interrelated but distinct components which include the following:

A **summer institute** which includes approximately 120 instructional clock hours prior to the beginning of the teaching assignment. The institute covers instructional strategies; assessment; classroom and behavior management; and adolescent development. School districts provide an orientation to the employing school/school district's policies, organization, and curriculum.

The first year of teaching is a full-time **practicum experience** requiring intensive on-the-job coaching by a trained mentor and supervision by a school administrator.

During the school year, candidates participate in approximately 120 instructional clock hours of **seminars on teaching** which provide additional skills needed by the teacher. These seminars include the areas of cultural diversity, teaching reading in the content areas, methods of teaching (content specific) and teaching exceptional students.

Learning experiences for the candidates are "co-taught" by university faculty and by practitioners experienced in teaching the content areas covered by the program.

NUMBER OF CREDIT HOURS TO COMPLETE:

Candidates take the equivalent of 15 credit hours of professional education coursework, designed to be completed within one calendar year. Candidates who need additional courses in their subject area may take longer to complete certification requirements. The specific amount of mentoring and supervision "hours" during the practicum experience are not prescribed.

WHO EVALUATES: Delaware Department of Education.

LENGTH OF TIME: One year.

DELAWARE

Class E

TITLE: Special Institute for Teacher Certification

HISTORY: Legislation approved in 1986.

MOTIVATION: The program was originally initiated in anticipation of projected teacher shortages, to recruit and support individuals seeking certification in areas identified as "critical needs.".

GRADE LEVELS AND/OR SUBJECT AREA(S) COVERED:

All areas identified by the state as "critical needs." These have included technology education, mathematics, science, foreign languages, business agriculture, English, library/media specialists and special education.

WHO OPERATES: Governed by the State Board of Education which makes the rules and regulations for the program, and the University of Delaware which administers the Institute.

REQUIREMENTS TO ENTER:

A bachelor's degree in a "critical needs" subject area and passing scores on Praxis I.

PROGRAM DESCRIPTION:

The state reimburses the tuition costs of participants taking courses required for teacher certification.

NUMBER OF CREDIT HOURS TO COMPLETE:

Depends on transcript analysis completed by the Department of Education Office of Professional Standards and Certification.

WHO EVALUATES: Delaware Department of Education.

LENGTH OF TIME: Varies according to number of credits needed for certification.

TITLE: Alternative Program -- Master's in Primary/K-4 or Middle Level/5-8 Education

HISTORY: Began in 1992.

MOTIVATION: Developed for individuals with bachelor's degrees who will meet content prerequisites for entry and complete a 36 semester hour master's degree program in Primary/K-4 or Middle Level/5-8 Education -- state developed and approved.

GRADE LEVELS AND/OR SUBJECT AREA(S) COVERED:

Primary/K-4 or Middle Level/5-8.

WHO OPERATES: IHE (Wilmington College); developed in conjunction with and with approval of SEA.

REQUIREMENTS TO ENTER:

This program is designed for candidates who already have a bachelor's degree in any field, who come from non-education backgrounds, and have an interest in primary or middle-level age children.

PROGRAM DESCRIPTION:

The program offers an accelerated means to earn both a master's degree and state teacher certification in two years. The individual must complete:

36 semester hours of courses, given during evening hours over about 18 months to accommodate those who hold a job while training.

12-15-weeks of student teaching. Candidates who have jobs must be available full-time during daytime hours to complete this requirement.

Additional coursework the summer after student teaching.

A three-week intensive research project.

There is an Internship requirement in order to complete the program for automatic State of Delaware certification.

NUMBER OF CREDIT HOURS TO COMPLETE:

36 semester hours.

WHO EVALUATES: IHE.

LENGTH OF TIME: Approximately two years.

TITLE: Master's in Secondary Education with Initial Certification

HISTORY: Established in 1996 at the request of the Delaware Department of Education. Number served to date: 13; 100 percent employment.

MOTIVATION: Designed to provide individuals who holds a bachelor's degree from a regionally-accredited college or university with the professional education courses necessary to become certified in an approved content area.

GRADE LEVELS AND/OR SUBJECT AREA(S) COVERED:

Grade levels: 7-12.

Subjects: Reading, English/Language Arts, Science, Mathematics, Social Studies.

WHO OPERATES: IHE; developed in conjunction with and with approval of the Delaware Department of Education.

REQUIREMENTS TO ENTER:

A bachelor's degree from a regionally-accredited IHE.

Overall undergraduate GPA of 2.75.

Content area GPA of 3.0.

Submission of scores for the Graduate Record Examination (GRE), and scores from one subject test in the teaching field.

Completed written application which includes a statement of professional goals.

One-page resume.

Two letters of recommendation, one of which must be from a college instructor in their major discipline.in an approved content area.

All supporting documentation must be received by July 30 of each year. No coursework may be taken in this degree program until formal acceptance into the program.

DELAWARE Class E

PROGRAM DESCRIPTION:

Candidates complete graduate university coursework, including: theories of learning; classroom management; models of curriculum and instruction design; and a student teaching experience.

NUMBER OF CREDIT HOURS TO COMPLETE:

30 graduate credits.

WHO EVALUATES: IHE.

LENGTH OF TIME: Full-time study: program can be completed in one year. Part-time: two years.

DELAWARE

Number of Teaching Licenses Issued

	1999-00	1998-99	1997-98	1996-97	1995-96	1994-95	1992-93	1991-92	1990-91
Persons who completed an approved college teacher preparation program	N/A	N/A	N/A	N/A	N/A	N/A	N/A	753	N/A
New elementary/secondary certificates a/	2,124	1,252	2,549	1,826	1,234	1,572	N/A	3,021	560
Internship program			1			4	N/A	8	
Emergency b/							2		
Temporary	198	161	177	54	129	56	N/A	69	
Limited Standard c/	768	582	645	246	330	303	N/A	913	
Provisional d/						e/	0	28	
Alternative Route f/ (Special Institute for Teacher Certification at the University of Delaware)			29	------	------	--- 204	since	1986 --	------
Other									

Number of Teachers Employed

	1999-00	198-99	1997-98	1996-97	1995-96	1994-95	1992-93	1991-92	1990-91
Total Teachers Employed in the State	7,311	7,023	6,849	6,593	6,417	6,366	N/A	6,046	5,908
Newly Hired Teachers in Each Year g/	927	474	606	405	263	350	N/A	i/ 1,010	h/ 418

a/ Includes Professional Status and Standard Certificates.

b/ No longer issued; title changed to Temporary.

c/ Issued only at the request of a school district to persons who meet requirements for a Standard Certificate and agree to complete remaining deficiencies toward full certification within a given time period, and issued until PPST scores are passing.

d/ Issued at the request of a school district to persons who have a college degree and are working for full certification. No longer issued, effective July 1, 1991.

e/ No longer issued.

f/ Since 1986, the Special Institute for Teacher Certification, based at the University of Delaware in Newark has had 204 completions. These figures do not include candidates who participated in the state's separate mathematics/science program, for which no numbers were available.

g/ Teachers new to Delaware or returning from a break in service; does not include new hires who moved from school-to-school or district-to-district within the state.

h/ Numbers represent the average of both years, 1990-91 and 1989-90.

i/ Early retirement in effect June 30, 1991.

Delaware Department of Education
P.O. Box 1402
Townsend Bldg.
Dover, DE 19903
Critical Areas Program (mathematics, science, & speech pathology)
Contact: (302) 739-4686
www.doe.state.de.us

Delaware Alternative Routes to Certification/Secondary Program
Contact: Linda Hughes, Ph.D.
University of Delaware
Delaware Center for Teacher Education
Willard Hall
Newark, DE 19711
(302) 831-4598 or 831-1100
artc-de@udel.edu
www.udel.edu/artc/

Special Institute for Teacher Certification
Contact: Barbara Van Dornick
University of Delaware
Delaware Center for Teacher Education
Willard Hall
Newark, DE 19711
(302) 831-3000
www.udel.edu/teachered/

Master's in Primary/K-4 or Middle Level/5-8 Education
Contact: Richard Gochenauer, EdD
Wilmington College
30 DuPont Highway
New Castle, DE 19720
(302) 328-9407
Masters in Secondary Education With Initial Certification
Contact: Thomas Sturgis, EdD
Wesley College
306 DuPont College Center
Dover, DE 19901
(301) 736-2352

DELAWARE

Institutions of higher education that have developed alternative teacher preparation programs leading to a teaching license:

Wilmington College (implemented 1992)
Delaware State University (implemented 1997)
University of Delaware (implemented 1997)

States with which the state has reciprocity of teacher licenses:

NASDTEC Interstate Contract.

Institutions of higher education that have *any* teacher preparation programs leading to a license to teach.

Delaware State University
University of Delaware
Wesley College
Wilmington College

Contact information for persons interested in finding a teaching position in the state:

Note: Employment is handled by local school districts. There is no one, central place to obtain vacancy information.

Applicants may be filed on-line at "Teach Delaware" from the Delaware Department of Education home page at www.doe.state.de.us

DISTRICT OF COLUMBIA — Class A

TITLE: D.C. Teaching Fellows

HISTORY: Initiated in Fall 2001.

MOTIVATION: The mayor and school superintendent called on 100 of the area's most outstanding young and mid-career professionals to commit two years to teach in D.C. Public Schools. These professionals from a variety of careers, bring their experience, knowledge, and record of achievement to positively impact the lives of students.

GRADE LEVELS AND/OR SUBJECT AREA(S) COVERED:

Elementary Education; Special Education (grades 1-6); English-as-a-Second Language (ESL)/Bilingual Education(1-6); Secondary Mathematics and Science.

WHO OPERATES: D.C. Teacher Education and Certification Branch and D.C. Public Schools.

REQUIREMENTS TO ENTER:

Candidates must:

Possess a bachelor's degree from an accredited institution; and

Submit an application, cover letter and resume.

PROGRAM DESCRIPTION:

D.C. Mayor Anthony Williams and D.C. Public Schools Superintendent Paul L. Vance are calling on 100 of the nation's most outstanding professionals to become Fellows and commit at least two years to teaching in D.C. Public Schools. They want young professionals from a variety of careers to bring their experience, knowledge, and record of achievement to the classroom, and positively impact the lives of students.

Fellows are trained at a comprehensive instructional summer institute, and are provided with an extensive support network to ensure success in the classroom.

Fellows receive a signing bonus and financial assistance toward completion of their teacher certification and/or master's degree.

NUMBER OF CREDIT HOURS TO COMPLETE:

18 semester credit hours.

WHO EVALUATES: D.C. Teacher Education and Certification Branch and local school administrators.

LENGTH OF TIME: Two-year commitment to teach in a D.C. public school.

TITLE: Provisional Teacher Program

HISTORY: Approved by the D.C. Board of Education on Jan. 15, 1992.

MOTIVATION: The program is designed to attract talented college graduates who have a strong academic background in a subject field, and persons from diverse fields such as private industry, government, and the military.

GRADE LEVELS AND/OR SUBJECT AREA(S) COVERED:

Bilingual Education; Elementary Education; Special Education; Early Childhood Education; English-as-a-Second Language, Mathematics, Science, and Foreign Language.

WHO OPERATES: D.C Office of Teacher Education and Certification.

REQUIREMENTS TO ENTER:

Possess at least a BA degree from an accredited institution.

Possess the equivalent of a 24-30 credit major in the appropriate subject field through applicable coursework and/or life experiences.

Submit a completed application.

An interview by select school officers.

PROGRAM DESCRIPTION:

This program was designed to increase the pool of eligible teacher applicants and to meet critical shortages in the areas of Bilingual Education, Early Childhood Education, Elementary Education; English-as-a-Second Language, and Special Education; .

The program consists of three basic components: professional education, field experience, and a support structure.

The field experience will be satisfied by one successful year of teaching in lieu of student teaching.

All participants will be evaluated for provisional certification at the end of the school year, based on the development of a portfolio, completion of the professional education component, and satisfactory completion of the field experience.

NUMBER OF CREDIT HOURS TO COMPLETE:

18 semester hours of Professional Education.

WHO EVALUATES: Office of Teacher Education and Certification Branch; local school administrators; IHE personnel.

LENGTH OF TIME: 18 months.

OTHER: Up to a five-year commitment.

TITLE: District of Columbia Alternative Certification Program: Teach for America

HISTORY: Implemented September 1992.

MOTIVATION: This national program was designed to attract talented college student graduates who have a strong desire to teach in urban/rural school districts.

GRADE LEVELS AND/OR SUBJECT AREA(S) COVERED:

Bilingual Education; Elementary Education; Special Education; Early Childhood Education; English-as-a-Second Language, Mathematics, Science, and Foreign Language.

WHO OPERATES: District of Columbia Teacher Education and Certification Branch.

REQUIREMENTS TO ENTER:

Possess at least a BA degree from an accredited institution.

Through regional Teach for America Office.

Submit a completed application.

An interview by select school administrators.

PROGRAM DESCRIPTION:

This program was designed to increase the pool of eligible teacher applicants and to meet critical shortages in the areas of Bilingual Education, Early Childhood Education, Elementary Education; English-as-a-Second Language, and Special Education; Mathematics and Science.

The program consists of three basic components: professional education, field experience, and a support structure.

The field experience will be satisfied by one successful year of teaching in lieu of student teaching.

NUMBER OF CREDIT HOURS TO COMPLETE:

18 semester credit hours.

WHO EVALUATES: Teacher Education and Certification Branch; local school administrators.

LENGTH OF TIME: One year.

DISTRICT OF COLUMBIA

Number of Teaching Licenses Issued

	1992-93	1991-92	1990-91	1989-90	1988-89
Persons who completed an approved college teacher preparation program	N/A	N/A	N/A		
Internship program					
Emergency					
Temporary	N/A	300			
Alternative Route	N/A	46			
Other	N/A	N/A	N/A	N/A	175

Number of Teachers Employed

	1992-93	1991-92	1990-91	1989-90	1988-89
Total Teachers Employed in the State	N/A	6,630	6,500	N/A	6,572
Newly Hired Teachers in Each Year	N/A	302	N/A	N/A	205

District of Columbia Dept. of Education
Educational Credentialing and
Standards Branch
825 North Capitol St., NE, Sixth Floor
Washington, DC 20002-4232
(202) 442-5377

States with which the state has reciprocity of teacher licenses:

NASDTEC Interstate Contract.

Institutions of higher education that have *any* teacher preparation programs leading to a license to teach.

American University
Catholic University
Gallaudet University
George Washington University
Howard University
Trinity College
University of the District of Columbia

TITLE: Alternative Certification Program

Florida has long used an "alternative" to certify non-education majors, by issuing Temporary Certificates to individuals who qualify for the subject area and giving them two/three years in which to complete the education coursework requirements.

In the 2002-03 school year, Florida began statewide implementation of competency-based alternative certification programs that satisfy the professional preparation so that individuals need not enroll at a college or university to qualify for a Professional Certificate.

The individuals participating in the programs already qualify for and hold nonrenewable three-year Temporary Certificates, which means subject area requirements have been met. In order to qualify for the five-year renewable Professional Certificate, the participants must pass the Florida Teacher Certification Examinations (tests of General Knowledge, Professional Knowledge, and Subject Area Knowledge), have their employing school district document their Professional Education Competence as a result of successful completion of an approved alternative certification program.

Beginning with the 2002-2003 school year, all school districts are required to offer a competency-based alternative certification program, either the program developed by the state or one developed by the district and approved by the state. In either case, the districts implement and run the programs. Florida has no alternative certification programs that are controlled by a college or university, but several institutions of higher education are collaborating with districts in the implementation of the approved programs.

TITLE: Temporary Certificate (includes Alternate Route)

HISTORY: Authorized by legislation in 1988.

MOTIVATION: To address teacher shortages and to provide a mechanism for persons who are not teacher-trained to consider becoming a teacher.

GRADE LEVELS AND/OR SUBJECT AREAS COVERED: All

WHO OPERATES: Florida Department of Education.

REQUIREMENTS TO ENTER:

A bachelor's degree.

The individual must meet specialized requirements in a subject in which Florida offers certification.

The individual must have a 2.5 grade point average on a 4.0 scale in each subject shown on the certificate.

The individual must obtain employment in a Florida public school or in a private school with a state-approved system for demonstration of professional education competencies.

PROGRAM DESCRIPTION:

The Temporary Certificate may be issued when the individual obtains employment in a public school or in a private school with a state-approved system for demonstration of professional education competencies.

The recipient then has two years to complete the requirements for the Professional Certificate, which are to:

- Satisfy professional education courses and practical experience requirements.
- Satisfy recency-of-credit requirement.
- Demonstrate professional education competencies.

Attain:

A passing score on the Professional Education Subtest of the Florida Teacher Certification Examination.

A passing score on the General Knowledge Test.

A passing score on the subject area examination for each subject or field shown on the certificate.

Operating under required competencies set by the state, a local school district works with the candidate to achieve the competencies, then verifies to the state that they have been demonstrated.

Operating under required competencies set by the state, a local school district works with the candidate to achieve the competencies, then verifies to the state that they have been attained.

LENGTH OF TIME: Valid for three years; non-renewable.

WHO EVALUATES: Florida Department of Education.

OTHER: Each school district must offer a competency-based alternative certification program by which members of its instructional staff who have not been trained as teachers but who meet state requirements for specialization in a coverage area may satisfy the professional education preparation requirements. Instead of taking college courses, program participants complete training only in those competencies, which are identified as deficient by the district. IF the district chooses to develop its own program in lieu of implementing the program developed by the state, then the Department of Education must approve each district-developed program.

TITLE: "Add-on Programs"

Florida also has offered what may qualify as a Class G program for teachers to add subjects on to a Professional Certificate. These "Add-on Programs" have been approved by the Department of Education and Implemented either by school districts, or the universities or a combination of these. Teachers who complete an approved Add-on Program complete only the specialization (content) requirements they are lacking as part of the Program.

Until July 1, 2002, completion of the approved add-on program was required in combination with a passing score on the corresponding subject area test to establish eligibility for the additional coverage. Now, a passing score on the appropriate subject area test is sufficient to establish eligibility for the coverages that do not require master's level training. A district may offer the training content of the add-on program as a means by which teachers can acquire the content knowledge and competencies that must be demonstrated on the subject area exam to qualify for the additional coverage.

FLORIDA

Number of Teaching Licenses Issued

45,477 teaching licenses were issued in 1995-96, an additional 36,376 in 1996-97, and 38,145 in 1997-98. The numbers decreased in 1996-97 and 1997-98, because Renewed Professional Certificates are now "issued" by school districts.

	2001-02	2000-01	1999-00	1998-99	1992-93	1991-92	1990-91	1989-90	1988-89
Persons who completed an approved college teacher preparation program	N/A	5,580	5,475	5,588	N/A	N/A	~5,000	~5,000	~5,000
Internship program									
Emergency									
Temporary (including Alternate Route) *	15,308	15,256	14,105	13,355	N/A	N/A	~7,000	~7,000	
Alternative Route (included in temporary)									
Other									

Number of Teachers Employed

					1998-99	1997-98	1996-97	1995-96	1994-95	1993-94
Total Teachers Employed in the State **	158,008	153,390	150,560	147,751	144,324	126,392	122,392	119,388	116,784	112,300
Newly Hired Teachers in Each Year	12,317	11,409	12,291	12,108	11,169	10,689	9,385	7,833	9,265	9,236

** Temporary licenses were primarily issued to teachers coming to Florida from out of state. The Alternate Route accounted for approximately 10 percent of the number for 1990-91 and 5 percent of the number for 1989-90.*

*** These figures include all instructional staff -- teachers, as well as librarians, guidance counselors, social workers, school psychologists.*

Florida Department of Education
Bureau of Educator Certification
325 W. Gaines St.
Tallahassee, FL 32399
Attn: Karen B. Wilde
(850) 488-2317

FLORIDA

States with which the state has reciprocity of teacher licenses:

Florida has signed NASDTEC Interstate Agreements with all other states. State Board of Education rules provide for additional consideration of out-of-state certificates and appropriate years of experience to satisfy some or all eligibility requirements (excluding the fingerprint requirement).

Institutions of higher education that have *any* teacher preparation program(s) leading to a license to teach.

Barry University
Bethune-Cookman College
Clearwater Christian College
Flagler College
Florida A&M University
Florida Atlantic University
Florida Gulf Coast University
Florida Institute of Technology
Florida International University
Florida Memorial College
Florida Southern College
Florida State University
Jacksonville University
Nova Southeastern University
Palm Beach Atlantic College
Rollins College
Saint Leo College
Southeastern College
St. Thomas University
Stetson University
University of Central Florida
University of Florida
University of Miami
University of North Florida
University of South Florida
University of Tampa
University of West Florida
Warner Southern College

TITLE: Georgia Teacher Alternative Preparation Program (TAPP)

HISTORY: Georgia is responding to the expected 2001-2002 teacher shortage with the introduction of the Georgia Teacher Alternative Preparation Program.

MOTIVATION: The goal of the alternative preparation program is to provide a University, Regional Education Service Agencies (RESA), and Public Schools collaborative non-traditional option for prospective post-baccalaureate teacher candidates to acquire the critical and essential knowledge and skills necessary for successful entry into the classroom.

GRADE LEVELS AND/OR SUBJECT AREA(S) COVERED:

WHO OPERATES: IHE, RESA and public schools.

REQUIREMENTS TO ENTER PROGRAM:

Bachelor's degree or higher from a regionally accredited college or university.

Graduate with an overall grade point average of 2.5 or higher.

Pass the Praxis I test requirements.

Pass the Georgia GCIC criminal background check.

Job offer as a beginning teacher from a local school system.

PROGRAM DESCRIPTION:

Phase One -- An instructional phase offered as an introduction to teaching during the summer.

Phase Two -- A two-year classroom based induction training period completed while teaching.

If the candidate has not passed the appropriate Praxis II content examination, he or she will be required to take it during the first year of teaching. The test scores will be used to determine whether or not one needs to take additional content in the subject area one is teaching.

This model requires that teacher candidates complete an intensive preparation program of approximately four weeks during the summer prior to entering the classroom in the fall. Additionally, it requires intensive monitoring, supervision and mentoring during a two-year induction period. (The model could be adjusted to accommodate teachers hired on provisional status after the school year has begun. In this model, the time required for pre-assignment training will be shortened with training classes held after school hours.)

The collaborative unit including the teacher preparation unit of a college or university, a RESA, and the cooperating public schools will be responsible for implementing the program and for recommending candidates for initial certification.

NUMBER OF CREDIT HOURS TO COMPLETE:

WHO EVALUATES: IHE, RESA and local school system.

LENGTH OF TIME: Two years.

GEORGIA — Class B

TITLE: Teach for America

HISTORY: Began July 1989.

MOTIVATION: Recognition of the high quality of individuals recruited into this program, and the design and delivery of professional preparation.

GRADE LEVELS AND/OR SUBJECT AREA(S) COVERED:

All.

WHO OPERATES: IHE, LEA, and Teach for America.

REQUIREMENTS TO ENTER PROGRAM:

Determined by Teach for America.

PROGRAM DESCRIPTION:

Program design by Teach for America.

IHE collaborates and provides a path through its approved programs for individuals to complete full professional certification in Georgia.

NUMBER OF CREDIT HOURS TO COMPLETE:

Varies and may not necessarily be based on credit hour generation.

WHO EVALUATES: Teach for America and IHE.

LENGTH OF TIME: Varies -- generally completed in two years.

GEORGIA

Class D

TITLE: Post-Baccalaureate Non-Degree Preparation Programs

HISTORY: Available since 1950.

MOTIVATION: To attract talented individuals with non-education degrees into the teaching profession.

GRADE LEVELS AND/OR SUBJECT AREA(S) COVERED:

All.

WHO OPERATES: IHE.

REQUIREMENTS TO ENTER PROGRAM:

A baccalaureate or higher degree from a regionally accredited institution.

A minimum grade point average of 2.5 on a 4.0 scale.

Other requirements determined by the IHE.

PROGRAM DESCRIPTION:

The program of study is developed by the IHE in fields in which it has approved programs.

The candidate's educational and experiential background is analyzed, and an individualized program is developed in the area in which certification is sought.

IHEs have the authority and flexibility to determine the programs.

Candidates must achieve a minimum grade point average of 2.5 and pass the required Praxis II Subject Assessment(s) to be recommended to the Professional Standards Commission for certification.

Some preparation may be completed in staff development programs offered by LEAs for those teaching on a Provisional Certificate.

NUMBER OF CREDIT HOURS TO COMPLETE:

Varies individually.

WHO EVALUATES: IHE.

LENGTH OF TIME: Determined by candidate and IHE.

TITLE: Post-Baccalaureate Non-Degree Preparation Programs for Transitioning Military Personnel

HISTORY: Began July 1, 1993.

MOTIVATION: Georgia has numerous military establishments, and the downsizing of the armed forces has made available a unique pool of talented individuals, covering a broad range of skills that could enhance the delivery system of education in Georgia.

GRADE LEVELS AND/OR SUBJECT AREA(S) COVERED:

All.

WHO OPERATES: IHE.

REQUIREMENTS TO ENTER PROGRAM:

A baccalaureate or higher degree from a regionally accredited institution.

A minimum grade point average of 2.5 on a 4.0 scale.

Other requirements determined by the IHE.

PROGRAM DESCRIPTION:

The program of study is developed by the IHE in fields in which it has approved programs.

The candidate's educational and experiential background is analyzed, and an individualized program is developed in the area in which certification is sought.

IHEs have the authority and flexibility to determine the programs.

Candidates must achieve a minimum grade point average of 2.5 and pass the required Praxis II Subject Assessment(s) to be recommended to the Professional Standards Commission for certification.

Some preparation may be completed in staff development programs offered by LEAs for those teaching on a Provisional Certificate.

NUMBER OF CREDIT HOURS TO COMPLETE:

Varies individually.

WHO EVALUATES: IHE.

LENGTH OF TIME: Determined by candidate and IHE. For example, one program has been developed using a cohort approach and field based, in which all requirements will be completed in 90 days.

GEORGIA — Class E

TITLE: Master's Degree Level Initial Preparation

HISTORY: Began July 1, 1993.

MOTIVATION: To offer opportunities for non-education baccalaureate degree holders to earn a master's degree in education, while at the same time completing state certification requirements.

GRADE LEVELS AND/OR SUBJECT AREA(S) COVERED:

All.

WHO OPERATES: IHE.

REQUIREMENTS TO ENTER PROGRAM:

Determined by the IHE.

PROGRAM DESCRIPTION:

These programs are individually designed by each IHE, and meet state initial preparation program standards. Programs are approved by the Professional Standards Commission.

NUMBER OF CREDIT HOURS TO COMPLETE:

Programs are designed within a 60 quarter hour framework, unless there are compelling reasons for a longer program.

WHO EVALUATES: IHE.

LENGTH OF TIME: Determined by IHE.

TITLE: Provisional Certification

HISTORY: Available since 1949.

MOTIVATION: To expand the pool of teachers by enabling individuals who meet requirements for the content of the teaching field to teach, while completing requirements for professional certification.

GRADE LEVELS AND/OR SUBJECT AREA(S) COVERED:

All.

WHO OPERATES: IHE.

REQUIREMENTS TO ENTER PROGRAM:

Satisfy minimum job entry content requirements.

Receive a passing score on the required Praxis II Subject Assessment(s).

Possess a bachelor's or higher degree from a regionally accredited IHE.

Have graduated with a cumulative undergraduate grade point average of 2.5 or higher on a 4.0 scale.

Be employed by a Georgia school and have the certificate requested by the employing superintendent.

PROGRAM DESCRIPTION:

An individual must affiliate with an IHE offering an approved program in his or her certification field.

College advisors will determine the requirements necessary to qualify for professional certification.

NUMBER OF CREDIT HOURS TO COMPLETE: Variable -- determined by the IHE.

WHO EVALUATES: IHE.

LENGTH OF TIME: The Provisional Certificate is valid for three years and cannot be renewed. The approved program and all applicable special Georgia requirements must be completed during the three-year validity period.

TITLE: Probationary Certification

HISTORY: Available since 1974.

MOTIVATION: To offer opportunities to professionally certified individuals to add a new field of certification, and to be able to work in the new field while completing requirements.

GRADE LEVELS AND/OR SUBJECT AREA(S): Not issued in some fields.

WHO OPERATES?: Professional Standards Commission, IHE, and, in some cases, LEA.

REQUIREMENTS TO ENTER PROGRAM:

Hold a valid professional certificate.

Be employed in a Georgia school and have the certificate requested by the employing superintendent.

Most teaching fields require 20 quarter hours of acceptable college credit to be issued a Probationary Certificate. Some endorsement and special education fields require 10 quarter hours. It is possible to complete some endorsement field requirements through LEA staff development programs.

PROGRAM DESCRIPTION:

Each certifiable field in Georgia that offers a Probationary Certificate clearly describes the requirements.

NUMBER OF CREDIT HOURS TO COMPLETE:

Varies. In some cases, credit hours are determined by a "Prescription" from the Professional Standards Commission. Other approaches include approved programs, and programs designed around staff development units.

WHO EVALUATES: IHE and/or LEA.

LENGTH OF TIME: Varies. The validity period is generally three years, with some opportunities for renewal of two additional years in some fields.

GEORGIA

Class H

TITLE: Permitted Personnel

HISTORY: Effective July 1, 1992.

MOTIVATION: To enable recognized experts -- such as artists, native speakers of less commonly taught languages, etc. -- to bring their knowledge and expertise into public schools.

GRADE LEVELS AND/OR SUBJECT AREA(S): Teaching fields and superintendent.

WHO OPERATES?: Professional Standards Commission.

REQUIREMENTS TO ENTER PROGRAM:

Established competence in field.

Three years experience in field.

Bachelor's or higher degree from a regionally accredited institution, except performing arts.

Permits granted to teaching fields and superintendent only.

There must be verified circumstances, including verification that there are no acceptable certified personnel available to serve in this capacity.

PROGRAM DESCRIPTION:

There are no program requirements.

NUMBER OF CREDIT HOURS TO COMPLETE: None

WHO EVALUATES: LEA.

LENGTH OF TIME: Permits are issued annually and may be renewed if the LEA verifies implementation of mentor support, induction, and professional development during the validity period of the previous permit. Additionally, the required Praxis II Subject Assessment(s) must be passed if one is available in the field.

GEORGIA

Number of Teaching Licenses Issued

Data Not Available

Georgia Professional Standards Commission
2 Peachtree Street, Suite 6000
Atlanta, GA 30303
Attn: Cynthia Stephens
(404) 657-9014

GEORGIA

Institutions of higher education that have developed alternative teacher preparation programs leading to a teaching license:

Agnes Scott College
Armstrong Atlantic State University
Breneau University
Georgia College & State University
Georgia Southern University
Georgia State University
Paine College
Valdosta State University
University of Georgia
State University of West Georgia

States with which the state has reciprocity of teacher licenses:

Georgia accepts all states' professional certificates, plus DODDS, NBPTS, Washington, D.C., and U.S. territory certificates. NASDTEC Interstate Contract.

Institutions of higher education that have *any* teacher preparation programs leading to a license to teach.

Agnes Scott College
Armstrong Atlantic State University
Albany State University
Augusta State University
Berry College
Breneau University
Brewton-Parker College
Clark Atlanta University
Clayton College & State University
Columbus State University
Covenant College
Emmanuel College
Emory University
Fort Valley State University
Georgia College & State University
Georgia Southern University
Georgia Southwestern State University
Georgia State University
Kennesaw State University
LaGrange College
Mercer University

Morris Brown College
North Georgia College & State University
Oglethorpe University
Paine College
Piedmont College
Shorter College
Spelman College
State University of West Georgia
Thomas College
Toccoa Falls College
University College of Mercer/Forsyth
University of Georgia
Valdosta State University
Wesleyan College

Home page for the Georgia Professional Standards Commission:

http://www.gapsc.com

For current information:

PRAXIS Testing

Certification rules/requirements

Application forms

TITLE: Alternative Program for Shortage Areas

HISTORY: Began in 1996.

MOTIVATION: To reduce the shortage of teachers in selected teaching fields or in geographic areas that are difficult to fill.

GRADE LEVELS AND/OR SUBJECT AREAS COVERED:

Hawaii Department of Education declared shortage fields (HDOE).

WHO OPERATES Brigham Young University-Hawaii (BYUH).

REQUIREMENTS TO ENTER PROGRAM:

Official transcript verifying the baccalaureate degree earned from an accredited institution.

Minimum of two semesters of satisfactory full-time contracted HDOE teaching experience in the content area for which licensing is sought.

Favorable letter of recommendation from applicant's principal as well as the completed form for the "Principal's Recommendation for Temporary Teacher."

Transcript evaluation to determine specific courses needed with a minimum of 2.7 GPA (on a 4.0 scale) on the baccalaureate degree.

PROGRAM DESCRIPTION:

Upon meeting the requirements outlined above, candidates are required to apply for admission to BYUH. Upon acceptance, candidates need to register for one semester of student teaching. Supervision during the semester will be the responsibility of BYUH. However, the principal or his/her designee will serve as the school-based mentor to fulfill the regular duties of a cooperating teacher in providing supervision and staff development support as well as working collaboratively with the BYUH supervisors.

Upon successful completion of the student teaching requirement, the applicant must complete prescribed professional education coursework with a GPA of 3.0 on a 4.0 scale.

Before licensing is recommended, applicants must show demonstrated competency in the following areas: *Assessment and lesson planning; Technology usage; Special education issues and strategies; and School law.* Special education applicants also need to demonstrate competency in writing individualized education programs (IEPs).

Upon successful completion of the program requirements, applicants must submit passing Praxis score reports for the appropriate tests to the Hawaii Department of Education.

NUMBER OF CREDIT HOURS TO COMPLETE:

To be established by BYUH in consultation with the principal and applicant.

WHO EVALUATES: BYUH.

LENGTH OF TIME: Varies, depending upon applicant's prescribed program.

TITLE: Respecialization in Special Education (RISE) Program -- Alternative Certification Program for Special Education

HISTORY: Began in 1990.

MOTIVATION: Response to the shortage of fully certified special education teachers in Hawaii.

GRADE LEVELS AND/OR SUBJECT AREAS COVERED:

Special Education, Kindergarten through grade 12.

WHO OPERATES Hawaii State Department of Education.

REQUIREMENTS TO ENTER PROGRAM:

Completion of a state approved teacher education program in a field other than special education.

Passing scores on the required Praxis assessments.

And a special education teaching position with the Hawaii State Department of Education.

PROGRAM DESCRIPTION:

RISE is a one-year, integrated, on-the-job training program consisting of formal coursework and field experience. The program is based on competencies identified as critical to become an effective special education teacher.

The courses are designed to provide teachers with the knowledge and skills that are necessary to provide appropriate services to students with disabilities.

Participants are provided with continuous on-site support from the RISE staff.

The formal instruction involves seminars covering Foundations of Special Education, Curriculum and Instruction, Classroom

Management, and Professional Development, as well as the on-the-job supervision.

During the supervised internship, knowledge and theory are integrated into practical classroom applications with an ongoing individual assessment component, supervision, on-site support, and the assessment of competencies.

NUMBER OF CREDIT HOURS TO COMPLETE:

No university credits are given. The applicant is given 6 workshop credits from the Department of Education upon successful completion of RISE requirements for the seminars, classroom observations, and Praxis.

WHO EVALUATES: Program Director.

LENGTH OF TIME: One year. Total of 20 sessions, from 8 a.m. to 4 p.m., as well as the one year of supervision while on-the-job.

TITLE: Alternative Licensing Program in Special Education (ABC-SE)

HISTORY: Began in 1991.

MOTIVATION: Response to the shortage of licensed special education teachers in Hawaii.

GRADE LEVELS AND/OR SUBJECT AREAS COVERED:

Special Education, Kindergarten through grade 12.

WHO OPERATES Hawaii State Department of Education, with Chaminade University of Honolulu.

REQUIREMENTS TO ENTER PROGRAM:

A baccalaureate degree from an accredited four-year college or university.

A special education full-time contracted teaching position with the Hawaii State Department of Education.

Minimum undergraduate and post-baccalaureate grade point average (GPA) of 2.75 on a 4.0 scale.

Complete admissions file at Chaminade University.

PROGRAM DESCRIPTION:

The alternative licensing option for special education is a two-year, integrated, on-the-job program consisting of formal coursework and field experiences. The program is based on competencies identified as critical to become an effective special education teacher.

Selection is on a competitive basis. All tuition fees and related program costs are the responsibility of each candidate.

Candidates are expected to satisfactorily complete 24 semester hours of prescribed special education coursework taken at Chaminade University and the seminars and supervised internship provided by the Hawaii Department of Education. During the supervised internship, knowledge and theory are integrated into practical classroom applications with an ongoing individual assessment component, supervision, on-site support, and the assessment of the competencies of the individuals.

NUMBER OF CREDIT HOURS TO COMPLETE:

24 semester credits of prescribed special education coursework.

WHO EVALUATES: Special education faculty at Chaminade University, and the Program Director from the Hawaii State Department of Education.

LENGTH OF TIME: Two years.

HAWAII

Number of Teaching Licenses Issued

	1998-99	1997-98	1996-97	1995-96	1994-95	1993-94	1992-93	1991-92	1990-91
Persons who completed an approved college teacher preparation program	542	N/A	N/A	N/A	557	636	698	763	1,040
Emergency									
Temporary	257	N/A	353	230*	379	395	417	393	176
Alternative Route/ Special Certification	209**	51	48	59	96	68	55	90	2

* *Initial appointments only*

** *158 SATE complete in regular ed/general ed.*

Number of Teachers Employed

	1998-99	1997-98	1996-97	1995-96	1994-95	1993-94	1992-93	1991-92	1990-91
Total Teachers Employed in the State	12,075	12,006	11,725	11,724	11,634	11,513	11,346	11,057	10,780
Newly Hired Teachers in Each Year	1,008	986	N/A	N/A	1,032	1,099	1,115	1,156	1,216

Hawaii Dept. of Education
Office of Personnel Services
P.O. Box 2360
Honolulu, HI 96804
Attn: Clara Burrows
(808) 586-3276
email: clara_burrows@notes.k12.hi.us

HAWAII

Institutions of higher education that have developed alternative teacher preparation programs leading to a teaching license:

Chaminade University of Honolulu, in conjunction with Hawaii State Department of Education
Brigham Young University-Hawaii

States with which the state has reciprocity of teacher licenses:

NASDTEC Interstate Contract.

Institutions of higher education that have *any* teacher preparation programs leading to a license to teach.

Brigham Young University-Hawaii
Chaminade University of Honolulu
University of Hawaii at Manoa
University of Hawaii at Hilo
University of Phoenix - Hawaii

Contact information for persons interested in finding a teaching position in the state:

John Hawkins, Personnel Specialist
Hawaii State Department of Education
P.O. Box 2360
Honolulu, HI 96804
Phone: (808) 586-3420

IDAHO — Class B

TITLE: Secondary Field Centered Teacher Training Program: An Alternate Route to Certification

HISTORY: Adopted by the State Board in February 1990.

MOTIVATION: To provide an alternative for individuals to become certificated secondary teachers in Idaho without following a standard teacher education program.

GRADE LEVELS AND/OR SUBJECT AREAS COVERED: Secondary only.

WHO OPERATES: Participating colleges and universities, the State Department of Education, and the employing local school district.

REQUIREMENTS TO ENTER PROGRAM:

A. Prior to application, the prospective trainee must:

1. Possess a baccalaureate or higher degree from an accredited college or university with a minimum grade point average of 2.0 on a 4.0 scale;

2. Have completed the degree at least five years previously;

3. Hold academic credits comparable with current major and minor requirements for secondary endorsement(s);

4. Meet all non-academic requirements of the State of Idaho, which includes fingerprinting and a background check.

B. Prior to admission, the applicant must:

1. Apply for a Teacher Trainee Certificate from the Office of Teacher Education and Certification;

2. Submit the required documents to the Office of Teacher Education and Certification: application, application fee, official transcripts and three letters of recommendation; and fingerprint cards.

4. Present the Teacher Trainee Certificate to potential employers and obtain a written statement from a school district declaring an intent to employ the applicant for the ensuing school year (full-time employment is expected).

5. Submit the statement of intent to employ to the Office of Teacher Education and Certification.

PROGRAM DESCRIPTION:

The teacher trainee must attend, participate in and successfully complete an individualized two year teacher trainee program as one of the conditions to receive recommendation for a Standard Secondary Teaching Certificate.

A formal teacher trainee plan will be developed by a consortium composed of the mentor teacher, a representative of the school district, a representative of the Office of Teacher Education and Certification, and a representative of the participating higher education institution with an approved secondary education program. Any deviation from the formal trainee plan must be approved by the consortium. The consortium will be responsible for the program design, supervision and evaluation of the training.

The teacher trainee program shall include:

1. Completion of a 9 semester credit hour program of pre-service training from an institution of higher education.

2. Completion of a 30 contact hour pre-service orientation presented by the school district prior to a classroom assignment. This orientation shall include district policies, procedures, curriculum, instructional model, community characteristics, and resources.

3. Completion of an internship of two academic years (four semesters) duration. The trainee shall be enrolled in 3 semester credit hours of internship each semester.

4. Completion of a 6 to 9 semester credit hour program during the second summer from an institution of higher education.

The pre-service and second summer program of 15 to 18 semester credit hours in total shall include: philosophical, psychological and methodological foundations of the profession, and reading in the content area. The consortium will determine the content required for the trainee, which may include both pedagogical and subject area course work. When designing the content necessary for the individual teacher trainee to complete the program, the consortium shall consider previous college credit, as documented in the official transcripts. Efforts will be directed to provide observation and clinical experiences during the time prior to being assigned to the classroom.

Each teacher trainee must be assisted by and guided throughout the two year training program by a certified employee of the district who has been designated as a mentor teacher. Principals must ensure that teacher trainees are provided with direct assistance from a mentor teacher and, where needed, other support personnel.

NUMBER OF CREDIT HOURS TO COMPLETE: 15-18 semester hours.

WHO EVALUATES: Principals are to provide assistance to teacher trainees regarding the purpose, expectations, and procedures involved in the evaluation process and with whatever guidance may be needed. The principal shall formally evaluate the teacher trainee at least once each quarter of the school year.

LENGTH OF TIME: Two years as a teacher under the teacher trainee program.

OTHER: Salary and benefits are established by the local district. All costs related to the college or university credits required will be the responsibility of the trainee. Other costs will be the responsibility of the respective agency involved in each trainee's program.

IDAHO

Number of Teaching Licenses Issued

	2000-01	1999-00	1998-99	1994-95	1993-94	1992-93	1991-92	1990-91	1989-90	1988-89
Persons who completed an approved college teacher preparation program	1,182	1,347	5,280	** 994	N/A	N/A	N/A	N/A	* 4,284	* 4,860
Emergency	442									
Alternative Route ***	3	5	8	10	7	8	4	N/A	N/A	N/A

* *Totals include all initial certificates and all renewals issued.*

** *Graduates from Idaho institutions*

*** *Nineteen (19) applicants applied for admission to the Alternate Route Program toward Idaho Secondary Certification from May 1, 1996, through April 30, 1997. Of these, 16 were eligible to receive a Teacher Training Certificates, which entitles the holder an opportunity to apply for a teaching position in a public or private secondary school.*

A total of 16 Teacher Trainees were employed, 10 of which were hired for the 1996-97 school year, and six of which completed the second of a two-year program. During this time period, four Teacher Trainees completed the requirements of the Alternate Route Program and subsequently received an Idaho Secondary Teaching Certificate.

Number of Teachers Employed

	2000-01	1999-00	1998-99	1997-98	1996-97	1994-95	1993-94	1992-93	1991-92	1990-91
Total Teachers Employed in the State	N/a	15,962	15,661			14,572	13,801	N/A	N/A	11,601
Newly Hired Teachers in Each Year	1,928	1,755	1,893	1,468	1,583	N/A	N/A	N/A	N/A	N/A

Idaho Department of Education
Teacher Education/Professional Standards
P.O. Box 83720
Boise, ID 83720-0027
Attn: Michael P. Stefanic
(208) 332-6800

IDAHO

Institutions of higher education that have developed alternative teacher preparation programs leading to a teaching license:

Albertson College of Idaho
Boise State University
Idaho State University
Lewis-Clark State College
Northwest Nazarene College
University of Idaho

States with which the state has reciprocity of teacher licenses:

NASDTEC Interstate Contract.

Institutions of higher education that have *any* teacher preparation programs leading to a license to teach.

Albertson College of Idaho
Boise State University
Brigham Young University -- Idaho
Idaho State University
Lewis-Clark State College
Northwest Nazarene College
University of Idaho

Contact information for persons interested in finding a teaching position in the state:

Each Idaho school district advertises its own vacancies and maintains its own employment procedures. District vacancies are often listed with college or university placement centers or with the Idaho Department of Employment. Questions about openings and salaries should be addressed to school districts.

Contact the following Idaho Teacher Placement Centers:

Teacher Placement Service, Employment Programs Section
State Department of Education
317 Main Street
Boise, ID 83735-0001
Phone: (208) 334-6137

Special Education Hotline
telephone toll-free (800) 247-0193

Albertson College of Idaho
Teacher Placement Service
Caldwell, ID 83686
(208) 459-5534

Boise State University
Career Planning & Placement
1910 University Drive
Boise, ID 83725
(208) 385-1747

Idaho State University
Career Planning & Placement Center
Campus Box 8108
Pocatello, ID 83209
(208) 236-2380

Lewis-Clark State College
Career Planning & Placement Center
Lewiston, ID 83501
(208) 799-2313

Northwest Nazarene College
Teacher Placement
Nampa, ID 83686
(208) 476-8258

University of Idaho
Career Planning & Placement Center
Moscow, ID 83843
(208) 995-6121

ILLINOIS

Class A

TITLE: Alternative Route to Teacher Certification

HISTORY: Illinois School code: 105 ILCS 5/21-5c Effective December 1999.

MOTIVATION: To provide alternative routes for certifying teachers in Illinois.

GRADE LEVELS AND/OR SUBJECT AREAS COVERED: All.

WHO OPERATES: The program must be provided by an approved teacher preparation institution and may be offered in conjunction with one or more not-for-profit organizations.

REQUIREMENTS TO ENTER:

An applicant must meet the following criteria:

Graduated from an accredited college or university with a bachelor's degree.

Employed for at least five years in an area requiring application of the participant's education.

Passed the Illinois Basic Skills Test.

PROGRAM DESCRIPTION:

The alternative teacher certification program must include the content and skills of the institution's approved preparation program and must be approved by the State Board of Education.

Phase I:

Successful completion of an intensive course of study in education theory, instructional methods, and practice teaching.

Passed the Illinois Subject Matter Knowledge Test.

A one-year nonrenewable provisional alternative teaching certificate will be issued when the participant meets the requirements of Phase I.

Phase II:

Full-time teaching position with one school year with the advice and assistance of a mentor teacher, and

Phase III:

A comprehensive assessment of the participant's teaching performance by school officials and program participants and recommendation for certification by the higher education institution.

A nonrenewable Initial Teaching Certificate, valid for four years, will be issued following completion of the three phases. After completing four years of teaching, individuals may apply for the Standard Teaching Certificate.

NUMBER OF CREDIT HOURS TO COMPLETE:

Determined by IHE.

LENGTH OF TIME: Varies (one to three years).

WHO EVALUATES: State Board of Education.

ILLINOIS

Class A

TITLE: Alternative Teacher Certification

HISTORY: Illinois School code: 105 ILCS 5/21-5b Effective December 1999.

MOTIVATION: To provide alternative routes for certifying teachers in Illinois.

GRADE LEVELS AND/OR SUBJECT AREAS COVERED: All.

WHO OPERATES: The program must be provided by a partnership that includes an approved teacher preparation institution, which offers baccalaureate and master's degree programs, and one or more not-for-profit organizations. The individual programs are limited to 260 participants per year.

REQUIREMENTS TO ENTER:

An applicant must meet the following criteria:

Graduated from an accredited college or university with a bachelor's degree.

Employed for at least five years in an area requiring application of the participant's education. (Work experience is not required for programs serving the city of Chicago.)

Passed the Illinois Basic Skills Test.

PROGRAM DESCRIPTION:

The alternative teacher certification program must include the content and skills of the institution's approved preparation program and must be approved by the State Board of Education.

Phase I:

Pass the Illinois Subject Matter Knowledge Test.

Successful completion of an intensive course of study in education theory, instructional methods, and practice teaching.

A one-year nonrenewable provisional alternative teaching certificate will be issued when the participant meets the requirements of Phase I.

Phase II:

Full-time teaching position with one school year with the advice and assistance of a mentor teacher.

Phase III:

A comprehensive assessment of the participant's teaching performance by school officials and program participants and recommendation for certification by the higher education institution.

A nonrenewable Initial Alternative Teaching Certificate, valid for four years, will be issued following completion of the three phases. After completing four years of teaching, individuals may apply for the Standard Teaching Certificate.

NUMBER OF CREDIT HOURS TO COMPLETE:

Determined by IHE.

LENGTH OF TIME: Varies (one to three years).

WHO EVALUATES: State Board of Education.

ILLINOIS

Number of Teaching Licenses Issued

	2001-02	2000-01	1999-00	1998-99	1997-98	1996-97	1995-96	1994-95	1993-94	1992-9
Persons who completed an approved college teacher preparation program	10,611	10,789	8,423	9,622	8,437	8,007	7,952	6,821	6,062	7,034
Emergency (Short-Term Emergency)	22	--	--	--	--	--	--	--	--	--
Temporary/Provisional	919	869	781	641	695	769	856	1,146	1,405	982
Alternative Route	274	157	21	24	--	--	--	--	--	--
Other (Transitional, Bilingual, Substitute, and Resident)	25,988	20,912	18,264	16,653	14,825	16,540	15,852	15,120	13,302	14,345

Number of Teachers Employed

	2001-02	2000-01	1999-00	1998-99	1997-98	1996-97	1995-96	1994-95	1993-94	1992-93
Total Teachers Employed in the State	138,485	137,826	134,826	131,528	128,292	125,204	122,319	119,535	117,194	117,713
Newly Hired Teachers in Each Year	13,090	14,397	13,305	11,759	10,448	9,645	9,975	14,930	10,487	8,162

Illinois State Board of Education
Division of Professional Preparation
and Recruitment
100 North First Street
Springfield, IL 62777-0001
Attn: Martha A. (Marti) Woelfle
Phone: (217) 782-4330
Fax: (217) 782-3687
e-mail: mwoelfle@isbe.net

ILLINOIS

Institutions of higher education that have developed alternative teacher preparation programs leading to a teaching license:

Aurora University
Benedictine University
Chicago State University
Concordia University
DePaul University
Governors State University
Illinois State University
National-Louis University
Northern Illinois University
Northwestern University
Roosevelt University
Southern Illinois University at Carbondale
University of Illinois at Chicago
University of St. Francis
Western Illinois University

For current information on Illinois' alternative certification programs, contact:

Michael J. Long
Marti Woelfle
Illinois State Board of Education
Division of Professional Preparation and Recruitment
100 N. First Street
Springfield, IL 62777
Phone: (217) 782-4330
http://www.isbe.net/profprep

States with which the state has reciprocity of teacher licenses:

Illinois has signed the Central States Teacher Exchange Agreement and the NASDTEC Interstate Contract with 36 states. As changes occur, the list is updated and posted on the state's Web site at: http://www.isbe.net/teachers/Services/interstateagree.htm.

Alabama
Arizona
California
Colorado
Connecticut
District of Columbia
Georgia
Indiana
Iowa
Kansas
Kentucky
Maine
Maryland
Massachusetts
Michigan
Missouri
Nebraska
New Hampshire
New Mexico
New York
North Carolina
Ohio
Oklahoma
Oregon
Pennsylvania
Rhode Island
South Carolina
South Dakota
Tennessee
Texas
Utah
Vermont
Virginia
Washington
West Virginia
Wisconsin

ILLINOIS

Institutions of higher education that have *any* teacher preparation program(s) leading to a license to teach.

Augustana College
Aurora University
Benedictine University
Blackburn College
Bradley University
Chicago State University
Columbia College
Concordia University
DePaul University
Dominican University
Eastern Illinois University
Elmhurst College
Erikson Institute
Eureka College
Governors State University
Greenville College
Hebrew Theological College
Illinois College
Illinois Institute of Technology
Illinois State University
Illinois Wesleyan University
Judson College
Keller Graduate School of Management
Kendall College
Knox College
Lake Forest College
Lewis University
Loyola University-Chicago
MacMurray College
McKendree College
Millikin University
Monmouth College
National-Louis University
North Central University
Northeastern Illinois University
Northern Illinois University
North Park University
Northwestern University
Olivet Nazarene University
Principia College
Quincy University
Rockford College
Roosevelt University
St. Xavier University
School of the Art Institute of Chicago
Southern Illinois University at Carbondale
Southern Illinois University at Edwardsville
Trinity Christian College
Trinity International University
University of Chicago
University of Illinois at Chicago
University of Illinois at Springfield
University of Illinois at Urbana-Champaign
University of St. Francis
VanderCook College of Music
Western Illinois University
Wheaton College

Contact information for persons interested in finding a teaching position in the state:

Illinois State Board of Education
Division of Professional Preparation
100 N. First Street
Springfield, IL 62777
Phone: 1-800-845-8749
http://www.isbe.net/teachers

INDIANA

Class I

Teacher preparation programs in the state offer alternative routes to full licensing.

State legislators are considering other alternative teacher certification.

Currently, a graduate of an accredited institution outside the state of Indiana must submit credentials for evaluation to the Division of Teacher Licensing or enroll in an approved teacher education program at an Indiana college or university. Those who have completed a teacher preparation program at an out-of-state institution should submit their credentials to the Teacher Licensing office.

All other candidates should contact the education licensing advisor at the university or college of their choice.

Number of Teaching Licenses Issued

	1999-00	1998-99	1997-98	1996-97	1995-96	1994-95	1993-94	1992-93	1991-92
Persons who completed an approved college teacher preparation program and were licensed	7,815	5,772	5,383	5,704	N/A	N/A	N/A	N/A	5,747
Internship program	3,440	3,438	2,624	2,921	2,607	2,292	2,035	1,927	1,375
Emergency	1,371	1,256	1,149	1,110	970	828	773	N/A	772
Temporary (reciprocal)						~1,200			
Alternative Route									
Other									

Number of Teachers Employed

	1999-00	1998-99	1997-98	1996-97	1994-95	1992-93	1991-92	1990-91	1989-90
Total Teachers Employed in the State	59,716	57,942	57,219	N/A	N/A	51,938	54,623	54,220	53,246
Newly Hired Teachers in Each Year	N/A	N/A	N/A	N/A	N/A	1,049	1,848	1,660	1,932

Indiana Professional Standards Board
251 E. Ohio St., Suite 201
Indianapolis, IN 46204
(317) 232-9010

INDIANA

States with which the state has reciprocity of teacher licenses:

NASDTEC Interstate Contract.

Institutions of higher education that have *any* teacher preparation program(s) leading to a license to teach.

Anderson University
Ball State University
Bethel College
Butler University
Calumet College
DePauw University
Franklin College
Goshen College
Grace College
Hanover College
Huntington College
Indiana State University
Indiana University
Indiana University-East
Indiana University-Kokomo
Indiana University-Northwest

Indiana University-Purdue-Ft. Wayne
Indiana University-Purdue-Indianapolis

Indiana University-South Bend
Indiana University-Southeast
Indiana Wesleyan University
Manchester College
Marian College
Oakland City University
Purdue University
Purdue University-Calumet
St. Francis College
St. Joseph's College
St. Mary's College
St. Mary of the Woods College
Taylor University
Tri-State University
University of Evansville
University of Indianapolis
University of Notre Dame
University of Southern Indiana
Valparaiso University
Wabash College

Purdue University North Central, and Earlham College offer coursework; their candidates are recommended for licensure through other institutions.

TITLE: Teacher Intern License

HISTORY: Authorized in 2002

MOTIVATION:

GRADE LEVELS AND/OR SUBJECT AREAS COVERED:

Middle school, junior high school, or high school.

WHO OPERATES: State Board of Education.

REQUIREMENTS TO ENTER PROGRAM:

The prospective intern must:

1. Hold a baccalaureate from an accredited institution with a minimum cumulative grade point average of 2.5 on a 4.0 scale.

2. Be admitted to a teacher intern program, which has been approved by the state board of education.

3. Meet the requirements of at least one of the board's secondary endorsement areas.

4. Possess a minimum of three years of post-baccalaureate work experience (an authorized official at a college or university with an approved teacher intern program will evaluate this experience).

6. Meet all non-academic requirements of the state, including fingerprinting and state and national criminal investigation background checks.

PROGRAM DESCRIPTION:

The Teacher Intern must successfully complete:

1. An introductory program of at least 12 semester hours of the teacher intern program prior to fall employment. The following areas shall be integrated into the introductory teacher intern program for delivery, and it is intended that the program shall

be developed further throughout the year of internship and during the summer following the internship year:

PROGRAM DESCRIPTION:

The Teacher Intern must successfully complete:

1. An introductory program of at least 12 semester hours of the teacher intern program prior to fall employment. The following areas shall be integrated into the introductory teacher intern program for delivery, and it is intended that the program shall be developed further throughout the year of internship and during the summer following the internship year:

   Learning environment/classroom management;

   Instructional planning;

   Instructional strategies;

   Student learning;

   Diverse learners;

   Collaboration, ethics, and relationships;

   Assessment;

   Integrated field experience.

2. Four semester hours of a teacher intern seminar during the teacher internship year. These seminars are intended to provide continued support for the teacher intern and provide an extension of the coursework taken during the first summer prior to employment.

3. 12 additional semester hours during the summer after the teacher intern year and in the following areas:

   Foundations, reflection, and professional development;

   Communication;

   Exceptional learner program;

   Preparation in the integration of reading strategies into the content area;

Computer technology related to instruction;

An advanced study of items 1 through 7 listed above.

After completing these requirements, the Teacher Intern may apply for issuance of an Initial License with the following:

1. Verification from a licensed evaluator that the teacher intern served successfully as a teacher intern for a minimum of 160 days.

2. Verification from a licensed evaluator that the teacher intern was deemed competent by means of a comprehensive evaluation.

3. Recommendation for an initial license by a college or university offering an approved teacher intern program. This recommendation includes the successful completion of the second summer coursework consisting of 12 semester hours.

At the request of the state board of education, the teacher intern shall provide to the board information regarding, but not limited to, the teacher intern selection and preparation programs, institutional support, local school district mentor, and local school district support.

The teacher intern year will count as one of the years needed to move from the initial license to the standard license if the above conditions are met.

NUMBER OF CREDIT HOURS TO COMPLETE: 24 semester hours.

WHO EVALUATES: Participating local school district and college or university offering an approved teacher intern program.

LENGTH OF TIME: One year.

OTHER:

IOWA

Number of Teaching Licenses Issued

	1999-00	1998-99	1997-98	1996-97	1995-96	1993-94	1992-93	1991-92	1990-91	1989-90
Persons who completed an approved college teacher preparation program *	2,846	2,800	2,788	3,100	3,000	N/A	4,105	~3,200	~3,200	N/A
Emergency										
Alternative Route										
Other										

Number of Teachers Employed

	2001-02	1999-00	1998-99	1997-98	1996-97	1995-96	1994-95	1992-93	1991-92	1990-91
Total Teachers Employed in the State	33,878	32,970	32,307	31,954	31,629	31,193	32,503	N/A	~31,000	~31,000
Newly Hired Teachers in Each Year **	1,443	1,616	1,258	1,133	1,014	920	1,529	***	~8-900	~8-900

*** Beginning full-time teachers with no prior experience.*

**** Newly Hired Teachers in 1992-93 ---*

	Full-time	Part-time	Total
Public	*671*	*129*	*800*
Non-public	*132*	*37*	*132*

Iowa Board of Educational Examiners
Grimes State Office Bldg.
East 14th and Grand
Des Moines, IA 50319
Attn: Anne E. Kruse
(515) 281-3611

IOWA

Institutions of higher education that have developed alternative teacher preparation programs leading to a teaching license:

States with which the state has reciprocity of teacher licenses:

No reciprocity with any state.

Iowa has a regional exchange agreement with six other states -- the Central States agreement, which links Missouri, Oklahoma, Iowa, Nebraska, Kansas, South Dakota, Illinois, Michigan, and Wisconsin. Through this agreement, each state's respective minimum standards are protected, but the applicant is guaranteed an initial two-year license in the receiving state.

Institutions of higher education that have *any* teacher preparation programs leading to a license to teach.

Briar Cliff University
Buena Vista University
Central University of Iowa
Clarke College
Coe College
Cornell College
Dordt College
Drake University
Emmaus Bible College
Faith Baptist Bible College
Graceland College
Grand View College
Grinnell College
Iowa State University
Iowa Wesleyan College
Loras College
Luther College
Maharishi University of Management
Maycrest International university
Morningside College
Mt. Mercy College
Mount Saint Clare College
Northwestern College
St. Ambrose University
Simpson College
University of Dubuque
University of Iowa
University of Northern Iowa
Upper Iowa University
Wartburg College
William Penn University

Contact information for persons interested in finding a teaching position in the state:

Note: Iowa does not have a state-level placement agency.

KANSAS

Class B

TITLE: Restricted Teaching License

HISTORY: Available after July 1, 2002. Proposed and designed as part of a total redesign of teacher preparation and licensure in Kansas that was initiated in 1992. The State Board of Education adopted the new licensure regulations in the summer of 2000.

MOTIVATION: Response to shortage of teachers in certain secondary teaching fields and the need to allow immediate access to practice to individuals who already hold degrees in the content field that they would teach.

GRADE LEVELS AND/OR SUBJECT AREA(S) COVERED:

Any secondary teaching area for which the participating higher education institution has an approved teacher preparation program.

WHO OPERATES: The teacher education institution in cooperation with the local school district

REQUIREMENTS TO ENTER:

1. An undergraduate or graduate degree in the content area in which the license is sought.

2. 2.5 grade point average (GPA).

3. Offer of employment from a local school district.

4. Documentation from the hiring district that they have exhausted reasonable attempts to fill the position with a licensed person.

PROGRAM DESCRIPTION:

If the candidate meets the above degree and GPA requirements and has an offer of employment, he/she may contact a Kansas teacher education institution for a plan of study that will qualify him/her for full licensure in the content area.

The plan must allow for completion of the approved teacher education program in not more than three years and must show specific requirements to be completed each year.

The teacher education institution provides the program through an alternative delivery system and supports the applicant on-site.

The local hiring district must collaborate with the teacher education institution on delivery of the program.

The school district must assign a mentor teacher with three or more years of experience to provide support to the individual.

The local district and the teacher education institution must submit a yearly progress report.

The individual is issued a three-year restricted teaching license while they are completing program requirements.

NUMBER OF CREDIT HOURS TO COMPLETE:

Will vary with individuals, the institutions they are working with and the program areas they are completing.

WHO EVALUATES: The teacher education institution, in cooperation with the local district, will evaluate and assess the individual as he/she progress through the program. Individuals will be required to complete all licensure assessments after completion of the program and prior to issuance of a conditional license.

LENGTH OF TIME: Three years under the restricted license will be allowed to complete the approved program requirements.

OTHER: Individuals who complete a program under a restricted license will be required to complete a content and pedagogy assessment to qualify for an initial conditional license. During the conditional licensing period, they will complete a performance assessment to move to a professional license.

TITLE: Post Baccalaureate Program to Alternative Certification

HISTORY: Approved in 1992 by the Kansas State Board of Education. The first applicants began the program in the summer on 1992.

Note: After July 1, 2003, this program will convert to the Restricted Teaching License requirements (see the listing for the Restricted Teaching License for details).

MOTIVATION: Wichita State University (WSU) is responding to a perceived shortage of teachers in the Wichita area.

GRADE LEVELS AND/OR SUBJECT AREA(S) COVERED:

All secondary 7-12 certification subject areas that have approved programs at WSU.

WHO OPERATES: Wichita State University.

REQUIREMENTS TO ENTER:

1. A baccalaureate degree from an accredited institution of higher learning.

2. A contract or offer of employment, to teach half-time or more at a state accredited middle or high school.

3. An academic major, or the equivalent, in an appropriate teaching field (it must be the field in which the student will have the majority of her/his teaching responsibilities).

4. A GPA of 3.00 in the last 60 hours on the student's transcript or a GPA of 2.75 combined with a Miller Analogies Test score of at least 40 or Graduate Record Exam total score of at least 917 on any two GRE subtests.

5. A GPA of 2.50 or higher in the student's anticipated academic major teaching field.

6. Evidence of success as a professional in a field other than teaching.

PROGRAM DESCRIPTION:

1. Contracted to teach half-time or more at a state accredited middle or high school.

2. Complete a core of courses in the summer prior to entering the classroom and become provisionally certified and teach a normal schedule while in the program.

3. Are advised by a team of professionals including a mentor-teacher who teaches in the same building as the alternative option student, a subject area specialist or the coordinator of the alternative teacher education program at WSU, and the building administrator or designee.

4. Complete a core of courses the second summer and pass the Principles of Learning and Teaching examination.

5. Become fully certified in one or more teaching fields at the conclusion of the second academic year.

6. Are able to finish a master's degree in curriculum and instruction by completing twelve to fifteen credit hours.

NUMBER OF CREDIT HOURS TO COMPLETE: 32 credit hours.

WHO EVALUATES: Wichita State University in conjunction with area school districts.

LENGTH OF TIME: Approximately two years.

KANSAS **Class I**

Currently, Kansas bases certification on the completion of state-approved programs. A minimum cumulative grade point average of 2.5 on a 4.0 grade point scale is required for all initial certificates issued after Sept. 1, 1985. Kansas does not base certification on a transcript analysis and is a member of the Central States Exchange Agreement (Illinois, Iowa, Kansas, Michigan, Missouri, Nebraska, Oklahoma , South Dakota, and Wisconsin).

The State Board has adopted the following:

I. Alternative Route to Certification, Higher Education Model -- Individuals could receive two one-year provisional certificates if a recommending IHE verified that they had met these requirements: a bachelor's degree; a cumulative GPA of 2.5 on a 4.0 scale; competence in an academic endorsement area through a major in that subject or equivalent coursework and experience; successful completion of pre-certification tests, including the Pre-professional Skills Test (PPST) and the PLT; a request from an employing LEA which has an approved application for Innovative Program Accreditation Waiver; and successful completion of an intensive eight-week summer Teacher Education Program Workshop -- with instruction in classroom management, instructional studies, exceptional child in the regular classroom, curriculum and instruction including methods, and child and/or adolescent psychology -- and a one-week orientation at the district and building levels. This would be followed by a year of classroom teaching, supervised and evaluated by a Certification Team, comprised of a school principal, district-appointed mentor, and college supervisor or adjunct clinical faculty member. After the first year, if the individual has completed all coursework requirements and demonstrated outstanding teaching ability, the Team can recommend award of the standard certificate. Otherwise, candidates would participate for a second year and complete the remaining coursework. They would receive college credit toward the 18 semester hours required for full certification. Currently, no university has sought to have a program approved under these guidelines. Note: This model will no longer be available after July 1, 2003. All programs will convert to the Restricted Teaching License requirements.

Alternative Certificate, State Board of Education Visiting Scholar Certificate -- This program would seek to tap the human resources found at the state's 22 IHEs, several military bases, and technology-based industries, targeting individuals with exceptional talent and/or outstanding distinction in an academic field. If an LEA identified an individual or the individual expressed an interest, the LEA could submit supporting documentation to the Commissioner of Education. Documentation includes an advanced course of study or extensive training in the area of certification requested; outstanding distinction or exceptional talent in the field of certification requested; significant recent occupational experience which is related to the field of certification. After review, the Commissioner could order issuance of a special certificate, valid for one year, specifying subjects the holder would be authorized to teach

TITLE: Master of Science in Teaching: Certification Emphasis

HISTORY: Approved by the Kansas State Board of Education in 2001. The first applicants began the program in the summer on 2001.

Note: After July 1, 2003, this program will convert to the Restricted Teaching License requirements (see the listing for the Restricted Teaching License for details).

MOTIVATION: Pittsburg State University (PSU) is responding to a shortage of teachers in the Kansas City, Kansas school district.

GRADE LEVELS AND/OR SUBJECT AREA(S) COVERED:

All secondary 7-12 certification subject areas that have approved programs at Pittsburg State and elementary education.

WHO OPERATES: Pittsburg State University in conjunction with the new Teacher Project.

REQUIREMENTS TO ENTER:

1. Bachelor's degree.

2. Graduate and program admission application.

3. A cumulative GPA of 2.50. A GPA of 2.5 in the major, and a 2.75 in the general education core.

4. A signed teaching contract half-time or more at a state-accredited school district.

5. Meet certificate requirements for an academic area in addition to the requirements for this degree.

6. Three letters of recommendation with at least one letter being from a previous employer.

7. Successfully complete an Interview and Evaluation session with the admission committee.

8. A commitment to complete an intensive course work segment prior to entering the classroom for the first semester.

Limited to 30 applicants per year.

PROGRAM DESCRIPTION:

The program offers three tracks; elementary, middle level, and secondary.

Participants complete a preservice summer institute offered through The New Teacher Project. Includes both teaching of students in summer school and completing graduate level coursework.

Enter their own classroom in the fall semester. They will teach while concurrently enrolled in the necessary graduate level coursework to fulfill the requirements of the Master's Degree in Teaching over the next two years, including the second summer.

Must successfully complete the PPST during the first year.

Must maintain a 3.0 grade point average throughout the program.

Participants meet with teacher mentors at least once each week and with the university supervisor at the designated time.

Candidates must achieve satisfactory evaluations from the mentor teacher, building principal and university supervisors.

WHO EVALUATES: Pittsburg State University in conjunction with the mentor teacher and building principal.

LENGTH OF TIME: Two years, including both summers.

KANSAS

Number of Teaching Licenses Issued

	2001-02	2000-01	1999-00	1996-97	1995-96	1994-95	1993-94	1992-93	1991-92
Persons who completed an approved college teacher preparation program at an IHE in Kansas	1,720	1,728	1,940	2,350	2,711	2,741	N/A	2,263	2,157
Total certificates issued	22,737	20,251	19,713	22,876	18,787	19,373	18,565	19,277	17,437
Initial certificates issued	3,104	2,884	3,272	3,610	3,683	4,396	4,533	4,899	4,226

Number of Teachers Employed

	2001-02	2000-01	1999-00	1997-98	1996-97	1995-96	1994-95	1992-93	1991-92
Total Teachers Employed in the State	41,545	41,058	41,250	39,760	b/ 33,795	e/ 36,273	30,578	35,831	35,276
Newly Hired Teachers in Each Year	1,769	1,919	2,025	1,284	c/ 1,053	f/ 1,732	1,396	1,339	c/ 1,138

a/ 1,611 of these completed approved programs at the undergraduate level.

b/ Total number of certified school employees.

c/ Figure is for first-year teachers, except for the largest district.

d/ State data showed that there were 1,143 first-year teachers, but that figure does not include first-year teachers hired in the four largest districts in the state.

e/ A new computer system for data collection with different data codes resulted in the drop.

f/ New data collection codes include only new teachers directly from college.

Kansas Dept. of Education
Division of Certification
120 East Tenth Street
Topeka, KS 66612
Attn: Dr. Martha Gage
Director of Certification and Teacher Education
(785) 296-8012

KANSAS

Institutions of higher education that have developed alternative teacher preparation programs leading to a teaching license:

States with which the state has reciprocity of teacher licenses:

Kansas is a signatory of the NASDTEC Interstate Contract Agreement

Kansas is a signatory of the Central States Exchange regional agreement.

Institutions of higher education that have *any* teacher preparation programs leading to a license to teach.

Baker University
Benedictine College
Bethany College
Bethel College
Emporia State University
Ft. Hays State University
Friends University
Haskell Indian Nations University
Kansas State University
Kansas Wesleyan University
McPherson College
Mid-America Nazarene University
Newman University
Ottawa University
Pittsburg State University
St. Mary College
Southwestern College
Sterling College
Tabor College
University of Kansas
Washburn University
Wichita State University

Contact information for persons interested in finding a teaching position in the state:

Visit the Web site at: http://www.kansasteachingjobs.com

TITLE: Alternative Route --- Local District Certification Option

HISTORY: Legislation enacted in 1990.

MOTIVATION: Legislative response to the growing number of adults who already have a bachelor's degree in a field other than education who want to become licensed to teach.

GRADE LEVELS AND/OR SUBJECT AREAS COVERED:

All, except special education.

WHO OPERATES: School district, which must show that it has sought collaboration with an IHE.

REQUIREMENTS TO ENTER PROGRAM:

To participate, a candidate must:

(a) Have a baccalaureate degree;

(b) Have a grade point average (GPA) of 2.5 overall (on a 4.0 scale), or a GPA of 2.0 with "exceptional life experience" related to teaching;

(c) Pass written tests of knowledge in the specific teaching field (must have completed a 30-hour major/minor, or have five years' experience in the field);

(d) Have been offered employment in a school district which has an alternative certification program approved by the state's Education Professional Standards Board (EPSB).

Upon completion of these requirements, the candidate shall be issued a one-year Provisional Certificate.

PROGRAM DESCRIPTION:

The candidate shall be issued a Professional Certificate upon satisfactory completion of:

(a) The program;

(b) The PRAXIS exam(s); and

(c) The teacher internship.

The candidate shall be placed on the local district salary schedule for the rank corresponding to the degree held.

Each local district alternative training program shall include:

(a) A full-time seminar and practicum of no less than eight weeks duration prior to the time the candidate assumes responsibility for a classroom;

(b) An 18-week period of classroom supervision, while the candidate assumes responsibility on a half-time basis for the classroom, including weekly visits by the professional support team, and three formal evaluations;

(c) An 18-week period of supervision, while the candidate assumes full responsibility for the classroom, including monthly visits and at least two evaluations by the professional support team;

(d) At least 250 hours of formal instruction;

(e) A comprehensive evaluation report by the support team, including a recommendation as to whether the candidate should be issued a one-year certificate of eligibility to complete the internship.

The district plan for operating an alternative certification program must include:

(a) Written evidence that the district has sought sponsorship of the program with an accredited college;

(b) The four-member professional support team (school principal, experienced teacher, instructional supervisor, and college/university faculty member);

(c) The persons who will provide the 250 hours of formal instruction;

(d) The training program for the support team;

(e) The training program for the candidate;

(f) A budget, not to exceed five years duration;

(g) A program director;

(h) An appeals process for the candidate; and

(i) Roles and expectations for the professional support team.

NUMBER OF CREDIT HOURS TO COMPLETE:

250 contact hours of direct instruction.

WHO EVALUATES: Professional support team.

LENGTH OF TIME Total of 44 weeks: eight weeks full-time seminar and practicum; 18 weeks half-time teaching; 18 weeks full-time teaching.

OTHER:

TITLE: Alternative Route --- Exceptional Work Experience Certification Option

HISTORY: Legislation enacted in 1998.

MOTIVATION: To bring into secondary school classrooms individuals who already have exceptional work experience in the field(s) in which they will teach.

GRADE LEVELS AND/OR SUBJECT AREAS COVERED:

Secondary level (grades 9-12).

WHO OPERATES: School district with candidate approval by EPSB.

REQUIREMENTS TO ENTER PROGRAM:

An individual who has been offered employment at the secondary level (grades 9-12) in a local school district shall be issued a one-year Provisional Certificate, if he/she has:

Documented 10 years' exceptional work experience in the area for which certification is being sought;

A bachelor's degree, with a GPA of at least 2.5 on a 4.0 scale; and

Submit an application, jointly with the employing school district, to the state's Education Professional Standards Board (EPSB).

PROGRAM DESCRIPTION:

"Exceptional experience" is defined as "recognized superiority as compared with others in rank, status, and attainment."

Verification shall include:

Documentation that the state's New Teacher Standards have been addressed; and

Professional recommendations.

Upon meeting the requirements, the candidate shall be issued a one-year Provisional Certificate. The Professional Certificate shall be issued upon satisfactory completion of the teacher internship. The candidate shall be placed on the local district salary schedule for the rank corresponding to the degree held.

NUMBER OF CREDIT HOURS TO COMPLETE:

No additional credit hours. See description of Alternative Certification Program for detailed information on the required internship program

WHO EVALUATES: EPSB evaluates candidate's initial application. Internship committee assesses first-year performance.

LENGTH OF TIME Candidates complete a one-year internship required of all new Kentucky teachers certified via alternative or traditional routes.

TITLE: Alternative Route --- College Faculty Certification Option

HISTORY: Legislation enacted in 1996.

MOTIVATION: To allow entry into secondary school classrooms for persons with experience teaching in colleges or universities.

GRADE LEVELS AND/OR SUBJECT AREAS COVERED:

Secondary level (grades 9-12).

WHO OPERATES: State (EPSB).

REQUIREMENTS TO ENTER PROGRAM:

To participate, a candidate must:

(a) Hold a master's or doctoral degree in the academic subject area for which certification is sought; and

(b) Have a minimum of five years of full-time teaching experience (or its equivalent of at least 90 semester credit hours taught) in the academic subject area for which certification is sought, in a regionally- or nationally-accredited IHE.

PROGRAM DESCRIPTION:

College faculty members applying for certification:

(a) Shall, contingent upon meeting the requirements, be issued a Statement of Eligibility, valid for five years;

(b) Shall, contingent upon confirmation of employment, be issued a Provisional Teaching Certificate for participation in the internship program;

(c) Shall, contingent upon successful completion of the teacher internship program, be issued the Professional Certificate, valid for an additional four years, and may renew the Professional Certificate for additional five-year periods, contingent upon three years of successful teaching experience or six semester hours of additional graduate credit.

(d) The candidate shall be placed on the local district salary schedule for the rank corresponding to the degree held.

NUMBER OF CREDIT HOURS TO COMPLETE:

No additional credit hours. See description of ACP for detailed information on the required internship program.

WHO EVALUATES: Internship committee assesses first year performance.

TITLE: Alternative Route --- Adjunct Instructor Certification Option

HISTORY: Legislation enacted in 1984.

MOTIVATION: To allow entry into part-time K-12 teaching for persons with training or expertise in specialty area(s).

GRADE LEVELS AND/OR SUBJECT AREAS COVERED:

All.

WHO OPERATES: State.

REQUIREMENTS TO ENTER PROGRAM:

Adjunct instructors:

(a) Shall be "of good moral character" and be at least 18 years of age;

(b) If employed for departmentalized instruction in grades 7-12, shall hold a bachelor's degree from a regionally-accredited institution with an overall minimum grade point average (GPA) of 2.5 (on a 4.0 scale), and a major, minor, or area of concentration in the subject to be taught with a minimum GPA of 2.5;

(c) If employed for vocational education, shall be a high school graduate, and have at least four years of appropriate occupational experience (or its equivalent, as approved by the Division of Secondary Vocational Education) for the specialty to be taught.

(d) If employed for teaching elementary or birth to primary, shall hold a bachelor's degree from a regionally-accredited institution with an overall 2.5 GPA (on a 4.0 scale) with a planned program in child development or a related area.

PROGRAM DESCRIPTION:

Adjunct instructors are those persons who:

(a) Have training or experience in a specific subject area;

(b) Are employed in a part-time position on an *annual contract basis* and shall not be eligible for continuing service status or retirement provisions;

(c) May contract with local school boards for part-time services on an hourly, daily, or other periodic basis;

(d) Shall not fill positions that will result in the displacement of qualified teachers with regular certificates who are already employed in the district;

(e) Shall be provided an orientation program developed and implemented for adjunct instructors by the local school board; and

(f) Shall be placed on the local district salary schedule for the rank corresponding to the degree held by the teacher.

NUMBER OF CREDIT HOURS TO COMPLETE:

N/A

TITLE: Minority Recruitment

HISTORY: Enacted in legislation by the General Assembly in 1990.

MOTIVATION: To bring minorities into teaching.

GRADE LEVELS AND/OR SUBJECT AREAS COVERED:

All.

WHO OPERATES: IHEs.

REQUIREMENTS TO ENTER PROGRAM:

PROGRAM DESCRIPTION:

Institutions may develop programs in accord with the alternative certification legislation or on an experimental basis to "identify, recruit, and prepare as teachers minority persons who already have earned college degrees in other job fields."

NUMBER OF CREDIT HOURS TO COMPLETE:

Determined by IHE.

WHO EVALUATES: IHE.

TITLE: Veterans of the Armed Forces

HISTORY: Enacted in legislation by the General Assembly in 2000.

MOTIVATION: Designed to:

(a) Help relieve overall teacher shortages, especially in the areas of math, science, special education, and vocational technology; and

(b) Improve the quality of education by attracting mature, highly-experienced personnel to the classroom.

GRADE LEVELS AND/OR SUBJECT AREAS COVERED:

All.

WHO OPERATES: State (EPSB).

REQUIREMENTS TO ENTER PROGRAM:

You are a candidate for this route if you:

- Were discharged or released from active duty under honorable conditions after six years of active duty immediately before the discharge or release;
- Have a bachelor's degree in the subject matter or related area for which certification is sought;
- Have a grade point average (GPA) of 2.5 (on a 4.0 scale) for a bachelor's degree or hold an advanced degree; and
- Have passing scores on EPSB-approved subject matter assessments.

PROGRAM DESCRIPTION:

A candidate meeting the above requirements receives a Statement of Eligibility.

After obtaining employment, the candidate is issued a one-year Provisional Certificate.

Upon successful completion of a Kentucky Teacher Internship Program (KTIP) during the first year of teaching, the teacher receives the Professional Certificate.

NUMBER OF CREDIT HOURS TO COMPLETE: N/A

WHO EVALUATES: N/A

KENTUCKY   Class H

TITLE: University-Based Alternative Teacher Certification

HISTORY: Enacted in legislation by the General Assembly in 2000.

MOTIVATION: Designed to relieve overall teacher shortages and provide a mechanism for recruitment of mid-career professionals into teaching.

GRADE LEVELS AND/OR SUBJECT AREAS COVERED: All.

WHO OPERATES: IHE.

REQUIREMENTS TO ENTER PROGRAM:

- Bachelor's or master's degree;
- Meet minimum teacher education admissions standards.

PROGRAM DESCRIPTION:

Allows completion of the teacher preparation program with concurrent employment in a school district.

After obtaining employment, the candidate is issued a Temporary Provisional Certificate.

Participates in the Kentucky Teacher Internship Program (KTIP).

The candidate must complete all requirements within two years and pass all required assessments.

The candidate then receives the Professional Certificate.

NUMBER OF CREDIT HOURS TO COMPLETE: N/A

WHO EVALUATES: IHE.

LENGTH OF TIME Not more than two years.

KENTUCKY

Number of Teaching Licenses Issued

	2001-02	2000-01	1999-00	1998-99	1997-98	1996-97	1995-96	1992-93	1991-92	1990-9
Persons who completed an approved college teacher preparation program	2,248	2,324	2,403	N/A	N/A	5,754	5,439	N/A	N/A	7,500
Internship program	2,876	3,035	3,369	2,920	2,782	N/A	N/A	N/A	N/A	1,800
Emergency	1,812	1,432	931	506	291	N/A	N/A	N/A	N/A	75
Temporary	99	11	N/A	N/A	N/A	N/A	N/A	N/A	N/A	N/A
Alternative Route ---	282	380	33	40	14	N/A	N/A	N/A	N/A	20

Number of Teachers Employed

	2000-01	1999-00	1998-99	1997-98	1992-93	1991-92	1990-91	1989-90	1988-89
Total Teachers Employed in the State	40,002	47,643	46,430	38,417	N/A	N/A	42,526	41,559	35,736
Newly Hired Teachers in Each Year	N/A	3,919	2,274	N/A	N/A	N/A	1,993	1,837	1,465

Kentucky Education Professional
Standards Board
1024 Capital Center Dr.
Frankfort, KY 40601
Attn: Dr. Susan Leib or
Mary Ellen Wiederwohl
(502) 573-4606
Fax: (502) 573-1610

KENTUCKY

Institutions of higher education that have developed alternative teacher preparation programs leading to a teaching license:

Asbury College
Bellarmine University
Eastern Kentucky University
Morehead State University
Murray State University
Northern Kentucky University
Spalding University
Thomas More College
Union College
University of Kentucky
University of Louisville
Western Kentucky University

States with which the state has reciprocity of teacher licenses:

NASDTEC Interstate Contract.

Institutions of higher education that have *any* teacher preparation programs leading to a license to teach:

Alice Lloyd College
Asbury College
Bellarmine University
Berea College
Brescia University
Campbellsville University
Centre College
Cumberland College
Eastern Kentucky University
Georgetown College
Kentucky Christian College
Kentucky State University
Kentucky Wesleyan College
Lindsey Wilson College
Mid-Continent College
Midway College
Morehead State University
Murray State University
Northern Kentucky University
Pikeville College
Spalding University
Thomas More College
Transylvania University
Union College
University of Kentucky
University of Louisville
Western Kentucky University

Contact information for persons interested in finding a teaching position in the state:

Jennifer Miller & Darryl Thompson
Kentucky Department of Education
Educator Recruitment & Retention
CPT 500 Mero Street, 17th Floor
Frankfort, KY 40601
Phone: (502) 564-1479

LOUISIANA

The Louisiana Alternative Teacher Certification Program providing alternative paths to teacher certification was adopted in September 2001. This program provides opportunities for individuals with non-education degrees to become certified public school teachers. Individuals seeking teacher certification under the Alternative Certification Program will follow one of three alternative certification paths: the *Practitioner Teacher Program*, the *Master's Degree Program*, or the *Non-Master's/Certification-Only Program.* (Descriptions of each of these programs follow on pages 197-203.)

Universities offering alternative certification are required to begin implementation of the newly adopted plans on or before July 2002.

No students should be accepted into the "old" post-baccalaureate alternate certification program after Spring Semester 2003. Candidates already in the "old" alternative certification programs (pages 204-209) would be given until August 31, 2006, to complete their programs.

TITLE: Practitioner Teacher Program

HISTORY: Began as a pilot 2001-02, with nine approved providers. Fully implemented in Summer 2002 with twelve approved providers.

MOTIVATION: Blue Ribbon commission Initiative -- a fast-track alternate option for certifying teachers.

GRADE LEVELS AND/OR SUBJECT AREAS COVERED: Elementary (grades 1-6), Middle School (grades 4-8), Secondary (grades 7-12; vary by provider), and Special Education Mild/Moderate.

WHO OPERATES: Universities and approved private providers.

REQUIREMENTS TO ENTER PROGRAM:

Submission of an official transcript for evaluation to a Louisiana college or university with an approved teacher education program or to a state-approved private practitioner program provider.

Baccalaureate degree from a regionally accredited university.

Have a 2.2 GPA on undergraduate work. Appropriate, successful work experience can be substituted for the required GPA, at the discretion of the program provider. However, in no case, may the GPA be less that 2.2. (note: State law requires that upon completion of the program the teacher candidate has a 2.5 GPA for certification).

Pass the Pre-Professional Skills Test (e.g. reading, writing, and mathematics) on the PRAXIS. (An exclusion from this requirement can be granted for a candidate who has an earned Master's Degree.)

Pass the content specific examinations for the PRAXIS

- Candidates for Grades 1-6 (regular and special education) pass the Elementary Education: Content Knowledge specialty examination;
- Candidates for Grades 4-8 (regular and special education): pass the Middle School Education: Content Knowledge specialty examination;
- Candidates for Grades 7-12 (regular and special education): pass the content specialty examination(s) (e.g. English, Mathematics, etc.) on the PRAXIS and in the content area(s) in which they intend to teach.

Meet the other non-course requirements established by the college or university

PROGRAM DESCRIPTION:

1. Teaching Preparation (Summer) 9 credit hours (or equivalent 135 contact hours)

    - Grades 1-6, 4-8 and 7-12 practitioner teachers will complete courses (or equivalent contact hours) pertaining to child-adolescent development/psychology, the diverse learner, classroom management, assessment, instructional design, and instructional strategies before starting their teaching positions.

    - Mild/moderate special education teachers will take courses (or equivalent contact hours) that focus upon the special needs of the mild/moderate exceptional child, classroom management, behavioral management, assessment and evaluation, methods/materials for mild/moderate exceptional children, and vocational and transition services for students with disabilities.

2. Teaching Internship and First-Year Teaching 12 credit hours (or equivalent contact hours)

    Practitioner teachers will assume full-time teaching positions in school districts.

    Participate in two seminars (one during the fall and one in the spring) that address immediate needs of the Practitioner Teacher program teachers.

    Receive one-on-one supervision through an internship program provided by the program providers.

    The Practitioner Teacher will also receive support from school-based mentor teachers (provided by the Louisiana Teacher Assistance and Assessment Program) and principals.

3. Teacher Performance Review (end of first year).

    Program providers, principals, mentors and practitioner teachers will form teams to review the first year teaching performance or practitioner teachers and determine the extent to which the practitioner teachers have demo9nstrated teaching proficiency.

types of instruction needed to address the areas of need. Prescriptive plans that require from 1 to 12 credit hours (or equivalent 15 - 180 equivalent contact hours) of instruction will be developed for practitioner teachers. In addition, the teams will determine if the practitioner teachers should participate in the new teacher assessment during the fall or if the practitioner teachers should receive additional mentor support and be assessed after the fall.

4. Prescriptive Plan Implementation 1-9 credit hours (15-135 contact hours)

   Practitioner teachers who demonstrate areas of need will complete prescriptive plans.

5. Louisiana Assessment Program

   Practitioner teachers will be assessed during the fall or spring of the second year of teaching depending upon their teaching proficiencies.

6. PRAXIS Review

   Program providers will offer review sessions to prepare practitioner teachers to pass remaining components of the PRAXIS.

NUMBER OF CREDIT HOURS TO COMPLETE: 21-30 (Varies)

WHO EVALUATES: Private providers and colleges or universities.

LENGTH OF TIME: Not specified

TITLE: Master's Degree Program

HISTORY: Summer 2002

MOTIVATION: Blue Ribbon Commission Initiative for alternative certification.

GRADE LEVELS AND/OR SUBJECT AREAS COVERED: Early Childhood (PK-3), Elementary (grades 1-6), Middle School (grades 4-8), Secondary (grades 7-12, secondary areas vary by provider), and Special Education Mild/Moderate.

WHO OPERATES: Approved University providers.

REQUIREMENTS TO ENTER PROGRAM:

Baccalaureate degree from a regionally accredited university.

Have a 2.5 GPA on undergraduate work.

Pass the Pre-Professional Skills Test (e.g. reading, writing, and mathematics) on the PRAXIS. (An exclusion from this requirement can be granted for a candidate who has an earned Master's Degree.)

Pass the content specific examinations for the PRAXIS

- Candidates for PK-3 (regular and special education): pass the Elementary Education: Content Knowledge specialty examination.
- Candidates for Grades 1-6 (regular and special education) pass the Elementary Education: Content Knowledge specialty examination.
- Candidates for Grades 4-8 (regular and special education): pass the Middle School Education: Content Knowledge specialty examination.
- Candidates for Grades 7-12 (regular and special education): pass the content specialty examination(s) (e.g. English, Mathematics, etc.) on the PRAXIS and in the content area(s) in which they intend to teach.

Meet the other non-course requirements established by the college or university

PROGRAM DESCRIPTION:

1. Knowledge of Learner and the Learning Environment 15 credit hours

   - Grades PK-3, 1-6, 4-8 and 7-12: Child-adolescent development/psychology, the diverse learner, classroom management, assessment, instructional design, and instructional strategies.

   - Mild/moderate special education 1-12: Special needs of the mild/moderate exceptional child, classroom management, behavioral management, assessment and evaluation, methods and materials for mild/moderate exceptional children, and vocational and transition services for students with disabilities.

2. Methodology and Teaching -- Methods courses and field experiences 12-15 credit hours

3 Student Teaching or Internship 6-9 credit hours

NUMBER OF CREDIT HOURS TO COMPLETE: 33-39 credit hours

WHO EVALUATES: Colleges or universities..

LENGTH OF TIME: Not specified

TITLE: Non-Master's/Certification-Only Program

HISTORY: Summer 2003

MOTIVATION: Blue Ribbon Commission Initiative for alternative certification.

GRADE LEVELS AND/OR SUBJECT AREAS COVERED: Early Childhood (PK-3), Elementary (grades 1-6), Middle School (grades 4-8), Secondary (grades 7-12; secondary areas vary by provider), and Special Education Mild/Moderate.

WHO OPERATES: Approved University providers.

REQUIREMENTS TO ENTER PROGRAM:

Baccalaureate degree from a regionally accredited university.

Have a minimum of 2.20 GPA on undergraduate work. (Note: State law requires that upon completion of the program the teacher candidate has a 2.5 GPA for certification).

Pass the Pre-Professional Skills Test (e.g. reading, writing, and mathematics) on the PRAXIS.

Pass the content specific examinations for the PRAXIS

- Candidates for PK-3 (regular and special education): pass the Elementary Education: Content Knowledge specialty examination.
- Candidates for Grades 1-6 (regular and special education) pass the Elementary Education: Content Knowledge specialty examination.
- Candidates for Grades 4-8 (regular and special education): pass the Middle School Education: Content Knowledge specialty examination.
- Candidates for Grades 7-12 (regular and special education): pass the content specialty examination(s) (e.g. English, Mathematics, etc.) on the PRAXIS and in the content area(s) in which they intend to teach.

LOUISIANA — Class D

PROGRAM DESCRIPTION:

1. Knowledge of Learner and the Learning Environment 12 credit hours

   - Grades PK-3, 1-6, 4-8 and 7-12: Child-adolescent development/psychology, the diverse learner, classroom management and organization, assessment, instructional design, and reading/instructional strategies.

   - Mild/moderate special education 1-12: Special needs of the mild/moderate exceptional child, classroom management, behavioral management, assessment and evaluation including IEP and ESYP, reading instruction, and vocational/transition services for students with disabilities.

2. Methodology and Teaching -- Methods courses and field experiences 6 credit hours

   - Methods courses, to include case studies and field experiences

3 Student Teaching or Internship 6 credit hours

NUMBER OF CREDIT HOURS TO COMPLETE: 24- 33 credit hours

WHO EVALUATES: Colleges or universities..

LENGTH OF TIME: Varies with individual candidates.

TITLE: Alternate Post-Baccalaureate Certification Program – Elementary Education (Grades 1-8)

HISTORY: March 1995. (Mandatory September 1, 2000)

MOTIVATION: Teacher shortage.

GRADE LEVELS AND/OR SUBJECT AREAS COVERED: Grades 1-8.

WHO OPERATES: IHE

REQUIREMENTS TO ENTER PROGRAM:

A bachelor's degree.

An overall grade point average of 2.5 on a 4.0 scale.

PROGRAM DESCRIPTION:

This program provides opportunities for individuals with non-education degrees to become certified public school teachers.

Certification requirements are:

General education – The general education component of the candidate's baccalaureate degree must meet the state minimum requirements.

Specialized Academic Education -- The candidate must have a degree with the major in the area of certification or meet the state minimum requirements. A baccalaureate degree from a regionally accredited institution will satisfy six hours of the specialized academic education requirements of Bulletin 746.

Professional Education -- 24 semester hours of coursework in pedagogy (professional education) as prescribed by the school/department/college of education. The professional education component should include courses in theories of teaching and learning, student achievement and evaluation, human growth and development, methods of instruction, reading diagnosis and remediation, and expectations of children or at-risk children.

Student teaching or a one-year internship in the area(s) of certification with supervision provided by faculty in the College of Education.

The applicant must have attained scores on the Praxis/NTE (National Teacher Examinations) that meet state requirements for certification.

NUMBER OF CREDIT HOURS TO COMPLETE:

Varies individually.

WHO EVALUATES: IHE.

LENGTH OF TIME: Not specified

OTHER: NOTE: No final grade below a "C" will be accepted for student teaching or any professional or specialized academic education course which is required for certification. In addition, no final grade below a "C" will be accepted for any other course specified as a deficiency under this plan.

The State Department of Education, Certification, and Higher Education unit, has the authority to waive the student teaching upon verification of three years of successful teaching experience in the area of certification.

TITLE: Alternate Post-Baccalaureate Certification Program -- Secondary

HISTORY: March 1990.

MOTIVATION: Teacher shortage.

GRADE LEVELS AND/OR SUBJECT AREAS COVERED: Secondary (grades 7-12)

WHO OPERATES: IHE

REQUIREMENTS TO ENTER PROGRAM:

A bachelor's degree.

An overall grade point average of 2.5 on a 4.0 scale.

PROGRAM DESCRIPTION:

This program provides opportunities for individuals with non-education degrees to become certified public school teachers.

Certification requirements are:

General education -- A baccalaureate degree will fulfill the general education requirements.

Specialized Academic Education -- The candidate must have a degree with the major in the area of certification or meet the state minimum requirements.

Professional Education -- 18 semester hours of coursework in pedagogy (professional education) appropriate to the level of certification as prescribed by the IHE teacher education program. The professional education component should include courses in theories of teaching and learning, student achievement and evaluation, human growth and development, and methods of instruction.

Student teaching or a one-year internship in the area(s) of certification with supervision provided by faculty in the College of Education.

The applicant must have attained scores on the Praxis/NTE, which meet state requirements for certification.

NUMBER OF CREDIT HOURS TO COMPLETE:

Varies individually.

WHO EVALUATES: IHE.

LENGTH OF TIME: Not specified

OTHER: NOTE: No final grade below a "C" will be accepted for student teaching or any professional or specialized academic education course which is required for certification. In addition, no final grade below a "C" will be accepted for any other course specified as a deficiency under this plan.

The State Department of Education, Certification, and Higher Education unit, has the authority to waive the student teaching upon verification of three years of successful teaching experience in the area of certification.

LOUISIANA

Class E

TITLE: Alternate Post-Baccalaureate Certification Program -- Special Education

HISTORY: March 1990

MOTIVATION: Teacher shortage.

GRADE LEVELS AND/OR SUBJECT AREA (S) COVERED: Special education areas.

WHO OPERATES: IHE

REQUIREMENTS TO ENTER:

A bachelor's degree.

An overall grade point average of 2.5 on a 4.0 scale.

PROGRAM DESCRIPTION:

This program provides opportunities for individuals with non-education degrees to become certified public school teachers.

Certification requirements are:

General Education -- A baccalaureate degree will fulfill the general education requirements.

Specialized Academic Education -- The candidate must have a degree with a major in the area of certification or meet the state minimum requirements.

Professional Education -- 18 semester hours of coursework in pedagogy (professional education) appropriate to the level of certification as prescribed by the IHE teacher education program. The professional education component should include courses in theories of teaching and learning, student achievement and evaluation, human growth and development, and methods of instruction.

Student teaching or a one-year internship in the area(s) of certification with supervision provided by faculty in the College of Education.

The applicant must have attained scores on the Praxis/NTE (National Teacher Examinations) which meet the state requirements for certification.

NUMBER OF CREDIT HOURS TO COMPLETE:

Varies individually.

WHO EVALUATES: IHE.

LENGTH OF TIME: Not specified.

OTHER: NOTE: No final grade below a "C" will be accepted for student teaching or any professional or specialized academic education course which is required for certification. In addition, no final grade below a "C" will be accepted for any other course specified as a deficiency under this plan.

The State Department of Education, Certification and Higher Education unit, has the authority to waive the student teaching upon verification of three years of successful teaching experience in the area of certification.

LOUISIANA

Number of Teaching Licenses Issued

	2001-02	2000-01	1999-00	1998-99	1997-98	1996-97	1995-96	1994-95	1993-94	1992-93
Persons who completed an approved college teacher preparation program Total Initial Standard Certificates Issued (Program Not Specified)	2,936	3,016	2,297	2,862	2,540	2,137	2,823	3,016	3,356	3,143
Internship program	N/A	N/A	N/A	N/A		N/A	N/A	N/A	N/A	N/A
Emergency	5	6	3	10	8	7	10	7	8	3
Temporary	5,950	5,868	4,826	4,675	4,698	4,717	4,784	4,775	4,681	4,514
Alternative Route	612	728	438	478	484	414	432	389	441	355
Other -- Out of State Provisional (1 Year)	240	344	198	409	331	175	155	152	153	176

Number of Teachers Employed

	2001-02	2000-01	1999-00	1998-99	1997-98	1996-97	1995-96	1994-95	1993-94	1992-93
Total Teachers Employed in the State	55,526	55,429	55,619	54,775	54,248	53,711	53,330	48,971	52,358	N/A
Newly Hired Teachers in Each Year	N/A	N/A	N/A	N/A	N/A	N/A	N/A	N/A	N/A	N/A

Louisiana Dept. of Education
Teacher Certification and
Higher Education
P.O. Box 44064
Baton Rouge, LA 70804
Attn: Mary Helen S. McCoy, Ph.D.
(504) 342-3490

LOUISIANA

Institutions of higher education that have developed alternative teacher preparation programs leading to a teaching license:

Centenary College
Dillard University
Grambling State University
Louisiana College
Louisiana State University, Baton Rouge
Louisiana State University-Shreveport
Louisiana Tech University
Loyola University
McNeese State University
Nicholls State University
Northeast Louisiana University
Northwestern State University
Our Lady of Holy Cross College
Southeastern Louisiana University
Southern University, Baton Rouge
Southern University in New Orleans
Tulane University*
University of New Orleans
University of Southwestern Louisiana
Xavier University

States with which the state has reciprocity of teacher licenses:

NASDTEC Interstate Contract.

Institutions of higher education that have *any* teacher preparation programs leading to a license to teach.

Centenary College
Dillard University
Grambling State University
Louisiana College
Louisiana State University, Baton Rouge
Louisiana State University-Shreveport
Louisiana Tech University
Loyola University
McNeese State University
Nicholls State University
Northeast Louisiana University
Northwestern State University
Our Lady of Holy Cross College
Southeastern Louisiana University
Southern University, Baton Rouge
Southern University in New Orleans
Tulane University*
University of New Orleans
University of Southwestern Louisiana
Xavier University

*Tulane University discontinued new enrollment into teacher preparation in October 1996.

Contact information for persons interested in finding a teaching position in the state:

Certification and Higher Education
P.O. Box 94064
Baton Rouge, LA 70804
Phone: (504) 342-3490

TITLE: Transcript Analysis

HISTORY: In effect for many years.

MOTIVATION: Shortage, to fill the needs of school districts, since only about 20 percent of newly hired teachers come through approved teacher education programs in Maine.

GRADE LEVELS AND/OR SUBJECT AREAS COVERED: All.

WHO OPERATES: State

REQUIREMENTS TO ENTER:

In applying for transcript analysis, an individual must provide a copy of undergraduate and/or graduate transcripts. Although official transcripts are preferred, legible photocopies of official transcripts are acceptable. These must show the individual's social security number and all courses for which credit has been received and the date that degrees were awarded. Continuing education units and teacher recertification credits are not acceptable for initial certification.

An applicant for a Conditional Certificate must have met the academic content area requirements and must meet passing scores on the PPST during the initial term of the certificate, as a prerequisite for renewal, further renewal, or issuance of a Professional Certificate.

If the individual is certified to teach in another state, he or she must submit a copy of out-of-state teaching certificate.

In order for a Conditional Certificate to be awarded, the local school district must have actively sought to employ a Provisional or Professional Certificate holder, but has been unable to do so.

PROGRAM DESCRIPTION:

If the state has determined, through transcript analysis, that the individual is eligible for a Conditional Certificate, he or she must complete all requirements for full certification while teaching under the Conditional credential. The transcript analysis determines which coursework deficiencies must be completed to qualify for full certification.

To renew the Conditional Certificate, the individual must demonstrate that he or she has annually completed the amount of approved study ordinarily required for renewal of a professional certificate. Approved study must consist of courses unless the Department gives advance approval for in-service training in lieu of courses, in whole or in part.

The individual's support system recommends that the Conditional Certificate be renewed or that a Provisional or Professional Certificate be issued.

NUMBER OF CREDIT HOURS TO COMPLETE:

For secondary level -- 18 semester hours of education coursework plus student teaching; for elementary level -- 27 semester hours plus student teaching.

WHO EVALUATES: State.

LENGTH OF TIME: The Conditional Certificate may be renewed for not more than two additional one-year terms.

OTHER: Transcript analysis is used for teachers coming from out of state, Maine teachers seeking additional endorsements to teach out of their subject areas, and for career changers.

MAINE

Number of Teaching Licenses Issued

	1999-00	1998-99	1995-96	1992-93	1991-92	1990-91	1989-90	1988-89
Persons who completed an approved college teacher preparation program	N/A	N/A	N/A	N/A	N/A	* N/A	400	
Internship program	N/A	N/A	N/A	N/A	N/A	N/A	N/A	
Emergency	N/A	N/A	N/A	N/A	N/A	N/A	178	
Other -- Conditional (Transcript Analysis)	335	495	N/A	468	N/A	285	424	300
Transitional Endorsement **	407	422	N/A	481	314	344	294	

Number of Teachers Employed

	1999-00	1998-99	1995-96	1992-93	1991-92	1990-91	1989-90	1988-89
Total Teachers Employed in the State	17,538	15,086	N/A	N/A	N/A	16,802	N/A	14,556
Newly Hired Teachers in Each Year	N/A	N/A	N/A	N/A	N/A	661	N/A	475

* *A state official said only about 10 percent of new teachers hired in Maine are produced by approved IHE programs in the state.*

** *Transitional Endorsement is issued upon the request of an employing superintendent and the teacher with a valid certificate who has accepted a teaching assignment out of the endorsed content area. The transitional teacher must complete 6 semester hours annually of prescribed coursework in order to renew the transitional endorsement.*

Maine Dept. of Education
Certification Office
23 State House Station
Augusta, ME 04333-0023
Attn: Nancy Ibarguen
(207) 624-6603
email: nancy.ibarguen@state.me.us

MAINE

Institutions of higher education that have developed alternative teacher preparation programs leading to a teaching license:

N/A.

States with which the state has reciprocity of teacher licenses:

NASDTEC Interstate Contract.

Note: Although Maine has reciprocity with the NASDTEC Interstate Contract states, this does NOT mean that someone certified in one of these states is automatically certified in Maine. There are conditions to certification.

Institutions of higher education that have *any* teacher preparation programs leading to a license to teach.

Bates College
Bowdin College
Colby College
College of the Atlantic
Husson College
Saint Joseph's College
University of Maine at Farmington
University of Maine at Fort Kent
University of Maine - Machias
University of Maine - Orono
University of Maine - Presque Isle
University of New England
University of Southern Maine

Contact information for persons interested in finding a teaching position in the state:

Nancy Ibarguen
Department of Education
23 State House Station
Augusta, ME 04333-0023
Phone: (207) 287-5944

MARYLAND

Class A

TITLE: Resident Teacher Certificate

HISTORY: This bylaw, which permits school systems to hire liberal arts graduates for teaching assignments, was passed by the State Board of Education on Dec. 20, 1990 and became effective on Apr. 1, 1991.

MOTIVATION: To increase the pool of highly qualified professional educators.

GRADE LEVELS AND/OR SUBJECT AREAS COVERED:

Secondary subjects and elementary education.

WHO OPERATES: Local School System

REQUIREMENTS TO ENTER:

A liberal arts bachelor's degree for the certification area of elementary education or a bachelor's degree in the subject to be taught at the secondary level.

3.0 grade point average in the major to be taught.

Employment.

Qualifying scores on the Praxis I and II tests. The professional education test is postponed until the end of the first year of teaching.

The skill areas of development in the 135 clock hours of study are: human growth and development, principles and theories of teaching and learning, strategies and models of teaching, planning and classroom management, and the Maryland reading requirements.

PROGRAM DESCRIPTION:

A school system will have a Resident Teacher Program (RTC) requiring a minimum of 135 hours of study prior to employment.

The program can be offered by a Local School System (LSS) or cooperatively with an IHE, or other approved educational course provider.

The Resident Teacher will be mentored by a certificated teacher.

Upon one additional year of successful teaching and additional hours of study (see below), the local superintendent may recommend that the Resident Teacher be issued the Standard Professional Certificate.

NUMBER OF CREDIT HOURS TO COMPLETE:

135 clock hours before employment -- 135 additional for elementary for a total of 270 hours for elementary teachers and 45 additional hours for secondary for a total of 180 hours for secondary teachers.

WHO EVALUATES: Local School System (LSS).

LENGTH OF TIME: The Resident Teacher Certificate will be valid for no less than one year and, at the request of the LSS, could be issued for a second year.

OTHER: As of September 2001, four LSS had RTC programs. Two of these systems are just beginning their programs. The other two began in 1999. One system has two programs in operation.

MARYLAND

Number of Teaching Licenses Issued

	2001-02	2000-01	1999-00	1998-99	1996-97	1995-96	1994-95	1993-94	1992-93	1991-92
Persons who completed an approved college teacher preparation program	2,332	2,354	2,550	2,546	2,566	2,179	2,395	865	N/A	1,695
Emergency	2,163									
Alternative Route	15	17	80	55	45	71	78	149	N/A	109
Other --Credit count (transcript analysis)	186	58	60	107	N/A	134	242	N/A	295	496

Number of Teachers Employed

	2001-02	2000-01	1999-00	1998-99	1996-97	1995-96	1994-95	1993-94	1992-93	1991-92
Total Teachers Employed in the State	55,021	66,187	52,302	51,077	** 53,846	* 53,726	52,404	45,187	48,707	43,665
Newly Hired Teachers in Each Year	7,385	7,649	7,329	6,033	** 4,588	3,623	3,774	2,955	3,120	2,802

* *Included guidance counselors, psychologists, therapists, administrative and supervisory staff.*

** *Includes therapists, media specialists, guidance counselors, psychologists, staff developers, teacher trainers, remedial specialists, athletic coaches, and other school-level professionals.*

Maryland Dept. of Education
Teacher Education/Certification
200 W. Baltimore St.
Baltimore, MD 21201
Attn: Norma Allen
or Virginia Pilato
Phone: (410) 767-0391
Fax: (410) 767-0390

MARYLAND

Institutions of higher education that have developed <u>post-baccalaureate</u> teacher preparation programs leading to a teaching license:

Bowie State University
College of Notre Dame of MD
Coppin State College
Hood College
Loyola College in MD
Morgan State University
Mount Saint Mary's College
Salisbury State University
Towson University
University of Maryland, Baltimore County
University of Maryland, College Park
University of Maryland, Eastern Shore
Western Maryland College

States with which the state has reciprocity of teacher licenses:

NASDTEC Interstate Contract.

Institutions of higher education that have *any* teacher preparation programs leading to a license to teach.

Bowie State University
College of Notre Dame of MD
Columbia Union College
Coppin State College
Frostburg State University
Goucher College
Hood College
Johns Hopkins University

Loyola College in Maryland
Maryland Institute College of Art
Morgan State University
Mount St. Mary's College
Peabody Institute
St. Mary's College of Maryland
Salisbury State University
Towson University
University of Maryland, Baltimore County
University of Maryland, College Park
University of Maryland, Eastern Shore
University of Maryland, University College
Villa Julie College
Washington College
Western Maryland College

Contact information for persons interested in finding a teaching position in the state:

Program Approval and Assessment Branch
Maryland State Department of Education
200 West. Baltimore St.
Baltimore, MD 21202
Phone: (410) 767-0390

TITLE: Massachusetts Institute for New Teachers (MINT)

HISTORY and MOTIVATION:

The Massachusetts Institute for New Teachers (MINT) grew out of the Massachusetts Signing Bonus Program, which was made possible by the commitment of Gov. Paul Cellucci, Senate President Thomas Birmingham, House Speaker Thomas Finneran, and other government and educational leaders, who passed Chapter 260 of the Acts of 1998, a comprehensive plan to enhance future teaching quality throughout the Commonwealth of Massachusetts. To learn about other state initiatives to recruit and retain quality educators, which is referred to as the "12 to 62 Plan," visit the Web site at: http://www.doe.mass.edu/eq/1262.html.

In 1999, MINT served as the training facility for the first cohort of 59 Signing Bonus recipients. Since 1999, MINT has expanded to include aspiring teachers who have received scholarships, paid tuition, and been sponsored by public school districts, in order to pursue their teaching credentials through this program. Over the past four years, the MINT program has received nearly 4,000 applications from candidates in 40 states and eight countries. More than 600 teachers have been trained through MINT, with more than half teaching in high-demand content areas. MINT graduates are now working in more than 225 schools in all regions of Massachusetts. In a telling sign of success, a study conducted by the University of Massachusetts -Amherst found that almost 90 percent of school principals who have hired MINT graduates would do so again, without reservation.

A typical MINT cohort offers a diverse range of experiences and perspectives. Approximately two-thirds of past participants identified themselves as "career-changers." The other one-third joined the program as recent college graduates from some of the state's most respected institutions of higher education. There is a very balanced age distribution within the program: through 2001, 23 percent of participants were aged 25 or younger; 22 percent were between 26 and 30; 25 percent were between 31 and 40; and 29 percent were aged 41 or older.

GRADE LEVELS and/or SUBJECT AREAS:

Middle and High School only in the following subject areas: mathematics, earth science, physics, chemistry, biology, general science, English, history, political science/political philosophy (social studies), foreign languages, English as a Second Language, health/family and consumer sciences, technology and engineering, business, transitional bilingual education.

WHO OPERATES: The Educator Quality Enhancement cluster of the state Department of Education is working to build a network of state-approved licensure programs, based in the high-need urban districts throughout Massachusetts.

REQUIREMENTS TO ENTER:

All MINT candidates must pass both sections (communication/literacy skills and a subject area) of the Massachusetts Test for Educator Licensure (MTEL).

In addition to this testing requirement, candidates must hold a bachelor's degree and meet any *one* of the following eligibility criteria:

1. Minimum of 3.0 grade point average (GPA) in the major area of study as designated by the college or university the candidate attended;
2. Minimum of 3.0 GPA overall from the college or university the candidate attended;
3. Ranking in the top tenth percentile overall on a nationally recognized examination designated by the Commissioner including, but not limited to, the GRE, MCAT, and LSAT.

Note: Mid-career professionals are not required to meet the academic eligibility outlined above.

A mid-career professional is defined as someone who graduated from an undergraduate program five or more years before applying.

PROGRAM DESCRIPTION:

MINT is an alternative route to initial licensure, designed for mid-career professionals, recent college graduates, and college seniors who aspire to teach at public middle or high schools, but do not have a traditional background in teacher preparation. MINT provides an accelerated certification process through an intensive seven-week training program.

As part of their training, each morning MINT participants teach middle or high school students in summer school programs at various sites across the state. All training sites are located in urban school districts. In the afternoon, participants engage in teacher training seminars to learn the skills -- such as lesson planning, classroom management, and goal setting -- that will help them to raise their students' academic achievement. MINT participants work to hone these skills, under the guidance of an experienced cooperating teacher, advisor, and site director.

Upon completion of the MINT program, participants are required to teach full-time in a Massachusetts public school district. MINT participants are highly encouraged to seek employment in urban school districts, where the need to fill vacancies with dedicated, talented educators is most pressing. Throughout their first year, MINT participants compile a portfolio that reflects how they meet the Department of Education's Professional Standard's for Teachers. MINT participants with satisfactory portfolios are granted an initial license.

Decisions on levels of acceptance are made by the Department of Education, after a rigorous selection process.

NUMBER of CREDIT HOURS to COMPLETE:

During the summer training, MINT participants complete approximately 200 “clock hours” of professional development seminars. During their first year of teaching, participants complete an additional 18 “clock hours” of support seminars.

WHO EVALUATES: The final portfolio assessment is evaluated by the Department of Education’s Portfolio Advisory Team, which is comprised of master teachers from various middle and high schools across the state.

TITLE: Certification Review Panel -- Alternative Route to Certification

HISTORY: Adopted by the State Board of Education in 1987.

Note: This Review Panel process will cease to exist by Oct. 1, 2003, when the Massachusetts 10/01/1994 Certification Regulations expire.

MOTIVATION: To provide flexibility in certification of applicants who have not followed the conventional route of teacher preparation, while adhering to high standards for competency spelled out in state regulations. For applicants who appear to meet certification standards, through both their experience and formal education, but do not meet all specified education requirements.

GRADE LEVELS AND/OR SUBJECT AREAS COVERED: All

WHO OPERATES: State

REQUIREMENTS TO ENTER:

Eligibility: A candidate's eligibility for review by the Certification Review Panel will be determined by the Department of Education. The Department will refer to the Panel any applicant for certification who:

Cannot be certified under other provisions;

appears to meet the requirements for the appropriate certificate, but does not necessarily hold any requisite certificate or meet all of the specific competencies for the certificate sought via traditional means;

Has at least five years or the equivalent of full-time professional experience relevant to the standards;

Has submitted proof of a bachelor's degree, sound moral character, the requisite score on any test required for certification, and any other statutory requirement.

The Panel will receive written information from the Department on each applicant referred to it, and will accept an applicant for full review unless a majority of the Panel members inform the Department of their objection.

Procedure: Full review of candidates accepted by the Panel will be carried out by three-member teams of the Panel which will, where possible, be composed of a teacher, an administrator, and a college faculty member. The team: will review the Department's conventional evaluation and other documentation and interview the candidate; may request additional information or supporting documentation from the candidate; may request or arrange any test, evaluations, or observations of performance it deems necessary; and may request outside advice or experts in areas not represented on the team.

PROGRAM DESCRIPTION:

The Certification Review Panel provides an alternative route to certification for candidates who appear to meet the certification standards (specified in the 1994 Massachusetts Regulations for Certification of Educational Personnel) through both their experience and their formal education, but who do not meet all of the specific certification requirements.

Candidates for the review panel must have at least five years full-time or the equivalent part-time professional experience relevant to the standards for certification. Whether an applicant is eligible for a Panel review is determined by the Department of Education, based upon an evaluation of the applicant's educational transcripts and work experience.

Upon completion of the Panel review, the Panel will deliberate and recommend to the Commissioner whether the candidate be waived of all the remaining requirements, or part of the requirements, or not be certified via the Review Panel process. The candidate may request that the Commissioner reconsider the Panel's recommendations not to issue a certificate. The decision of the Commissioner shall be final.

NUMBER OF CREDIT HOURS TO COMPLETE: Individually determined.

WHO EVALUATES: Certification Review Panel.

LENGTH OF TIME: Not applicable.

TITLE: Waiver

HISTORY: Since the 1950s.

MOTIVATION: A waiver allows an uncertified person to teach in shortage areas when a local school district, after a bona fide effort, has been unable to fill a position with a certified and qualified candidate.

GRADE LEVELS AND/OR SUBJECT AREAS COVERED:

Shortage areas, such as bilingual and special education.

WHO OPERATES: LEA.

REQUIREMENTS TO ENTER:

A bachelor's degree.

Qualification in the specialty area to be taught.

Application for a waiver by the local school superintendent.

PROGRAM DESCRIPTION:

The individual is issued a waiver, but not a teaching credential.

The Office of Educator Certification specifies requirements which must be completed, based upon its review of the applicant's educational transcripts.

The individual must make continuous progress toward completion of regular certification requirements in order to continue in this program.

Typically, a waiver might be issued to individuals who have completed a teacher education program or were certified out-of-state, until they can show they have attained the competencies required for licensure.

NUMBER OF CREDIT HOURS TO COMPLETE:

For renewal of the waiver, the individual must make continuous progress toward completing regular license requirements.

WHO EVALUATES: State.

LENGTH OF TIME: The waiver is valid for one academic year.

Additional waivers may be requested by the school district if the shortage still exists, without a time limit -- but usually, licensure can be obtained within three years.

Some school districts impose a time limit on the number of years a waiver request will be made.

For subsequent waivers to be considered, the teacher must make continuous toward completing regular licensure requirements.

MASSACHUSETTS — Class G

TITLE: Internship

HISTORY: Began under revised state regulations, September 1982.

MOTIVATION: For applicants who have not completed a Massachusetts approved or registered education program. This program is not shortage based and interns may be hired, regardless of whether or not a school district has available a qualified, certified teacher who could fill a position.

GRADE LEVELS AND/OR SUBJECT AREAS COVERED: All

WHO OPERATES: IHE or LEA.

This option will cease to exist by Oct. 1, 2003, when the Massachusetts 10/01/1994 Certification Regulations expire.

REQUIREMENTS TO ENTER:

The individual files an application for licensure.

The Massachusetts Office of Educator Certification and Licensure evaluates and notifies the individual whether he/she is ready to undertake an internship.

The internship may be used in lieu of the previously required completion of a half practicum -- the traditional student teaching experience, which is college sponsored and evaluated.

Internships are available when the applicant is no more than two courses away from certification.

For internships sponsored by local school districts, the applicant must find a district willing to accept him/her as an intern.

This program is often used by already-certified teachers wishing to gain certification in a new subject area and by those licensed teachers from out-of-state who are not covered by reciprocal agreements.

PROGRAM DESCRIPTION:

The state does not issue the intern a teaching credential, but the individual is permitted to enter the classroom under the internship process.

The school district determines whether the intern will be paid.

If the internship is sponsored by a college, the institution may require the intern to take additional coursework, at its option.

Interns must be assigned to teach at least one-fifth of the time of a regular teacher in the local school district.

NUMBER OF CREDIT HOURS TO COMPLETE:

The internship is 150 clock hours (compared to 75 clock hours of a half practicum in a college) of indirectly supervised teaching, sponsored either by a college (for credit) or by a local school district (not for credit).

WHO EVALUATES: The intern will be indirectly supervised by two evaluators:

If college-sponsored, one evaluator comes from the college, one from the local school district;

If district-sponsored, both evaluators are designated by the school district, and may be head teachers, administrators, etc.

LENGTH OF TIME: Not specified.

OTHER: State officials say this is a popular route to certification. It is currently used by persons receiving an estimated 45 percent of all initial certificates issued by the state.

MASSACHUSETTS

Number of Teaching Licenses Issued

	1999-02	1997-98	1996-97	1995-96	1994-95	1993-94	1992-93	1991-92	1990-91
Persons who completed an approved college teacher preparation program		1/	2/	3/	4/	5,347	3,637		5,598
Internship program			N/A	N/A	98	183	~250+	169	45%
Alternative Route -- MINT	> 600								
Apprentice Teacher Cards issued (no longer available)					256	553	502	593	665
Fully certified by Certificate									
Review Panel		326	285	96	23	81*	77	65	65
Waivers		575	549	649	409	268	597	641	606
Applicants evaluated		24,124	22,219	23,814	24,930	19,520	21,632	21,792	
Areas of certification evaluated		41,138	38,468	42,389	46,029	36,592	41,357	41,465	

** 366 individuals were fully certified by the Certificate Review Panel in March 1994. Includes June 1995 special English as a Second Language Review Panel.*

Number of Teachers Employed

	1997-98	1994-95	1992-93	1991-92	1990-91	1989-90	1988-89
Total Teachers Employed in the State	N/A	N/A	N/A	N/A	N/A	N/A	60,395
Newly Hired Teachers in Each Year	N/A	N/A	N/A	N/A	N/A	N/A	N/A

MASSACHUSETTS

1/ *In 1997-98, 18,999 certificates issued to 12,677 people.*

2/ *In 1996-97, 18,061 certificates were issued to 12,265 people.*

3/ *In 1995-96, 18,801 certificates were issued to 13,273 people.*

4/ *Total 10,085 certificates issued to 9,138 people.*

Massachusetts Dept. of Education
Bureau of Educator Certification
and Licensure
350 Main St.
Malden, MA 02148
Attn: Dennis DiCarlo
(781) 338-8000
Web site:
http://www.doe.mass.edu/educators

MASSACHUSETTS

Institutions of higher education that have developed alternative teacher preparation programs leading to a teaching license:

States with which the state has reciprocity of teacher licenses:

NASDTEC Interstate Contract.

Institutions of higher education that have *any* teacher preparation programs leading to a license to teach.

EARLY CHILDHOOD

American International College
Anna Maria College
Atlantic Union College
Bay Path College
Becker College
Boston College
Boston University
Bridgewater State College
Eastern Nazarene College
Elms College
Endicott College
Fitchburg State College
Gordon College
Lasell College
Lesley College
Mount Holyoke College
Mount Ida College
North Adams State College
Northeastern University
Pine Manor College
Salem State College
Shady Hill School
Simmons College
Smith College
Springfield College
Stonehill College
Tufts University
University of Massachusetts/ Amherst
University of Massachusetts/ Boston
University of Massachusetts/ Lowell
Westfield State College
Wheaton College

ELEMENTARY

American International College
Anna Maria College
Assumption
Atlantic Union College
Bay Path College
Becker College
Boston College
Boston University
Bradford College
Brandeis University
Bridgewater State College
Cambridge College
Clark University
Curry College
Eastern Nazarene College
Elms College
Emmanuel College
Endicott College
Fitchburg State College
Framingham State College
Gordon College
Hellenic College
Lasell College
Lesley College
Merrimack College
Mount Holyoke College
North Adams State College
Northeastern University
Pine Manor College
Regis College
Salem State College
Shady Hill School
Simmons College
Smith College
Springfield College

MASSACHUSETTS

Stonehill College
Suffolk University
University of Massachusetts/ Amherst
University of Massachusetts/ Boston
University of Massachusetts/ Dartmouth
University of Massachusetts/ Lowell
Westfield State College
Wheaton College
Wheelock College
Worcester State College

MIDDLE SCHOOL
Bridgewater State College
Eastern Nazarene College
Fitchburg State College
Gordon College
Lesley College
North Adams College
Salem State College
Shady Hill School
University of Massachusetts/ Boston
University of Massachusetts/ Lowell
Westfield State College

STUDENTS WITH SPECIAL NEEDS
American International College
Assumption College
Boston College
Boston University
Bridgewater State College
Curry College
Eastern Nazarene College
Elms College
Fitchburg State College
Framingham State College
Gordon College
Lesley College
North Adams State College
Northeastern University
Salem State College
Simmons College
University of Massachusetts/ Amherst
University of Massachusetts/ Boston
Westfield State College
Wheelock College

STUDENTS WITH INTENSIVE SPECIAL NEEDS
Boston College
Boston University
Fitchburg State College
Lesley College
Northeastern University
Simmons College
Westfield State College

For other areas, please contact the Massachusetts Department of Education/Bureau of Educator Certification and Licensure, Phone (781) 338-3000, Web site: http://www.doe.mass.edu/educators

Contact information for persons interested in finding a teaching position in the state:

Note: Positions are handled through each local school district.

TITLE: Michigan's Alternative Routes to Teacher Certification (MARTC)

HISTORY: In May 1993, the State Board of Education approved "A Model Process and Standards for Alternative Routes to Teacher Certification" (MARTC).

MOTIVATION: MARTC is designed to address local/regional teacher shortages (1) in specific grade levels, (2) in subjects or geographic settings, (3) and to promote diversity of culture and gender by expanding the pool of minority and underrepresented teacher candidates. It will allow Michigan citizens who have been professionally active in specialized areas and who are interested in teaching to come into the teaching profession in non-traditional ways.

GRADE LEVELS AND/OR SUBJECT AREAS COVERED:

All grade levels, Pre K-12, and all teacher certification endorsement areas where there is a critical need , identified by: an LEA or consortium of LEAs and verified by the appropriate teacher bargaining organization(s) to assure that there is no existing pool of appropriately certified teachers; an approved teacher preparation institution or consortium of such IHEs; and the Michigan Department of Education; as approved by the State Board of Education.

WHO OPERATES: Collaborative: SEA, IHEs, LEAs, teachers' unions.

REQUIREMENTS TO ENTER PROGRAM:

The MARTC program is a system through which an individual -- who (a) possesses a bachelor's degree from a regionally or nationally accredited IHE, and (b) has a major or a graduate degree in the field of specialization in which he or she will teach -- may become certified to teach to address local/regional teacher shortages (1) in specific grade levels, (2) in subject areas or geographic settings, and (3) in order to expand the pool of minority and underrepresented teacher candidates to promote diversity of culture and gender.

For grades 6-12, the candidate must have a major or graduate degree in the field of specialization in which he or she wishes to teach.

For grades Pre K-5, he or she must have a major in the liberal arts, the humanities, the social sciences, the mathematical and natural sciences, the arts, or sciences, and in addition to such major, a minor of at least 20 semester hours in another field deemed appropriate for elementary education.

The individual must:

Have an awareness that Michigan's constitution and laws guarantee the right to equal educational opportunity without discrimination because of race, religion, color, national origin or ancestry, age, gender, sexual orientation, marital status, or handicap.

Have an overall 2.5 grade point average and a 2.5 grade point in the major and/or minor or graduate program on a 4.0 scale or the equivalent.

Pass both the basic skills examination and the comprehensive elementary examination for elementary candidates, or the appropriate subject area examinations for secondary candidates, offered through the Michigan Test for Teacher Certification (MTTC) program.

Pass a criminal history check.

Be employed by a qualified LEA, with a letter of acknowledgment issued by the State Department of Education.

Except in the case of persons engaged to teach a foreign language, have not less than two years of occupational experience within the last five years in the field of specialization in which he or she will teach.

For elementary, have documented relevant work experience (voluntary or paid), or experience with children of elementary school age.

Participate in a structured interview used for screening or diagnostic purposes.

Meet all cost obligations related to participation in the MARTC program.

PROGRAM DESCRIPTION:

The individual will become certified by successfully completing required coursework and supervised practical experience offered under conditions which vary from the traditional state approved teacher preparation program.

Alternative routes may also be used to enable currently certified teachers to acquire additional endorsements in areas of critical needs.

Those with no Pre K-12 teaching experience must successfully complete appropriate initial pedagogy coursework prior to classroom placement.

Those certified candidates seeking an additional certificate or endorsement, and who do not possess a teachable major or minor, must successfully complete appropriate subject area coursework prior to classroom placement.

NUMBER OF CREDIT HOURS TO COMPLETE: Not specified.

WHO EVALUATES: LEA and IHE.

LENGTH OF TIME: Six months to two years.

TITLE: Limited License to Instruct (Mid-career Model)

HISTORY: Authorized for pilot to support the outplacement of retired or released business and industry personnel.

MOTIVATION: Especially developed to assist the entry of mid-career changers into teaching.

GRADE LEVELS AND/OR SUBJECT AREAS COVERED:

Initially, secondary level Mathematics and Science, then all levels and subject areas as needed.

WHO OPERATES: Collaborative among state, school district and university.

REQUIREMENTS TO ENTER PROGRAM:

Base requirements include at least a bachelor's degree from an accredited institution with a major or graduate degree in the field of specialization to be taught (Foreign language, Chemistry, Engineering, Robotics, Physics, Music).

Have, within the past 5 years, at least 2 years of occupational experience in the field of specialization to be taught. Those who will teach in the area of Foreign Language are exempted from this requirement.

PROGRAM DESCRIPTION:

A qualified individual must complete an Michigan Department of Education (MDE) approved orientation (4-8 week) after which he/she may be employed for one year with no additional academic requirements.

During years 2-5, an individual may continue to be employed on this restricted license track based on annual recommendation of the employing district. If the person remains on this track, he or she becomes unemployable under this license unless they convert to a regular certificate track leading to Michigan's initial Provisional certificate.

WHO EVALUATES: Employing district/school..

LENGTH OF TIME: 4-8 weeks.

TITLE: Limited License to Instruct (General Model)

HISTORY: Authorized for pilot to assist a large urban district.

MOTIVATION: Developed to assist in reducing the number of uncertified teachers employed and for recruiting individuals with significant academic and occupational experience into teaching.

GRADE LEVELS AND/OR SUBJECT AREAS COVERED:

Secondary, especially Science and Mathematics.

WHO OPERATES: Collaborative among state, school district and university.

REQUIREMENTS TO ENTER PROGRAM:

An applicant must:

1. Possess a bachelor's or higher degree from a regionally or nationally accredited college or university.*
2. Have completed a major and/or a minor or a graduate degree in the field of specialization in which the applicant wishes to instruct or has one year of occupational experience in that specialization field.

OR

Have completed at least 120 semester hours of satisfactory college credit in an approved teacher preparation program, including a major and a minor or the equivalent and at least 15 semester hour credits in professional education.**

3. Have an overall 2.5 grade point average and a 2.5 grade point in the major and/or minor, on a 4.0 scale or the equivalent or is between 2.0 - 2.5 grade point average and passes the MTCC test in the area of specialization by the second request for renewal.
4. Pass a criminal history check.

* Except in the case of an applicant to teach foreign language, have completed the program of study/degree in the field of specialization within the last 5 years or have at least 2 years of occupational experience in the field of specialization within the last 5 years.

** Professional education credit is coursework that is part of the professional education sequence of a K-12 teacher preparation program. Counselor education courses, educational leadership courses, and psychology courses that are not required, as part of an approved teacher education program may not be counted as professional education credit.

PROGRAM DESCRIPTION:

Validity period: The initial Limited License to Instruct (LLI) is valid for one academic year and will expire on June 30th of the academic year during which it was issued.

Renewal Requirements:

1. The initial LLI can only be renewed through the recommendation of the employing district/school.

2. Have taken the MTTC Basic Skills examination, including reading, writing and mathematics and passed one of the three within Year One. To receive consideration for a second renewal must have passed 2/3. To receive consideration for a third renewal, must pass 3/3.

3. Have taken and passed the appropriate teacher certification examination(s) for the field(s) of specialization for which the LLI was issued, by the second request for renewal.

4. Have received a rating no less than "satisfactory" on the Annual Performance Evaluation, based on at least 2 observations of classroom teaching.

5. Must have on file with the employing district evidence of admission to the partner University and an approved plan of work for earning a Michigan Provisional certificate, which may include the completion of an MDE-approved fast track teacher preparation program.*

6. Have successfully completed a professional orientation to teaching offered by the local district/school or ISD in collaboration with a teacher preparation college or university.

7. Annual renewals up to 3 additional academic years may be recommended at the discretion of the employing district/school if the licensee provides evidence of annual progress towards completion of the Individual Development Plan, and progress on the approved university plan of work.

* A licensee who has completed all by the student/practice teaching experience for a Michigan Provisional certificate is exempt from this requirement.

NUMBER OF CREDIT HOURS TO COMPLETE: Determined on a case-by-case basis, depending on academic/experience background..

WHO EVALUATES: LEA and IHE.

LENGTH OF TIME: 1-3 years with successful completion resulting in a Michigan Provisional teaching certificate..

TITLE: Emergency Permit

HISTORY: In existence for many years.

MOTIVATION: A local or intermediate school district or nonpublic school must justify on the basis of an emergency shortage.

GRADE LEVELS AND/OR SUBJECT AREAS COVERED: All

WHO OPERATES: State

REQUIREMENTS TO ENTER PROGRAM:

A local or intermediate school district or nonpublic school must request and the district or nonpublic school, not the individual, is granted an Emergency Permit.

The district or nonpublic school must show the state that an emergency situation exists which will affect the education of the children if the permit is not authorized.

The district or nonpublic school must provide evidence that it has advertised at the colleges which have teacher education programs and in the mass media.

The individual must:

Have a baccalaureate or higher degree from a regionally or nationally accredited IHE.

OR

Currently be enrolled in and have completed at least 90 semester hours in a teacher preparation program which, when completed, will result in Michigan certification.

MICHIGAN

Number of Teaching Licenses Issued

	2001-02	1999-00	1998-99	1997-98	1996-97	1995-96	1994-95	1993-94	1992-93	1991-92	1990-91	1989-90
Persons who completed an approved college teacher preparation program	6,400	6,471	5,636	5,372	6,562	6,417	6,246	5,847	5,623	6,630	5,398	6,046
Internship program												
Permits (Full year) / Emergency	2,241	1,421	935	714	269	170	126	98	95	109	183	160
Temporary												
Alternative Route	40	40										
Other												

Number of Teachers Employed

	1998-99	1997-98	1996-97	1995-96	1994-95	1993-94	1992-93	1991-92	1990-91	1989-90	1988-89
Total Teachers Employed in the State	101,623	92,651	* 87,374	98,250	96,368	101,871	92,509	92,332	92,592	90,250	90,928
Newly Hired Teachers in Each Year **	3,422	4,108	5,183	4,289	3,940	2,784	3,048	3,066	2,683	2,095	2,110

* *These data are inaccurate, due to reporting errors. Approximately 12,000 records are missing from the 1996-97 data set.*

** *With zero years of experience*

Michigan Dept. of Education
Office of Professional Preparation Services
P.O. Box 30008
Lansing, MI 48909
Attn: Frank Ciloski
Phone: (517) 373-6791
Fax: (517) 373-0542
e-mail: ciloski@michigan.gov

MICHIGAN

Institutions of higher education that have developed alternative teacher preparation programs leading to a teaching license:

Oakland University
Wayne State University
University of Michigan - Dearborn Campus
Saginaw Valley State University
Western Michigan University

States with which the state has reciprocity of teacher licenses:

Michigan will certify a holder of a valid teaching certificate from any state to teach in comparable grade levels and endorsement areas. Those with less than three years of teaching experience and/or do not meet the academic requirements for certificate advance must take and pass the Michigan Test for Teacher Certification.

Institutions of higher education that have *any* teacher preparation programs leading to a license to teach.

Adrian College
Albion College
Alma College
Andrews University
Aquinas College
Calvin College
Central Michigan University
Concordia College
Cornerstone College
Eastern Michigan University
Ferris State University
Grand Valley State University
Hillsdale College
Hope College
Kalamazoo College
Lake Superior State University
Madonna University
Marygrove College
Michigan State University
Michigan Tech University
Northern Michigan University
Oakland University
Olivet College
Saginaw Valley State University
Siena Heights College
Spring Arbor College
University of Detroit Mercy
University of Michigan, Ann Arbor
University of Michigan-Dearborn
University of Michigan-Flint
Wayne State University
Western Michigan University

Contact information for persons interested in finding a teaching position in the state:

Note: There are 555 local districts in Michigan and 171 Public School Academies (charter schools). Therefore, the State Department of Education does not provide employment services.

TITLE: Alternative Preparation to Teacher Licensure Program

HISTORY: The 1990 Legislature authorized the Board of Teaching to establish this program. Implementation is stalled due to budget cuts.

MOTIVATION: "1) To augment the current high quality teacher corps with individuals whose backgrounds would be especially relevant in today's classrooms, but who might not otherwise seek the preparation needed to be licensed; especially individuals of color.

2) Foster closer relationships between school districts and colleges with teacher preparation programs."

According to the state, "Although Minnesota does not have a shortage of licensed teachers, data on issuance of 'provisional' and 'limited' permits indicate relatively few candidates for certain areas (e.g., special education and bilingual-ESL [English as a second language] positions."

GRADE LEVELS AND/OR SUBJECT AREAS COVERED:

Grades 1-6.

WHO OPERATES: The Minnesota Board of Teaching approves all alternative preparation programs. A school district, group of schools, or an educational district must be affiliated with a postsecondary institution to offer an alternative preparation program.

REQUIREMENTS TO ENTER PROGRAM:

To participate in the program, a candidate must:

be hired by a school district;

have a bachelor's degree;

pass Pre-Professional Skills Tests in reading, writing, and mathematics;

have experience in a field related to the subject to be taught; and document successful experiences working with children.

PROGRAM DESCRIPTION:

Approved programs have these characteristics:

Staff development conducted by a Resident Mentorship Team made up of administrators, teachers, and postsecondary faculty members.

An instruction phase involving intensive preparation of a candidate for licensure before the candidate assumes responsibility for a classroom.

Formal instruction and peer coaching during the school year.

Assessment, supervision, and evaluation of a candidate to determine the candidate's specific needs and to ensure satisfactory completion of the program.

A research-based and results-oriented approach, focused on skills teachers need to be effective.

Assurance of integration of education theory and classroom practices.

The shared design and delivery of staff development.

NUMBER OF CREDIT HOURS TO COMPLETE:

No credit. Programs may not be driven by credit hours. Upon successful completion, a candidate will have the requirements for a Minnesota initial teaching license.

WHO EVALUATES: The Resident Mentorship Team (classroom teacher, administrator, higher education faculty) must prepare for the Board of Teaching an evaluation report on the candidate's performance.

LENGTH OF TIME: Program is one year in duration (June - June).

OTHER:

Only one site is offering an alternative preparation licensing program in Minnesota. Since the start of the program in 1991, approximately 163 candidates have completed.

Fellowship awards of up to $5,000 are available to candidates of color, with funds paid over two-year periods.

Several other alternative programs are anticipated in the next few years.

MINNESOTA

Number of Teaching Licenses Issued

	1999-00	1998-99	1997-98	1996-97	1995-96	1994-95	1993-94	1992-93	1991-92	1990-91	1989-
Persons who completed an approved college teacher preparation program --											
First time license issue, Minnesota & non-Minnesota Initial License	5,841	5,416	5,325	4,793	5,074	5,755	6,000	5,903	5,638	5,926	4,76
Persons who completed an approved program in Minnesota		N/A	N/A	3,500	3,546	3,779	N/A	3,517	3,550		
Internship program											
Emergency		316	540	384	279	245	207	115	173	147	9
Temporary											
Alternative Route	9	29	28	26	25	32	22	22	18		

Number of Teachers Employed

	1998-99	1996-97	1994-95	1992-93	1991-92	1990-91	1989-90	1988-89
Total Teachers Employed in the State	59,320	49,845	46,686	N/A	43,753	N/A	43,101	42,752
Newly Hired Teachers in Each Year	2,000	N/A	1,700	N/A	1,700	1,685	1,554	1,482

Minnesota Board of Teaching
1500 Highway 36 West
Roseville, MN 55113
Attn: Dr. George Maurer
(651) 582-8833

MINNESOTA

Institutions of higher education that have developed alternative teacher preparation programs leading to a teaching license:

Minneapolis Public Schools and St. Paul Public Schools, working with St. Thomas University.

States with which the state has reciprocity of teacher licenses:

None.

Institutions of higher education that have *any* teacher preparation programs leading to a license to teach.

Augsburg College
Bemidji State University
Bethel College
Carleton College
College of St. Benedict
College of St. Catherine
College of St. Scholastica
Concordia College-Moorhead
Concordia University-St. Paul
Crown College
Gustavus Adolphus College
Hamline University
Macalester College
Martin Luther College
Metropolitan State University
Minnesota State University-Mankato
Moorhead State University
North Central College
Northwestern College
St. Cloud State University
St. John's University
St. Mary's University
St. Olaf College
Southwest State University
University of Minnesota, Duluth Campus
University of Minnesota, Morris Campus
University of Minnesota, Twin Cities Campus
University of St. Thomas
Winona State University

Contact information for persons interested in finding a teaching position in the state:

Note: No placement services available at state level.

TITLE: Teach Mississippi Program

HISTORY: The Teach Mississippi Institute was mandated by the Mississippi Legislature during the 2002 legislative session, but the Institute did not begin until Jan. 1, 2003.

MOTIVATION:

GRADE LEVELS AND/OR SUBJECT AREAS COVERED:

Limited to these 15 areas:

Biology
Business
Chemistry
English
French
German
Home Economics
Marketing
Mathematics
Physics
Social Studies
Spanish
Special Education (grades 7-12 only)
Speech Communication
Technology Education

WHO OPERATES: Mississippi State Department of Education.

REQUIREMENTS TO ENTER:

The institute is available to applicants who hold a minimum of a bachelor's degree from a regionally/nationally accredited institution of higher education, but have not completed a state- or NCATE-approved teacher education program.

PROGRAM DESCRIPTION:

Teach Mississippi Institute is an eight (8) week , nine (9) semester hour summer program which shall include, but is not limited to, the following:

Instruction in education;

Effective teaching strategies;

Classroom management;

State curriculum requirement;

Planning and instruction;

Using tests to improve instruction; and

A one (1) semester, three (3) semester hour, supervised internship, to be completed while the teacher is employed as a full-time teacher intern in the school district.

NUMBER OF CREDIT HOURS TO COMPLETE:

Nine (9) semester hours of course work and three (3) semester hours of internship.

WHO OPERATES: Mississippi State Department of Education.

LENGTH OF TIME: Five (5) years; renewable.

TITLE: Mississippi Alternate Path to Quality Teachers

HISTORY: The Office of Teacher Certification analyzes applicant transcripts and makes evaluations, compared to requirements in various areas of certification.

Candidates must have a bachelor's degree, meet required Praxis I scores, and pass the Praxis II Specialty Area test within a specified amount of time.

MOTIVATION:

GRADE LEVELS AND/OR SUBJECT AREAS COVERED:

Limited to these 18 areas:

Art Education
Biology
Business
Chemistry
English
French
German
Home Economics
Marketing
Mathematics
Music
Physical Education
Physics
Social Studies
Spanish
Special Education
(grades 7-12 only)
Speech Communication
Technology Education

WHO OPERATES: Mississippi State Department of Education.

REQUIREMENTS TO ENTER:

A candidate for this license must have a bachelor's degree (non-education) from a regionally/nationally accredited institution of higher learning.

Individuals who graduated from college 7 years or more ago must have a minimum 2.0 overall grade point average.

Individuals who graduated from college less than 7 years ago must have a minimum 2.5 overall grade point average or a 2.75 grade point average in their major.

PROGRAM DESCRIPTION:

The Mississippi Alternate Path to Quality Teachers is an alternate route program in which the candidate must:

Attain a passing scores on the Praxis I and the Praxis II Specialty Area Test in the subject to be taught, or provide a score that is within one standard error of measurement of the passing score.

Complete the Teach Mississippi Training Institute, a two- or three-week session that introduces new teachers to the profession by providing training and hands-on field experiences.

Complete new teacher practicums, new teacher training models, and a local school district evaluation during the first year of employment. (Note: The local school district should provide an intensive induction program and provide a mentor for the new teacher.)

NUMBER OF CREDIT HOURS TO COMPLETE: N/A

WHO OPERATES: Mississippi State Department of Education.

LENGTH OF TIME: Teachers who pass the Praxis II Specialty Area Test at the end of the third year will be issued a Standard Five-Year License.

MISSISSIPPI

Class D

TITLE: Alternate Route License

HISTORY: The Office of Teacher Certification previously analyzed applicant transcripts and made evaluations compared to requirements in various areas of certification. However, the system was changed and this responsibility was assumed by Mississippi colleges with approved teacher education programs after 1986.

Effective July 1, 1997, candidates must have a bachelor's degree and must meet required Praxis I. Must pass Praxis II Specialty Area test.

MOTIVATION: Not specified.

GRADE LEVELS AND/OR SUBJECT AREAS COVERED:

Limited to these 18 areas:

Art Education
Business Education
English
Home Economics
Music
Physics
Spanish
German
Marketing
Biology
Chemistry
French
Mathematics
Physical Education
Social Studies
Library Media
Technology Education
Speech Communication

WHO OPERATES: The Office of Educator Licensure of the Mississippi Department of Education.

REQUIREMENTS TO ENTER:

Hold a baccalaureate degree from a regionally accredited institution of higher learning.

(Official transcript must be filed with the Office of Educator Licensure.)

Meet minimum score requirements on the subject area examination of Praxis II and meet the minimum score requirements on the Praxis I.

PROGRAM DESCRIPTION:

Complete, with a grade of "C" or higher, nine (9) semester hours of course work in pedagogy (Educational Psychology or curriculum, Classroom Management, Tests and Measurements). These courses must be completed through an accredited senior college with an approved teacher education program.

All nine (9) semester hours must be completed within the three-year validity period.

Alternate route candidates completing these requirements will receive a standard certificate valid for five (5) years.

NUMBER OF CREDIT HOURS TO COMPLETE:

Nine (9) semester hours of course work.

WHO OPERATES: Mississippi Department of Education.

LENGTH OF TIME: Three years. Non-renewable. All coursework must be completed by the end of the three-year period.

TITLE: Master of Arts in Teaching Program

HISTORY:

The Office of Teacher Certification previously analyzed applicant transcripts and made evaluations compared to requirements in various areas of certification. However, the system was changed and this responsibility was assumed by Mississippi colleges with approved teacher education programs after 1986.

Effective July 1, 1997, candidates must have a bachelor's degree, meet the required Praxis I scores, and pass the Praxis II Specialty Area test.

MOTIVATION:

GRADE LEVELS AND/OR SUBJECT AREAS COVERED:

Limited to these 18 areas:

Art Education
Biology
Business Education
Chemistry
Elementary Education
grades 4-8 only)
English
French
German
Home Economics
Marketing
Mathematics
Music
Physical Education
Physics
Social Studies
Spanish
Speech Communication
Technology Education

WHO OPERATES: The college or university administers the MAT through the graduate program.

REQUIREMENTS TO ENTER:

A candidate must:

Hold a bachelor's degree in a non-education major from a regionally/nationally accredited institution of higher learning.

Enroll in a Master of Arts program.

PROGRAM DESCRIPTION:

The Master of Arts in Teaching Program is an alternate route program.

A candidate must pass both the Praxis I (Pre-Professional Skills Test [PPST]) and the Praxis II (Specialty Area Tests).

A candidate must complete a total of 30 to 33 semester hours of specified graduate coursework over a period of three years.

This coursework includes six (6) semester hours of pre-teaching course requirements from an approved Master of Arts in Teaching Program, including an internship prescribed by the participating college or university. And the candidate must provide program verification.

NUMBER OF CREDIT HOURS TO COMPLETE:

30 to 33 semester hours of coursework.

WHO OPERATES: The college or university administers the MAT through the graduate program.

LENGTH OF TIME: Three years; non-renewable.

MISSISSIPPI

Number of Teaching Licenses Issued

	2001-02	1999-00	1998-99	1997-98	1994-95	1993-94	1992-93	1991-92	1990-91	1989-90
Persons who completed an approved college teacher preparation program	1,448	1,432	N/A	1,386	N/A	N/A	N/A	N/A	1,909	1,987
Internship program										
Emergency	0	1,684	636	586	N/A	839	N/A	N/A	702	787
Temporary										
Alternative Route	354	561	N/A	554	N/A	N/A	N/A	N/A	229	199

Number of Teachers Employed

	2001-02	1999-00	1998-99	1997-98	1994-95	1993-94	1992-93	1991-92	1990-91	1989-90
Total Teachers Employed in the State	32,569	31,017	35,199	29,574	N/A	N/A	N/A	35,000	32,900	27,367
Newly Hired Teachers in Each Year	2,010	2,048	1,956	N/A	N/A	N/A	N/A	N/A	N/A	N/A

Mississippi Dept. of Education
Office of Educator Licensure
P.O. Box 771
Jackson, MS 39205
Attn: Regina Ginn, Director
(601) 359-3483
email: rginn@mde.k12.ms.us

MISSISSIPPI

Institutions of higher education that have developed alternative teacher preparation programs leading to a teaching license:

States with which the state has reciprocity of teacher licenses:

All. NASDTEC Interstate Contract.

Institutions of higher education that have *any* teacher preparation programs leading to a license to teach.

Alcorn State University
Belhaven College
Blue Mountain College
Delta State University
Jackson State University
Millsaps College
Mississippi College
Mississippi State University
Mississippi University for Women
Mississippi Valley State University
Rust College
Tougaloo College
University of Mississippi
University of Southern Mississippi
William Carey College

Contact information for persons interested in finding a teaching position in the state:

Daphne Buckley, Director
Mississippi Teacher Center
Mississippi Department of Education
P.O. Box 771
Jackson, MS 39205
Phone: (601) 359-3631

MISSOURI

Class D

TITLE: An Alternative Certification Program

HISTORY: Approved October 26, 1989.

MOTIVATION: To provide entry into the teaching profession by individuals who have not completed a traditional teacher education program and to certificate special assignment teachers.

GRADE LEVELS AND/OR SUBJECT AREAS COVERED:

Secondary level and where there is a critical need as identified by the district and approved by the Department of Elementary and Secondary Education.

WHO OPERATES: Missouri colleges/universities with State approved teacher education programs.

REQUIREMENTS TO ENTER:

Present evidence of employment by a school district in the State of Missouri contingent upon certification prior to acceptance into the Missouri Alternative Certification Program.

A bachelor's degree from a regionally accredited institution in the area of the proposed certificate with a cumulative grade point average no lower than the Missouri requirement for teacher certification (2.5) and a grade point average no lower than 2.5 in the major (teaching) area.

Verify the completion of a general education background satisfactory to the teacher education institution.

Document a minimum of five years of successful employment during which the content of the bachelor's degree major is significantly applied. Documentation shall be defined and required by the college or university offering the Alternative Teacher Certification Program.

Participate in a structured interview selected by the teacher education institution. This interview would assess the candidate's beliefs regarding the nature of teaching, the nature of students and the goals and mission of education as a profession. The interview may be utilized for screening purposes (e.g., The Missouri Pre-Professional

Teacher Interview) or for diagnostic and counseling purposes (e.g., The Selection Research, Incorporated Preserve Teacher Perceiver).

Enter into a four-party contract with a higher education institution which has a teacher education program approved by the State Board of Education, with the local school district, and with the Department of Elementary and Secondary Education. This contract (an Alternative Teaching Contract) will permit the candidate to enroll in coursework which will require demonstrated understanding of the following:

1. Adolescent Development.

2. The Psychology of Learning.

3. Teaching Methodology in the Content Area.

This coursework must be completed prior to provisional certification and employment.

PROGRAM DESCRIPTION:

Upon successful completion of the coursework outlined above and upon recommendation of the higher education institution, candidates will receive a two-year provisional certificate. The candidate will:

1. Be assigned a mentor by the school district.

2. Receive follow-up assistance from the higher education institution.

3. Participate in the employing district's professional development program.

4. Successfully participate in the district's Performance Based Teacher Evaluation (PBTE).

Candidates will enroll in 8 to 9 semester hours of professional education coursework no later than the summer following the awarding of the provisional certificate.

Prior to entrance to the second year of the provisional certificate, the candidate must take the appropriate exit test required of all pre-service teacher candidates seeking certification in the state of Missouri. This test, plus the provision outlined in Subsection (G), must be completed successfully prior to moving to a Professional Certificate II (PCII).

Should this not occur within the designated two years, the contract and certificate will be void.

NUMBER OF CREDIT HOURS TO COMPLETE:

Determined by IHE.

WHO EVALUATES: IHE and LEA.

LENGTH OF TIME: Two years

OTHER: The state department office of Teacher Certification has a publication entitled, "Teacher Information Packet and Applications" that includes detailed information about certification requirements, supply and demand data, names and addresses of colleges and universities that have approved teacher education programs and facts about schools in Missouri.

MISSOURI

Number of Teaching Licenses Issued

	1997-98	1996-97	1995-96	1993-94	1992-93	1991-92	1990-91	1989-90
Persons who completed an approved college teacher preparation program	3,800	3,790	3,800	3,600	N/A	N/A	2,580	3,200
Internship program			N/A					
Emergency a/								
Temporary								
Alternative Route b/		4	N/A	N/A	23	25		
Other								

Number of Teachers Employed

	1997-98	1996-97	1995-96	1993-94	1992-93	1991-92	1990-91	1989-90
Total Teachers Employed in the State	52,400	63,100	63,100	62,691	54,011	52,302	52,304	51,361
Newly Hired Teachers in Each Year	2,350	3,471	3,482	3,330	2,030	2,031	c/ 2,376	c/ 2,349

a/ State does not issue.

b/ State officials estimated that at least 23 candidates were in training or teaching in Fall 1992.

c/ First year teachers who were new to teaching. In addition, there were about 1,800 teachers new to their school districts, including those who were returning to teaching and those who were coming from out of state.

Missouri Dept. of Education
Teacher Ed/Certification
Dept. of Elementary/Secondary Education
P.O. Box 480
Jefferson City, MO 65102
Attn: John Miller
(573) 751-0051

MISSOURI

Institutions of higher education with approved alternative teacher preparation programs leading to a teaching license:

Central Missouri State University
Park College
Southeast Missouri State University

States with which the state has reciprocity of teacher licenses:

Note: No reciprocity. Limited exchange agreement only. Missouri is a signatory to the MOINKSA regional exchange agreement – with Arkansas, Iowa, Kansas, Nebraska, Oklahoma, and South Dakota.

Institutions of higher education that have *any* teacher preparation programs leading to a license to teach.

Avila College
Central Methodist College
Central Missouri State University
College of the Ozarks
Columbia College
Culver-Stockton College
Drury College
Evangel College
Fontbonne College
Hannibal LaGrange College
Harris-Stowe State College
Lincoln University
Lindenwood College
Maryville College
Missouri Baptist College
Missouri Southern State College
Missouri Valley College
Missouri Western State College
Northeast Missouri State University
Northwest Missouri State University
Park College
Rockhurst College
St. Louis University
Southeast Missouri State University
Southwest Baptist University
Southwest Missouri State University
Stephens College
University of Missouri-Columbia
University of Missouri-Kansas City
University of Missouri-St. Louis
Washington University
Webster College
William Woods College
William Jewell College

Contact information for persons interested in finding a teaching position in the state:

John Miller, Director, Teacher Certification
Department of Elementary and Secondary Education
P.O. Box 480
Jefferson City, MO 65102
Phone: (573) 751-0051

TITLE: Class 5 (Provisional) Teaching Certificate (redefined as an Alternate Route)

HISTORY: Enacted 1975, Amended 1976,1978, 1980, 1982, 1984, 1985, 1986, 1995.

MOTIVATION: May be issued to applicants who have major preparation toward regular certification, but have minor discrepancies such as lack of recent credits or program deficiencies. Initiated to provide additional avenue for certification for the non-traditional applicant.

SUBJECT AREAS COVERED: Elementary and Secondary Teaching Areas.

WHO OPERATES: Office of Public Instruction, Certification Services.

REQUIREMENTS TO ENTER:

Approval usually depends on the written recommendation of the appropriate higher education official(s) with whom the applicant has outlined a plan of professional intent which commits the applicant to a program leading to regular certification.

Provisional elementary level: Elementary level endorsement is granted to an applicant who submits acceptable evidence of a partially completed elementary education program, and that the following minimum requirements have been met:

Bachelor's degree.

Minimum of 90 quarter (60 semester) credits of academic preparation in acceptable balance in language arts and literature, history, government and related social science, mathematics, and any two of the following: art, music, foreign languages, speech, dramatics, library science or health.

Professional preparation to include human growth and development, the teaching of reading or language arts, social science and arithmetic, and student teaching or appropriate intern experiences.

Provisional secondary level: Secondary level endorsement is granted to an applicant who submits acceptable evidence of a partially completed secondary education program, and that the following minimum requirements have been met:

Bachelor's degree.

Major preparation of at least 45 quarter (30 semester) credits in an area commonly offered in high school programs in Montana and approved by the Board of Public Education for endorsement;

8 quarter (6 semester) credits in a planned program of professional teacher education, and admission to the secondary teacher education program of an accredited college or university.

PROGRAM DESCRIPTION:

The individual must make yearly progress toward completing deficiencies for full certification.

NO. OF CREDIT HOURS TO COMPLETE:

Depends on the college program the individual plans to complete

WHO EVALUATES: The state certification office evaluates for initial certification; the college must verify completion of program before further certification is available.

LENGTH OF TIME: Three years, not renewable.

May be extended up to two years under special circumstances, if an individual provides verification from the school district or college that the special circumstances were not the fault of the individual and were the result of involvement with the district or college.

MONTANA

Number of Teaching Licenses Issued

	1997-98	1996-97	1995-96	1994-95	1993-94	1992-93	1991-92	1990-91
Persons who completed an approved college teacher preparation program	N/A	N/A	N/A	N/A		State not able to provide any data		
Internship program								
Emergency	1	N/A	N/A	6	5	7	4	
Temporary	N/A	N/A	N/A	N/A		State not able to provide any data		
Alternative Route	N/A	N/A	N/A	N/A		State not able to provide any data		
Total Certificates Issued --	5291	6,166	6,230	6,927	6,610	* 6,020	* 6,942	

Number of Teachers Employed

	1997-98	1996-97	1995-96	1994-95	1993-94	1992-93	1991-92	1990-91
Total Teachers Employed in the State	N/A	** 10,349	N/A	** 10,086	***	** 10,135	** 9,883	** 10,295
Newly Hired Teachers in Each Year	N/A	N/A	N/A	N/A	N/A	N/A	N/A	N/A

* *Includes added endorsements.*

***Full-time equivalents (FTEs), not individuals.*

**** Because there is an overlap of FTE at the 7-8 grade level, an accurate number is not available.*

Teacher Education/Certification
Office of Public Instruction
P.O. Box 202501
Helena, MT 59601-2501
Attn: Marilyn Roberts
Phone: (406) 444-3150
Fax: (406) 444-2893
marilynr@state.mt.us

MONTANA

Institutions of higher education that have developed alternative teacher preparation programs leading to a teaching license:

N/A.

States with which the state has reciprocity of teacher licenses:

NASDTEC Interstate Contract.

Note: No reciprocity. Although Montana has contracts with these other states, candidates must still meet Montana's minimum requirements. Advantage is to expedite applications from qualified candidates.

Institutions of higher education that have *any* teacher preparation programs leading to a license to teach.

Carroll College
Montana State University - Billings
Montana State University - Bozeman
Montana State University - Northern
Rocky Mountain College
University of Great Falls
University of Montana
Western Montana College

Contact information for persons interested in finding a teaching position in the state:

Contact the Career Placement offices of the Montana universities. Also, access the Internet at the following address: http://jsd.dli.mt.gov.

NEBRASKA — Class D

TITLE: Alternative Route to Regular Teacher Certification

HISTORY: To begin implementation in 2003.

MOTIVATION: 1. Shortage in some teaching areas.

2. Mid-life career changers needing access to the profession.

GRADE LEVELS AND/OR SUBJECT AREAS COVERED:

Shortage areas: mathematics, science, and others to be announced.

WHO OPERATES: SEA, IHE, LEA -- collaboratively.

REQUIREMENTS TO ENTER:

This program is not yet in operation. See the following section for available information. More information will become available in Spring 2003.

PROGRAM DESCRIPTION:

According to the state:

"An alternative route to regular certification is expected to be implemented in Spring 2003. It will provide for the person who holds a degree in specified areas to begin teaching with none of the pedagogical hours of teacher education having been completed. This provides access to teaching much earlier than the older 'provisional' certificate, which required half or more of the pedagogy to be completed. The new plan, however, does not excuse the applicant from eventually completing the teacher education program in its entirety. It also requires substantial participation and up-front commitment from an employer and a teacher education institution. It is not available in elementary education, nor in some other areas. It attempts to address areas of critical and continuous shortage. The Department of Education hopes to have printed informational tracts and instructions for making an application available in early 2003.

NO. OF CREDIT HOURS TO COMPLETE: Various.

WHO EVALUATES: IHE.

LENGTH OF TIME: Five years -- one year each; renewable.

TITLE: Provisional Commitment Teaching Certificate

HISTORY: Effective November 12, 2000.

GRADE LEVELS AND/OR SUBJECT AREAS COVERED: All

WHO OPERATES: IHE and SEA.

REQUIREMENTS TO ENTER:

The holder of the certificate is limited to the school requesting its issuance.

The individual must:

Submit a written request for issuance of the certificate from the superintendent or governing body of the local school district;

Have received a baccalaureate degree;

Have completed at least one-half of the pre-student teaching requirements of an approved teacher education program, including a course in teaching methods;

Have fulfilled three-quarters of the requirements for a subject or full endorsement;

Submit a statement of intent to fulfill his/her remaining program and endorsement requirements during the period in which the certificate is in effect or to make sure progress (at least six semester hours) which fulfills some or all of the remaining requirements.

The applicant must have achieved a minimum score on the Pre-Professional Skills Test or Content Mastery Examination for Educators (CMEE) unless he/she has previously held a regular (not provisional) Nebraska teaching certificate.

The applicant must complete a qualifying course in human relations training.

The applicant must complete a qualifying three-hour course in special education.

The applicant must submit to a criminal history background check (fingerprints) if not a five-year or longer Nebraska resident or holder of a previous Nebraska certificate.

PROGRAM DESCRIPTION:

While teaching with a Provisional Certificate, the individual must complete 6 semester hours of credit for college coursework which fulfills some or all of his/her remaining program or endorsement requirements.

Each year, the individual must submit an application and a written request for renewal of the certificate from his/her employing school district.

NO. OF CREDIT HOURS TO COMPLETE:

Six (6) semester hours per year toward completing certification requirements.

WHO EVALUATES: IHE and SEA.

LENGTH OF TIME: Valid for one year. Renewable if specified progress toward completion of an IHE teacher education program is being made.

TITLE: Provisional Re-Entry Teaching Certificate

HISTORY: Effective November 12, 2000.

MOTIVATION: To provide that teachers who have been long-absent from the classroom are re-tooled to be successful in today's classroom.

GRADE LEVELS AND/OR SUBJECT AREAS COVERED: All

WHO OPERATES: SEA, IHE, and LEA.

REQUIREMENTS TO ENTER:

Have held a lapsed regular Nebraska or other state certificate.

Have teaching employment in a school.

PROGRAM DESCRIPTION:

The individual must complete 15 semester hours of specified credit to return to a regular certificate -- 6 semester hours per year -- if the regular certificate is lapsed by five or more years.

Coursework includes school law, issues in education, curriculum updating, and 100 hours of in-class practicum.

NO. OF CREDIT HOURS TO COMPLETE:

15 semester hours -- 6 hours per year. A structured program, not free choice.

WHO EVALUATES: SEA and IHE.

LENGTH OF TIME: One year. Renewable if progress is made.

OTHER: The human relations training course -- which is mandatory for all certificate holders -- may be included in the required 15 semester hours.

TITLE: Provisional Trades Teaching Certificate

HISTORY: Effective April 29, 1997.

MOTIVATION: Shortage of coaching staff; shortage of industrial-construction trades teachers; former military teaching ROTC.

GRADE LEVELS AND/OR SUBJECT AREAS COVERED:

High school only. Coaching; ROTC; industrial-construction trades, welding, drafting, metals, engineer, graphic arts, electricity, electronics, auto.

WHO OPERATES: SEA and LEA.

REQUIREMENTS TO ENTER:

Requirements for the first issuance of the Professional Trades Certificate, regardless of endorsement, are:

The holder of the certificate is limited to the school requesting its issuance and may teach only in the subject, subject field, or area of specialization and at the grade level specified.

The individual must:

1. Complete the application form.
2. Pay the application fee.
3. Submit, with the application, a written request for the issuance of the certificate from the superintendent of the employing school system or from the governing body of the school system or from the personnel director of the employing school system.
4. Pass one of the prescribed basic skills competency tests required of teachers, and have a score report sent to the Department of Education, Teacher Certification Office.
5. Successfully complete a qualifying human relations training class required of all Nebraska teachers and have the official transcript (not the grade report) sent to the Teacher Certification Office. (A list of approved courses will be provided by the Teacher Certification Office, upon request.)

6. Successfully complete a three semester hour course in a four-year college which trains teachers on special education (this must be a survey course covering all handicapping conditions).

7. If fingerprinting is required (see the application form for more information) submit fingerprints as specified in the special fingerprint memo and use the special fingerprint envelope, available from the Department of Education, and pay the additional $40 for fingerprinting.

* The renewed Provisional Trades Certificate is valid for three years and may be renewed for an unlimited number of times by meeting requirements 1, 2 and 3, and the verification of experience or the completion of three semester hours of credit.

** Persons who have not completed one, two, or all three requirements (4, 5 and 6) but who are employed in a Nebraska school system may be eligible to receive a one-year temporary certificate which can usually be renewed for one more year. The requirements which are not met must be completed to receive any further certification.

*** Persons who have submitted fingerprints but for whom the report of the fingerprint investigation by the Nebraska State Patrol and the Federal Bureau of Investigation is not yet completed may be eligible to receive a conditional permit, allowing teaching to be done. A self-reporting form must be submitted with the certificate application. This form is available from the Teacher Certification Office, upon request.

PROGRAM DESCRIPTION:

Requirements for the Coaching Endorsement (applicants must meet the requirements for the certificate, as well as for this endorsement):

1. Complete American Sport Education Program / National Federation of Interscholastic Coaches Education Program (SE / NFICEP) -- this program consists of coaching principles and sports first aid . . . OR

2. Complete Program for Athletics Education (PACE) . . . OR

3. Complete the following six courses from a college with an approved teacher education program: (a) Prevention, care, and management of injuries; (b) Risk management; (c) Growth,

development, and learning; (d) Training, conditioning, and nutrition; (e) Psychology of coaching; (f) Coaching theory and methods.

Submit a certificate of completion of these coaches education programs or an official transcript showing completion of the appropriate college hours with the application for certification.

No 'coaching on trade' certificate will be issued unless at least one of these training programs is completed. A partial completion of the chosen programs of training will not result in certification.

To learn when these training sessions will be offered in your area, contact: Nebraska School Activities Association, 8230 Beechwood Drive, Lincoln, NE 69510, telephone (402) 489-0386.

Requirements for OTHER ENDORSEMENTS on the Professional Trades Certificate:

Other trade or industrial endorsements, such as welding, auto body, construction trades, and other true 'trades areas' are based on one or more of the following qualifiers:

- Completion of a prescribed course of study in a community college or other technical trade institution

OR

- Completion of an apprenticeship program in the trade;

OR

- Passing a proficiency examination approved by the particular trade or industry;

OR

- Demonstrated proficiency in the trade over five years of employment in the trade;

OR

- Current employment by a community college as an instructor to teach the specific trade or skill.

Unlike coaching, these endorsements generally are NOT available through traditional teacher training and do not appear on a regular teaching certificate.

🗣 Requirements for the Reserve Officers Training Corps (ROTC) endorsement:

This endorsement requires four years of full-time experience in the military, as well as a recommendation from a former military supervisor.

NO. OF CREDIT HOURS TO COMPLETE: N/A.

WHO EVALUATES: SEA.

LENGTH OF TIME: One year (1st certificate); three years (subsequent).

NEBRASKA

Number of Teaching Licenses Issued

	2001-02	2000-01	1997-98	1996-97	1995-96	1994-95	1993-94	1992-93	1991-92	1990-91
Persons who completed an approved college teacher preparation program	1,650	1,658	2,000	2,000	2,000	2,000	2,000	2,000	2,000	2,000
Emergency										
Temporary	350	317	161	605	430	311			224	175
Alternative Route	*		58			50			45	14

** New definition / program for Alternative Route.*

Number of Teachers Employed

	2001-02	2000-01	1997-98	1994-95	1993-94	1992-93	1991-92	1990-91	1989-90	1988-89
Total Teachers Employed in the State	27,430	27,850	est. 20,000	20,000	20,000	20,000	est. 20,000	20,000	N/A	17,896
Newly Hired Teachers in Each Year	1,300	1,312	est. 800	est. 700	est. 700	700	est. 700	700	N/A	855

Nebraska Dept. of Education
Teacher Education/Certification
P.O. Box 94987
301 Centennial Mall Square
Lincoln, NE 68509
Robert Crosier
(402) 471-2496 or 471-0739
FAX (402) 471-9735

NEBRASKA

Institutions of higher education that have developed alternative teacher preparation programs leading to a teaching license:

Chadron State College -- Accelerated Certification
University of Nebraska-Lincoln -- Project Experience

States with which the state has reciprocity of teacher licenses:

Note: Nebraska is a signatory to the MOINKAS regional exchange agreement -- with Arkansas, Illinois, Michigan, Missouri, Iowa, Kansas, Oklahoma, South Dakota and Wisconsin-- for two-year temporary certificate only.

Nebraska is a signatory of the NASDTEC Interstate teacher reciprocity agreement 2000-2005.

Institutions of higher education that have *any* teacher preparation programs leading to a license to teach.

Chadron State College
College of St. Mary
Concordia Teachers College
Creighton University
Dana College
Doane College
Grace University
Hastings College
Midland Lutheran College
Nebraska Wesleyan University
Peru State College
Union College
University of Nebraska-Kearney
University of Nebraska-Lincoln
University of Nebraska-Omaha
Wayne State College
York College

Contact information for persons interested in finding a teaching position in the state:

Teach in Nebraska Web site: http://www.nebraskaeducationjobs.com

Note: Contact the personnel office of the school system in which employment is desired.

To obtain a copy of the Nebraska Educational Directory, download it from the state's Web page at: http://www.nde.state.ne.us. (It is not available in printed form.)

The Directory contains lists of school districts, county education officials, enrollments by grade in every school district in the state, faculty names by school building, and a wealth of similar and related data. Current year data are available after November.

The Nebraska Department of Education Publications Catalog is available free of charge. Order from:

Nebraska Department of Education
Information & Publications Section
P.O. Box 94987
Lincoln, NE 68509-4987

TITLE: Non-Renewable License

MOTIVATION: For individuals who are within 6 semester hours of meeting licensing requirements.

GRADE LEVELS AND/OR SUBJECT AREAS COVERED: All

WHO OPERATES: SEA.

REQUIREMENTS TO ENTER:

All applicants are granted a Three-Year Non-Renewable License, if they are within 6 semester hours of meeting credit requirements.

PROGRAM DESCRIPTION:

The recipient of the Three-Year Non-Renewable License must remove all provisions by the expiration date of the License.

NUMBER OF CREDIT HOURS TO COMPLETE: 6 semester hours.

WHO EVALUATES: SEA.

LENGTH OF TIME: Three years.

OTHER: Officials said the state currently has no way for a person to teach without first completing an approved teacher education program and student teaching.

A Professional Development Degree in Science & Education, offered by the University of Nevada-Las Vegas, is considered to be above a bachelor's but below a master's, but counts for state purposes only as a bachelor's. This degree is designed for persons who already hold a bachelor's degree (not in education), and provides a means for them to complete the required education coursework, including student teaching. A state official said that persons going through this program do not enter a classroom to teach until after they have completed the degree program.

NEVADA

Number of Teaching Licenses Issued

	1997-98	1993-94	1992-93	1991-92	1990-91	1989-90	1988-89
Persons who completed an approved college teacher preparation program	N/A	2,300	1,800	N/A	N/A	1,500	1,000
Internship program							
Emergency/ Temporary (Provisional)	N/A	N/A	N/A	N/A			
Alternative Route	21						
Other							

Number of Teachers Employed

	1997-98	1993-94	1992-93	1991-92	1990-91	1989-90	1988-89
Total Teachers Employed in the State	18,431	15,351	14,000	13,027	10,384	9,175	8,699
Newly Hired Teachers in Each Year	N/A	N/A	N/A	2,643	1,750	931	N/A

Nevada Dept. of Education
State Mail Room
1820 E. Sahara #205
Las Vegas, NV 89104-3746
Attn: Chopin Kiang
(702) 486-6458

NEVADA

Institutions of higher education that have developed alternative teacher preparation programs leading to a teaching license:

University of Nevada-Las Vegas

States with which the state has reciprocity of teacher licenses:

NASDTEC Interstate Contract.

Institutions of higher education that have *any* teacher preparation programs leading to a license to teach.

Sierra Nevada College
University of Nevada-Las Vegas
University of Nevada-Reno

Contact information for persons interested in finding a teaching position in the state:

Note: Each school district must be contacted.

ALTERNATIVES FOR CERTIFICATION IN NEW HAMPSHIRE

The New Hampshire State Board of Education recognizes that persons may become qualified as educators through a variety of educational and life experiences.

Therefore, the following alternatives to becoming a certified educator in New Hampshire are made available to applicants.

Alternative 1: Approved Programs in New Hampshire

Alternative 2: States Other Than New Hampshire

Alternative 3: Demonstrated Competencies and Equivalent Experiences

Alternative 4: Individual Professional Development Plan (Restricted)

Alternative 5: Site-Based Certification Plan

Note: As of Sept. 1, 1998, all applicants for initial certification must take and pass Praxis I (Pre-Professional Skills Test, PPST, or Computer Based Test, CBT) before receiving a New Hampshire credential.

As of July 1, 1999, all applicants for initial certification must take and pass Praxis I and Praxis II (Content tests -- Math, Science, Social Studies, or English), if applicable. Other content areas will be added in the future.

This affects Alternatives 1, 2, 3, 4, and 5 candidates for certification.

TITLE: Alternative 5: Site-Based Certification Plan

HISTORY: Effective Nov. 20, 1990.

MOTIVATION: Response to growing number of adults who already have a bachelor's degree in a field other than education and who want to become licensed to teach.

GRADE LEVELS AND/OR SUBJECT AREA(S) COVERED:

Elementary and secondary content areas.

WHO OPERATES: State determines eligibility; LEA recommends candidate for certification.

REQUIREMENTS TO ENTER:

The candidate shall possess a bachelor's degree from an institution approved by the New Hampshire Post Secondary Education Commission or a regional accrediting agency such as, but not limited to, the Northeast Regional Association of Schools and Colleges; and the candidate shall meet one of the following criteria:

a. For secondary education, candidates shall possess the equivalent of a 30 credit collegiate major in the subject to be taught and an overall grade point average of 2.5 or equivalent.

b. For elementary education, candidates shall possess a four-year arts and sciences background, including a major, and an overall grade point average of 2.5 or the equivalent.

An individual who fails to meet the grade point average requirement may still qualify for the provisional certification plan providing:

a. All other requirements are met; and

b. Collegiate graduation occurred more than five years prior to application for the provisional plan, and

c. Five years of occupational experience directly related to the area to be taught is documented.

Candidates who meet the requirements of part (b) of this section shall be issued a letter of eligibility by the Bureau of Credentialing, Division of Program Support. The Bureau of Credentialing shall maintain a list of individuals who have been issued letters of eligibility.

Equivalence of credits shall be determined through analysis of such information as number of contact hours, course titles, course syllabi, required projects, and data of official transcripts. The required level of academic performance shall be equivalent to a 2.5 in a 4.0 system and shall be determined by mathematical computation or by analysis of such documents as academic recommendations.

Documentation of experience may consist of, but not be limited to, letters from previous employers, employment contracts and letters of commendation and recommendations from parties knowledgeable about the candidate's background and experience.

PROGRAM DESCRIPTION:

Superintendents or their designees may hire those individuals who possess a letter of eligibility, provided that the employing district agrees to the following conditions:

1. The superintendent or his/her designee shall appoint a mentor teacher or a mentoring team to work with the provisional teacher for at least one school year;

2. The mentor teacher shall receive a minimum of 12 hours training in the mentoring process which shall include, but not be limited to:

    a. theories of adult development and learning models and tools for classroom observation;

    b. techniques for providing feedback to the candidate;

    c. ways of providing emotional support to the candidate;

3. Mentor training shall be provided by the Department of Education or other persons or institutions under contract to the Department;

4. The mentor, building principal, teacher candidate, and others who may be designated by the Superintendent to be responsible for the work of the candidate shall develop the candidate's education plan;

5. The plan shall be comprised of pre-service and in-service components.

6. The pre-service component of the plan shall contain study of the following:

    a. Knowledge of the processes of human growth, development and learning, including the characteristics of the applicable age group;

b. techniques to determine the learning needs of students;

c. techniques for using available resources to meet those needs;

d. techniques for establishing orderly classroom routines;

7. An assessment of the candidate's background may determine that some or all of this study has been completed prior to employment.

8. The superintendent shall file with the BUREAU OF CREDENTIALING a copy of the completed pre-service education program and a description of the candidate's teaching assignment. The Superintendent shall include a statement in which he/she testifies to the fact that pre-service training has been completed.

9. The in-service component of the plan shall be completed during the first year of service and address requirements as deemed necessary by an assessment of the candidate's previous training and experience.

10. The in-service education plan shall be developed and filed with the BUREAU OF CREDENTIALING prior to the teaching assignment. The in-service education plan may be modified by those responsible for the work of the candidate, but any modifications shall be filed with the BUREAU OF CREDENTIALING.

11. The pre-service and in-service components of the candidate's education program shall provide for performance evaluations, which may be the same as that used for other staff, and performance evaluations shall be filed with the BUREAU OF CREDENTIALING.

12. The superintendent may request an extension of time for the completion of the education plan from the Commissioner of Education citing the reasons for such as request. An extension shall be for no longer than one year.

13. Any incomplete plan shall be terminated and the candidate's employment shall be terminated at the end of the extension year. Extensions may be granted for reasons such as but not limited to ill health or unavailability of coursework.

14. Upon completion of the in-service component of the plan, the Superintendent shall submit to the Director, Division of Standards and Certification a statement verifying that all portions of the in-service plan have been implemented by the district and satisfactorily completed by the candidate. This statement shall include a recommendation for certification. A positive recommendation shall not obligate a school district to continue the employment of a candidate.

15. Failure by a candidate to complete the in-service component shall result in a negative certification recommendation.

16. Upon receipt of the completed plan and the superintendent's positive recommendation, the Director, Division of Standards and Certification, or his/her designee, shall issue a beginning educator certificate.

17. Costs of the Provisional Certification Plan shall be borne by the candidate unless such expenses are otherwise provided.

NUMBER OF CREDIT HOURS TO COMPLETE: N/A

WHO EVALUATES: State and LEA

LENGTH OF TIME: One year.

TITLE: Alternative 4: Individual Professional Development Plan (Restricted)

HISTORY: New Hampshire Code of Administrative Rules, effective Nov. 1, 1989.

MOTIVATION: Critical shortage.

GRADE LEVELS AND/OR SUBJECT AREAS COVERED:

WHO OPERATES: State

REQUIREMENTS TO ENTER:

Employment in the area for which certification is sought and a bachelor's degree from a college or university approved by an accrediting agency or state with a collegiate major area of study compatible with the prospective teaching assignment.

PROGRAM DESCRIPTION:

In March, the state conducts a survey of school district superintendents to see if they are having difficulty employing teachers in any areas.

On the basis of these data, the state decides if there are critical needs and, if so, in what areas, and prepares a list of specialties needed.

An LEA can request a letter of eligibility to employ a candidate on the basis of his or her background or potential.

The LEA assigns a mentor certified in the content area to monitor and develop a Professional Development Plan for the teacher -- giving him or her three years to complete; the teacher is also given assessments on the basis of competencies.

The teacher may be required to complete additional preparation at a college, but in the Field-Based Special Education Teacher Training Program, non-college credit training is provided on the campus of Plymouth State College.

NO. OF CREDIT HOURS TO COMPLETE: N/A

WHO EVALUATES: State

LENGTH OF TIME: Three years from the time the Professional Development Plan is approved.

NEW HAMPSHIRE

Class E

TITLE: Conversion Programs

HISTORY: The New Hampshire Code of Administrative Rules, effective Nov. 1, 1989.

MOTIVATION: "Conversion programs shall be specifically designed to prepare for teacher certification persons who hold baccalaureate degrees."

GRADE LEVELS AND/OR SUBJECT AREA(S) COVERED: Not specified

WHO OPERATES: IHE

REQUIREMENTS TO ENTER:

Programs must meet the following criteria:

Responsibility for assuring the quality of programs will be centralized in a single specifically designated administrative unit.

Conversion programs shall be consistent with the philosophy and objectives upon which all other education programs are based. Data should be available to indicate that consistency exists.

One person shall be responsible for coordinating conversion programs within each administrative unit.

There will be published criteria for admission to the program.

Life experience may be accepted by the institution subject to the following provisions:

1. No more than one-third (1/3) of the total work required for any individual conversion program may be satisfied by life experience.

2. A system for evaluation of life experience shall assure that:

a. experience is related to specific areas in general education, professional education, or specialty area competency. These are listed in Ed 609, 610, 611 and 612.

b. documentation must be provided for any life experience.

PROGRAM DESCRIPTION:

STANDARDS FOR CONVERSION PROGRAMS

The program involves individuals being given transcript evaluation by an IHE, which determines coursework and student teaching which must be completed. Conversion programs are approved by the State Department of Education.

Student Teaching. Student teaching procedures must conform to the following.

1. Any student admitted to student teaching must be competent in the basic skills of reading, writing, and mathematics according to the same criteria established for the school's undergraduate programs.

2. Student teaching or other major practicum must meet all the provisions of Ed 610.07.

Previous Collegiate Training. A process must exist to assure that any previous collegiate training is consistent with recent developments in general education, professional education, and any specialty area.

Counseling and Advising Students. Advisors must assist students in structuring individual programs designed to maximize strengths, overcome weaknesses, and reflect attention to a variety of backgrounds and potential.

NO. OF CREDIT HOURS TO COMPLETE:

Varies according to background and training.

WHO EVALUATES: College officials.

LENGTH OF TIME: Varies.

NEW HAMPSHIRE — Class F

TITLE: Emergency Permission to Employ

MOTIVATION: Shortage.

GRADE LEVELS AND/OR SUBJECT AREA(S) COVERED: Not specified.

WHO OPERATES: State

REQUIREMENTS TO ENTER:

The local school district must request because of emergency need.

PROGRAM DESCRIPTION:

The individual has one year in which to become certified. This permission may not be renewed.

NO. OF CREDIT HOURS TO COMPLETE: N/A

WHO EVALUATES: N/A

LENGTH OF TIME: One year.

TITLE: Alternative 3: Demonstrated Competencies and Equivalent Experiences

HISTORY: New Hampshire Code of Administrative Rules, effective Oct. 5, 1996.

MOTIVATION:

GRADE LEVELS AND/OR SUBJECT AREA(S) COVERED: Not specified

WHO OPERATES: State

REQUIREMENTS TO ENTER:

No transcript analysis.

Individual must pass written and verbal tests, showing the same level of competencies required of a beginning educator who has been through a teacher education program.

PROGRAM DESCRIPTION:

The state agency sets up a half-day verbal interview by three board examiners -- a state officer and two specialists in the subject field.

The examiners may recommend to the state that the individual be licensed if he or she has the same beginning level of competency as a traditionally trained educator.

NO. OF CREDIT HOURS TO COMPLETE: Not applicable

WHO EVALUATES: State

LENGTH OF TIME: Not applicable.

NEW HAMPSHIRE

Number of Teaching Licenses Issued

	1999-2000	1998-99	1997-98	1996-97	1995-96	1994-95	1993-94	1992-93	1991-92	1990-9
Persons who completed an approved college teacher preparation program	1,224	1,749	2,241	* 1,475	* 1,040	* 2,461	2,104	1,750	983	2,134
Emergency		N/A	N/A	N/A	N/A	N/A	N/A	N/A	62	72
Alternative Route --										
Alternative # 2 & #3 */**		N/A	N/A	N/A	N/A	N/A	N/A	N/A	251	292
Alternative #2	470	993	1,348	1,523	1,472	1,122	1,103	955	870	N/A
Alternative #3 *	38	77	177	112	107	183	98	102	97	N/A
Alternative #4 *	49	70	80	123	113	121	185	176	182	187
Alternative #5 *	36	63	41	53	58	88	55	34	22	N/A
Other -- Permission to Employ	74***	381	172	62	48	77	86	37	44	

Number of Teachers Employed

	1999-2000	1998-99	1997-98	1996-97	1995-96	1994-95	1993-94	1992-93	1991-92	1990-91
Total Teachers Employed in the State	10,240	16,391	16,410	17,321	16,461	16,311	14,301	11,187	10,879	10,519
Newly Hired Teachers in Each Year	N/A	N/A	N/A	N/A	N/A	N/A	N/A	N/A	N/A	N/A

* *These numbers do not reflect individuals, since teachers may received second endorsements for new, additional specialties through the approved program route, or through Alternatives 3, 4, and 5.*

** *Includes persons certified after completing written or verbal tests and persons who were licensed under an interstate agreement after* ***completing*** *an approved teacher education program in another state.*

*** *96 individuals in process of certification.*

New Hampshire Dept. of Education
Bureau of Credentialing
101 Pleasant Street
Concord, NH 03301
Attn: Kathleen M. Moulis
(603) 271-2407

NEW HAMPSHIRE

Institutions of higher education that have developed alternative teacher preparation programs leading to a teaching license:

States with which the state has reciprocity of teacher licenses:

NASDTEC Interstate Contract.

Institutions of higher education that have *any* teacher preparation programs leading to a license to teach.

Antioch/New England Graduate School
Colby Sawyer College
College for Lifelong Learning (UNH)
Dartmouth College
Franklin Pierce College
Keene State College
New England College
New Hampshire College
Notre Dame College
Plymouth State College
Rivier College
Saint Anselm College
University of New Hampshire
Upper Valley Institute

Contact information for persons interested in finding a teaching position in the state:

TRACE Educational Services
24 Airport Road, Unit 15
West Lebanon, NH 03784
Phone: (603) 298-5525

TITLE: Provisional Teacher Program

HISTORY: Adopted by the State Board of Education in Sept. 1984.

MOTIVATION: The Provisional Teacher Program is intended to enhance both the quantity and quality of teaching candidates.

GRADE LEVELS AND/OR SUBJECT AREAS COVERED:

All, except special education, English as a Second Language, and Bilingual Education.

WHO OPERATES: LEAs, supported by colleges of education that are providing formal instruction, with coordination and authority provided by the State Department of Education.

REQUIREMENTS TO ENTER:

To be eligible for employment in the Provisional Teacher Program, applicants must present completion of the following:

1. Bachelor's degree from an accredited institution.

2. For secondary candidates: a major in the subject teaching field (e.g. English, mathematics). For elementary candidates: a major in the liberal arts or sciences.

3. Test requirement -- Applicants for certification in a subject teaching field must pass the appropriate Praxis II Subject Assessment/NTE Programs Specialty Area tests. Applicants for certification in elementary education must pass the NTE General Knowledge test of the Core Battery. Candidates in the following subject teaching fields available through the Alternate Route are exempt from the test requirement: foreign languages other than French, German, and Spanish; earth science; health education; psychology; and vocational education.

4. Cumulative grade point average (GPA) requirement of 2.5 or higher on a 4.0 scale. Candidates graduating on or after Sept. 1, 2004, will be required to hold a GPA of 2.75 or higher.

Upon completion of the above requirements, a candidate receives a Certificate of Eligibility, which provides the opportunity to seek employment through the Provisional Teacher Program.

When offered employment, applicants are advised of documents required before a provisional license can be issued. A provisional license is required to legalize employment during the 34-week Provisional Teacher Program.

PROGRAM DESCRIPTION:

Provisional teachers attend a program of formal instruction that takes place concurrently with employment during the first year. This instruction supplements a program of on-the-job mentoring, support, and evaluation, aimed at developing and documenting the teacher's instructional competency.

Formal instruction consists of approximately 200 hours of study in essential professional knowledge and skills. It is presented after school and/or on Saturdays at a district-operated or state-operated training center.

Mentoring is arranged by the local district and provided by an experienced mentor teacher. Other professionals, as determined by the district, may also participate.

After successful completion of the program, provisional teachers are eligible to be recommended for standard licensure in the teaching area(s) listed in the Certificate of Eligibility. Certificates are issued in subject teaching fields (N-12) and elementary education (N-8).

NO. OF CREDIT HOURS TO COMPLETE:

Approximately 200 clock hours of instruction and 34 weeks of full-time classroom competency development.

WHO EVALUATES: Evaluations are conducted by the school principal or administrative designee. The teacher is evaluated on at least three occasions during the initial year. The first two evaluations are used to aid the teacher's development.

The third and final evaluation is conducted after the provisional teacher has completed 34 weeks of full-time teaching. This last evaluation will contain the principal's recommendation regarding licensure. Recommendations for standard licensure are made by the principal (on forms provided by the New Jersey Department of Education), and are submitted for final action to the State Board of Examiners.

LENGTH OF TIME: 34 weeks of full-time employment.

NEW JERSEY

Number of Teaching Licenses Issued

	2001-02	2000-01	1999-00	1998-99	1997-98	1996-97	1995-96	1993-94	1992-93	1991-92
Persons who completed an approved college teacher preparation program	4,412	4,260	3,830	4,617	N/A	3,110	2,640	N/A	N/A	N/A
Internship program										
Emergency	0	0	0	0	0	0	0	0	0	0
Alternative Route -- *										
Provisional	2,180	1,836	1,142	1,190	N/A	691	746	668	606	N/A
Regular	1,826	1,981	1,832	1,223	N/A	627	701	702	458	N/A

Number of Teachers Employed

	2001-02	2000-01	1999-00	1998-99	1997-98	1993-94	1992-93	1991-92	1990-91
Total Teachers Employed in the State	102,723	98,072	94,415	85,844	91,236	N/A	N/A	N/A	79,886
Newly Hired Teachers in Each Year	*** 7,527	6,856	6,356	** 5,371	N/A	N/A	N/A	N/A	4,112

* *The first row of numbers shows the numbers of provisional certificates issued to persons when they began the alternative program; the second row of numbers shows the numbers of regular certificates issued in each year to persons who entered the alternative program under provisional certification in any prior year.*

** *This number represents the total number of alternate and traditional route first-year teachers hired from September 1998 to June 1999. It does not include special education teachers or veteran teachers new to the school district.*

*** *This number represents the total number of alternate and traditional route first-year teachers hired from September 2001 to June 2002. It does not include special education teachers or veteran teachers new to the school district.*

New Jersey Dept. of Education
Office of Licensure and Credentials
P.O. Box 500
Trenton, NJ 08625-0500
Attn: Joan E. Brady
(609) 292-2045

NEW JERSEY

Institutions of higher education that have developed alternative teacher preparation programs leading to a teaching license:

Montclair State University (T.R.U.S.T. Program)

States with which the state has reciprocity of teacher licenses:

NASDTEC Interstate Contract.

Institutions of higher education that have *any* teacher preparation programs leading to a license to teach.

Caldwell College
Centenary College
College of New Jersey
College of St. Elizabeth
Fairleigh Dickinson University
Felician College
Georgian Court College
Kean University
Monmouth University
Montclair State University
New Jersey City University
Princeton University
Rabbinical College of America
Ramapo College of New Jersey
Rider University
Rowan University
Rutgers State University-Camden
Rutgers State University-Cook College
Rutgers State University Graduate School
Rutgers State University-Newark
Saint Peter's College
Seton Hall University
The Richard Stockton College of New Jersey
Westminister Choir College of Rider University
William Paterson University

Contact information for persons interested in finding a teaching position in the state:

Office of Licensure and Credentials
New Jersey Department of Education
100 Riverview Executive Plaza
P.O. Box 500
Trenton, NJ 08625-0500

TITLE: Alternative Licensure

HISTORY: New State Board of Education regulation effective July 1, 2000, supercedes earlier one filed July 14, 1986. Governs alternative licensure programs for persons who have earned at least a baccalaureate degree but have not completed educator preparation programs and seek alternative routes to licensure in early childhood education, elementary education, middle level education, K-12 education, secondary education, or special education.

MOTIVATION: Expand the pool of qualified teachers.

GRADE LEVELS AND/OR SUBJECT AREAS COVERED: All

WHO OPERATES: State Department of Education.

REQUIREMENTS TO ENTER PROGRAM:

An applicant for alternative licensure must

- Possess a bachelor of arts or science degree from a regionally accredited college or university including completion of a minimum of 30 semester hours of graduate or undergraduate credit in a particular field that appertains and corresponds to the subject area of instruction and level of instruction that will enable the applicant to teach in a competent manner as determined by the State Board.

OR

- Possess a master of arts or science from regionally accredited college or university including completion a minimum of 12 graduate hours in a particular field that appertains and corresponds to the subject area of instruction and level of instruction that will enable the applicant to teach in a competent manner as determined by the State Board.

OR

- Possess a doctor of philosophy or doctor of education degree from a regionally accredited college or university. The degree shall appertain and correspond to the subject area of instruction and level of instruction that will enable the applicant to teach in a competent manner as determined by the State. Board.

PROGRAM DESCRIPTION:

Complete a minimum of 12 semester hours of credit earned through a regionally accredited college or university.

- The credits must include the State Board's competencies for entry level teachers that correspond to the license being sought
- Credits must be in a program approved by the State Board
- Program must include student teaching or field-based component.

OR

The applicant for alternative licensure must successfully demonstrate approved competencies for entry level teachers that correspond to the license being sought. An applicant shall, prior to assuming teaching duties, demonstrate the necessary teaching competencies by submitting to a portfolio assessment through a process approved by the State Board of Education.

All applicants for alternative licensure must pass all of the New Mexico Teacher Assessments.

Completion of the program will lead to a Level 1, 3-year alternative license.

In order to receive a standard license, all holders of alternative licenses must then complete additional requirements, including a one to three year mentorship program approved by the State Board and verification from the local school district where the applicant has most recently been employed that the applicant has satisfactorily demonstrated the State Board's competencies for level of license and type sought.

NO. OF CREDIT HOURS TO COMPLETE:

12-18 semester hours of Secondary Education; 12-18 semester hours of Elementary Education and Special Education.

WHO EVALUATES: State Board of Education.

LENGTH OF TIME: One to three years.

NEW MEXICO

Number of Teaching Licenses Issued

	2001-02	2000-01`	1999-00	1998-99	1997-98	1996-97	1995-96	1994-95	1993-94	1992-93
Persons who completed an approved college teacher preparation program	1,296	1,400	N/A	N/A	N/A	N/A	N/A	N/A	N/A	N/A
Internship program *										
Emergency / Temporary	1,356	1,806	1,301	1,076	1,030	1,020	946	N/A	1,298	1,241
Alternative Route	60	N/A	N/A	73	65	78	85	89	115	77

* *Included in Alternative Route figures.*

Number of Teachers Employed

	2001-02	2000-01	1999-00	1998-99	1997-98	1994-95	1993-94	1992-93	1991-92	1990-91
Total Teachers Employed in the State	25,827	27,092	25,934	23,416	21,374	18,997	19,396	17,412.6	17,155.	N\A
Newly Hired Teachers in Each Year	N/A	N/A	N/A	N/A	N/A	N/A	N/A	571	N\A	N\A

New Mexico Dept. of Education
Asst. Director, Professional Licensure
300 Don Gasper
Santa Fe, NM 87501-2786
Attn: James Ball
Phone: (505) 827-1200
Fax: (505) 827-4148
e-mail: jball@sde.state.nm.us

NEW MEXICO

Institutions of higher education that have developed alternative teacher preparation programs leading to a teaching license:

College of Santa Fe
Eastern New Mexico University
New Mexico Community College
Northern New Mexico State University
Santa Fe Community College

States with which the state has reciprocity of teacher licenses:

NASDTEC Interstate Contract. New Mexico has signed the NASDTEC Interstate Contract in the areas of teaching and school administration.

In addition, any applicant who has a valid out-of-state license and has taken a licensure exam or has teaching experience may receive a comparable license in New Mexico.

Institutions of higher education that have *any* teacher preparation programs leading to a license to teach.

College of Santa Fe
College of Southwest
Eastern New Mexico University
New Mexico Highlands University
New Mexico Mining
New Mexico State University
University of New Mexico
Western New Mexico University

Contact information for persons interested in finding a teaching position in the state:

New Mexico School Boards Association
Educator Placement Service
300 Galisteo St., Ste. 204
Santa Fe, NM 87501
Phone: (505) 983-5041

TITLE: Alternative Teacher Certification - Transitional B

HISTORY: Instituted through action of the Board of Regents in July 2000.

GRADE LEVELS AND/OR SUBJECT AREAS COVERED: All

WHO OPERATES: IHE and LEA

REQUIREMENTS TO ENTER PROGRAM:

Secondary teaching: Baccalaureate degree with major in subject appropriate to the certificate.

Elementary teaching: Baccalaureate degree with any liberal arts and sciences major.

A 3.0 cumulative grade-point average or written recommendation of officer of the college program.

PROGRAM DESCRIPTION:

Introductory component of 200 clock hours of pedagogical study, including 40 hours of field experiences, prior to beginning mentored teaching with a Transitional B certificate.

The introductory component is followed by part-time collegiate study in pedagogy, while teaching, to qualify for the provisional or initial certificate.

To begin mentored teaching with a Transitional B certificate, the candidate must pass the New York State Liberal Arts and Sciences test and the Content Specialty Test, in addition to successfully completing the 200-hour introductory pedagogical component.

The individual must complete an approved two clock-hour course in the identification and reporting of suspected child abuse or maltreatment and an approved two-hour workshop on school violence prevention and intervention.

NEW YORK **Class A**

NUMBER OF CREDIT HOURS TO COMPLETE:

Determined by the college and approved by the state, but sufficient for meeting all requirements for a provisional or initial certificate.

WHO EVALUATES: IHE and LEA collaborate; IHE awards degree and recommends the candidate to the New York State Education Department for certification.

LENGTH OF TIME: Valid for three years.

OTHER: A similar alternative program is available for candidates holding graduate degrees in subjects appropriate to the certificate. These candidates may begin at least two years of mentored teaching with a Transitional C certificate upon passing the NYS Liberal Arts and Sciences Test and the Content Specialty Test. While teaching with the Transitional C certificate, candidates must complete a registered teacher education program meeting all the requirements for an initial or provisional certificate.

NEW YORK   Class E

TITLE: Internship Certificate

HISTORY: In effect for 32+ years. To be amended effective February 2004.

MOTIVATION: To enable persons to provide professional services during and as a part of their program of study for any graduate program leading to teacher certification which includes an internship experience.

GRADE LEVELS AND/OR SUBJECT AREAS COVERED: All

WHO OPERATES: IHE and LEA

REQUIREMENTS TO ENTER PROGRAM:

A baccalaureate degree in an appropriate field.

The individual applies for admission to a registered master's degree program that includes an internship and leads to certification.

The college applies to the state for issuance of the internship certificate for the individual's specific school assignment.

PROGRAM DESCRIPTION:

Following completion of at least one half of the degree program, the institution of higher education places the individual in a professional position in a local school district under appropriate supervision.

The length of classroom teaching is determined by the participating institution of higher education and is reviewed and approved by the State Education Department.

The internship is the culminating graduate program activity.

The certificate enables the individual to receive remuneration for the services provided, as well as to legalize the individual's employment.

The individual must complete an approved two clock-hour course in the identification and reporting of suspected child abuse or maltreatment and an approved two-hour workshop on school violence prevention and intervention.

NUMBER OF CREDIT HOURS TO COMPLETE:

Determined by the college and approved by the State Education Department, but at least 30 semester hours for the award of a master's degree.

WHO EVALUATES: IHE and LEA

LENGTH OF TIME: The internship certificate is valid for two years.

TITLE: Temporary License

HISTORY: In existence since 1966, but to be terminated effective February 2004.

MOTIVATION: To ensure the presence of a classroom teacher when no certified teacher is available after extensive and documented recruitment.

GRADE LEVELS AND/OR SUBJECT AREA(S) COVERED: All.

WHO OPERATES: State

REQUIREMENTS TO ENTER PROGRAM:

A baccalaureate degree, other than those instances where a baccalaureate degree is not required for an entry-level certificate.

Request from the school district superintendent.

PROGRAM DESCRIPTION:

The local school board draws up a plan for staff development and professional support for the uncertified teacher. This plan must include assurances that an individual who has no previous teaching experience will work under the guidance of a permanently certified mentor teacher, who will be given either a 20 percent reduction in assignment or additional compensation. The uncertified teacher will spend 20 percent of his/her assignment in planning, preparation, and training.

To satisfy the requirement for an initial certificate, the individual may substitute one year of appropriately supervised full-time teaching for the student teaching requirement.

The individual must complete required coursework in professional education at an institution of higher education that has an approved teacher education program prior to the provisional certification.

The individual must achieve passing scores on the Liberal Arts and Sciences Test (LAST), the Assessment of Teaching Skills-Written (ATS-W), and the appropriate Content Specialty Test (CST) of the New York State Teacher Certification Examinations (NYSTCE) prior to provisional certification.

The individual must complete an approved two clock-hour course in the identification and reporting of suspected child abuse or maltreatment and an approved two-hour workshop on school violence prevention and intervention.

NUMBER OF CREDIT HOURS TO COMPLETE:

Must fulfill all academic, pedagogical and assessment requirements for a Provisional Certificate within four years:

For elementary -- 30 semester hours of professional education, including 6 hours in the teaching of reading, and student teaching, if necessary;

For secondary -- 18 semester hours of professional education, plus 36 semester hours in subject content coursework, and student teaching, if necessary.

The individual may substitute one year of full-time appropriately supervised teaching on the appropriate level for the student teaching requirement.

WHO EVALUATES: The State evaluates the request and identifies the applicant's deficiencies.

LENGTH OF TIME: Valid for one year; renewable up to three times; individual must fulfill all requirements for a provisional certificate within four years.

NEW YORK   Class G

TITLE: Alternative Completion of Requirements (formerly Transcript Analysis)

HISTORY: More than 60 years. To be amended effective Feb. 1, 2004.

MOTIVATION: To enable persons who have not completed a state-approved teacher education program to establish eligibility for a state certificate.

GRADE LEVELS AND/OR SUBJECT AREAS COVERED: All

WHO OPERATES: State

REQUIREMENTS TO ENTER PROGRAM:

Baccalaureate degree.

Applicants submit an application, fee, and official transcripts of collegiate-level study for evaluation.

PROGRAM DESCRIPTION:

The applicant must fulfill all academic, pedagogical, and assessment requirements for a provisional certificate similar to graduates of registered teacher preparation programs.

If there are deficiencies, the applicant is so informed, and must complete those requirements before a certificate may be issued.

Evaluation is conducted and certificates issued by the Office of Teaching of the New York State Education Department.

The individual must complete an approved two clock-hour course in the identification and reporting of suspected child abuse or maltreatment and an approved two-hour workshop on school violence prevention and intervention.

NUMBER OF CREDIT HOURS TO COMPLETE: Varies by certificate title.

WHO EVALUATES: State or Regional Certification Offices.

LENGTH OF TIME: N/A

TITLE: Visiting Lecturer

HISTORY: Available since the early 1960s.

MOTIVATION: To supplement a local school district's regular program of instruction.

GRADE LEVELS AND/OR SUBJECT AREAS COVERED: All

WHO OPERATES: LEA

REQUIREMENTS TO ENTER PROGRAM:

Applicant must have unusual qualifications and expertise in a specific subject area.

Examples of persons who have received Visiting Lecturer credentials include higher education faculty, persons from the arts, the judiciary, legal profession, bank officers, etc.

PROGRAM DESCRIPTION:

The individual works under the general supervision of a certified teacher.

The individual does not replace a regular, certified, full-time teacher.

NUMBER OF CREDIT HOURS TO COMPLETE: Not applicable

WHO EVALUATES: LEA.

LENGTH OF TIME: Valid for one year, but renewable.

NEW YORK

Number of Teaching Licenses Issued

	2001-02	2000-01	1999-00	1998-99	1997-98	1996-97
Persons who completed an approved college teacher preparation program	18,619	16,666	24,692	27,400	24,,443	25,400
Internship program -- Figures included in above	609					
Emergency / Temporary	15,347	19,151	18,566	15,498	14,973	12,960
Alternative Route	951					
Other -- Transcript evaluation	27,205	16,166	22,795	24,708	20,081	24,367

Number of Teachers Employed

	2001-02	2000-01	1999-00	1998-99	1997-98	1996-97
Total Teachers Employed in the State	212,495	220,865	216,452	209,007	207,938	202,976
Newly Hired Teachers in Each Year	10,287	10,173	11,145	6,338	6,525	5,751

Office of College and University Evaluation
5N Mezzanine, Education Building
Albany, NY 12234
Attn: Ruth L. Pagerey
(518) 474-1914

NEW YORK

Institutions of higher education that have developed alternative teacher preparation programs leading to a teaching license:

Transitional B Certificate Programs:

Adelphi University
Bank Street College
City College
City University of New York-Brooklyn
College of Staten Island
Fordham University
Herbert H. Lehman College
Hunter College
Iona College
Long Island University-Brooklyn
Mercy College-Bronx
New York University
Pace University
Queens College
Roberts Wesleyan College
St. John's University
Utica College

Internship Certificate Programs:

Long Island University-Brooklyn
Pace University

States with which the state has reciprocity of teacher licenses:

NASDTEC Interstate Contract and Northeast Common Market.

Institutions of higher education that have *any* teacher preparation programs leading to a license to teach.

Adelphi University
Alfred University
Bank Street College of Education
Barnard College
Boricua College
Canisius College
Cazenovia College
Colgate University
College of Mount St. Vincent
College of New Rochelle-Main Campus
College of St. Rose
Concordia College
CUNY-Brooklyn College
CUNY-City College
CUNY-College of Staten Island
CUNY-Herbert H. Lehman College
CUNY-Hunter College
CUNY-Medgar Evers College
CUNY-New York City Technical College
CUNY-Queens College
CUNY-York College
Daemen College
Dominican College of Blauvelt
Dowling College
D'Youville College
Elmira College
Five Towns College
Fordham University
Hartwick College
Hobart & William Smith Colleges
Hofstra University
Houghton College
Iona College
Ithaca College
Keuka College
Le Moyne College
Long Island University
Manhattan College
Manhattanville College
Marist College
Marymount Manhattan College
Medaille College
Mercy College
Molloy College

NEW YORK

Mount St. Mary's College
Nazareth College
New York Institute of Technology
New York University-Main Campus
Niagara University
Nyack College
NYS College of Agriculture and Life Sciences at Cornell
Pace University
Pratt Institute
Roberts Wesleyan College
Rochester Institute of Technology
Sarah Lawrence College
School of Visual Arts
Siena College
Skidmore College
St. Bonaventure University
St. Francis College
St. John Fisher College
St. John's University
St. Joseph's College
St. Lawrence University
St. Thomas Aquinas College
State University of New York (SUNY) College-Brockport
SUNY College-Buffalo
SUNY College-Cortland
SUNY College-Fredonia
SUNY College-Genesco
SUNY College-New Paltz
SUNY College-Old Westbury
SUNY College-Oneonta
SUNY College-Oswego
SUNY College-Plattsburgh
SUNY College-Potsdam
SUNY-Albany
SUNY-Binghamton
SUNY-Buffalo
SUNY Stony Brook
Syracuse University
Teachers College
The King's College
The Sage Colleges
Touro College
Union College
University of Rochester
Utica College of Syracuse University
Vassar College
Wagner College
Wells College
Yeshiva University

Contact information for persons interested in finding a teaching position in the state:

Visit the Web site at: http://www.nysed.gov.

For New York City, call 1-800-TEACH NY.

TITLE: Lateral Entry Provisional License

HISTORY: Effective July 1, 1985.

MOTIVATION: The 1984 session of the North Carolina General Assembly approved an amendment, stating that: "It is the policy of the State of North Carolina to encourage lateral entry into the profession of teaching by skilled professionals from the private sector."

The State Board of Education has adopted policies to implement lateral entry which limits such licensure to individuals who have been selected for employment by a North Carolina school system.

GRADE LEVELS AND/OR SUBJECT AREA(S) COVERED:

Major areas for which the state has established licensure

WHO OPERATES: The Local Education Agency (LEA).

REQUIREMENTS TO ENTER:

Relevant professional work experience (optional).

Selected employment by a North Carolina school system.

A bachelor's degree from a regionally accredited college or university in the subject area in which they are employed to teach, and, have a minimum cumulative grade point average (GPA) of at least 2.5 (on a 4.0 scale),

Or have passed the Praxis I test ***and*** one of the following

- A GPA of 3.0 in the major field of study **or**
- a GPA of 3.0 on all work relevant to the teaching area completed in the senior year **or**
- a GPA of 3.0 on a minimum of 15 semester hours of course work (relative to licensure) completed during the preceding five years..

An employer for an individual who has satisfied all major degree requirements but may still have some minor deficiency or technical requirement may file application for licensure. Such a deficiency cannot exceed 6 semester hours and must be corrected during the first year of licensing.

PROGRAM DESCRIPTION:

An initial license is issued for up to 2 school years. It can be extended on a yearly basis for up to 3 years, if the holder earns a minimum of 6 semester hours of appropriate course work per year.

The Praxis II subject area assessment must be met by the end of the initial two-year lateral license.

The individual must complete professional education and/or other requirements for clear licensure through an approved teacher education program at a participating college.

Successful teaching experience in the program for initially licensed personnel will be accepted for the student teaching requirement.

Other appropriate professional training activities in this program must be reflected in the evaluation for full licensure.

NUMBER OF CREDIT HOURS TO COMPLETE:

Six semester hours must be completed each year.

WHO EVALUATES: IHE.

LENGTH OF TIME: For a lateral entry license to remain valid an individual must meet the testing and progressive credit requirements within the 5-year limit, whether or not employment continues in a north Carolina system..

TITLE: Alternative Entry Licensure

HISTORY: Adopted November, 1998.

The Alternative Entry policy expires September 1, 2002, except that it remains effective for any teacher employed under this act before September 1, 2002.

MOTIVATION: To provide an alternative method for local boards to hire lateral entry teachers and to employ teachers who are legally certified in other states.

GRADE LEVELS AND/OR SUBJECT AREA(S) COVERED:

All teaching areas.

WHO OPERATES: The Local Education Agency (LEA) and the Department of public Instruction Teacher Licensure Section.

REQUIREMENTS TO ENTER:

A bachelor's degree from a regionally accredited college or university.

Be eligible for re-employment by a prior employer; **and**

Hold a valid out-of-state certificate with a minimum of one year classroom teaching experience considered relevant by the local board to the grade or subject to be taught.

Or

Have at least one year of full-time classroom teaching experience, considered relevant by the local board to the grade or subject to be taught, as a professor, associate professor, assistant professor, instructor, or visiting lecturer at a regionally accredited college or university.

Or

Have three years of other experience provided the local board determines that both the individual's experience and postsecondary education are relevant to the grade or subject to be taught.

PROGRAM DESCRIPTION:

Local Education Agencies (LEAs) using the alternative entry policy to employ teachers are required to:

- Determine shortage or "anticipated" shortage license areas.
- Develop a plan to determine competence as a teacher including a review of the performance of students taught.
- Report semi-annually to the State Board of Education the number of individuals employed in each category.

NUMBER OF CREDIT HOURS TO COMPLETE:

No applicable.

WHO EVALUATES: During the period of employment with an alternative entry license, the individual receives an annual evaluation and multiple observations as prescribed by GS 115C-333(a).

The individual's competence as a teacher, including review of the performance of students taught by the individual, is assessed according to the plan developed by the local board.

If the individual does not have one year of classroom teaching experience, the local board will provide a mentor teacher..

LENGTH OF TIME: The alternative entry license is a one-year (maximum) provisional license.

TITLE: Emergency Permit

HISTORY: Adopted by the State Board of Education in June 1998.

MOTIVATION: To provide teachers where shortages exist in a critical need teaching area.

GRADE LEVELS AND/OR SUBJECT AREA(S) COVERED:

All teaching areas.

WHO OPERATES: The Local Education Agency (LEA).

REQUIREMENTS TO ENTER:

A bachelor's degree from a regionally accredited college or university.

Not qualified for licensure under any other licensure approach.

PROGRAM DESCRIPTION:

A Local Education Agencies (LEA) superintenent or designee may request the issuance of an Emergency Permit to Practice for a teacher by submitting a statement of critical need.

No extensions are available for an Emergency Permit to Practice.

NUMBER OF CREDIT HOURS TO COMPLETE: Not applicable.

WHO EVALUATES: Not applicable.

LENGTH OF TIME: An Emergency Permit to Practice may be issued for one school year..

NORTH CAROLINA

Number of Teaching Licenses Issued

	1992-93	1991-92	1990-91	1989-90	1988-89
Persons who completed an approved college teacher preparation program *	1,786	N/A	2,689	2,509	2,143
Internship program					
Emergency					
Temporary	N/A	3,365	3,219	3,660	
Alternative Route ---					
Lateral Entry	222	322	432	318	243
Modified Licensure	1	3	0		
Other					

Number of Teachers Employed

	1992-93	1991-92	1990-91	1989-90	1988-89
Total Teachers Employed in the State	74,065	75,102	68,492	67,528	66,877
Newly Hired Teachers in Each Year	5,775	7,400	5,940	6,373	7,170

* *Graduates of approved programs in North Carolina IHEs.*

North Carolina Dept. of Public Instruction
Division of Teacher Education Services
114 West Edenton Street
Raleigh, NC 27611
Attn: Van Brock Murray
(919) 733-4125

NORTH CAROLINA

Institutions of higher education that have developed alternative teacher preparation programs leading to a teaching license:

States with which the state has reciprocity of teacher licenses:

ILA; NASDTEC Interstate Contract; NCATE.

Out-of-state applicants from non-reciprocal states are eligible for provisional licensure upon employment in North Carolina, if they have completed an education program approved by their states, although not accredited by NCATE or based on NASDTEC standards.

Institutions of higher education that have *any* teacher preparation programs leading to a license to teach.

Appalachian State University
Barton College
Barber-Scotia College
Belmont Abbey College
Bennett College
Campbell University
Catawba College
Davidson College
Duke University
East Carolina University
Elizabeth City State University
Elon College
Fayetteville State University
Gardner-Webb University
Greensboro College
Guilford College
High Point University
Johnson C. Smith University
Lees-McRae College
Lenoir-Rhyne College
Livingstone College
Mars Hill College
Meredith College
Methodist College
Montreat-Anderson College
North Carolina A&T State University
North Carolina Central University
North Carolina State University
North Carolina Wesleyan College
Pembroke State University
Pfeiffer College
Queens College
Salem College
Shaw University
St. Andrews College
St. Augustine's College
University of North Carolina-Asheville
University of North Carolina-Chapel Hill
University of North Carolina-Charlotte
University of North Carolina-Greensboro
University of North Carolina-Wilmington
Wake Forest University
Warren Wilson College
Western Carolina University
Wingate College
Winston-Salem State University

Contact information for persons interested in finding a teaching position in the state:

Licensure Section
301 N. Wilmington St.
Raleigh, NC 27601-2825
Phone: (919) 733-4125

TITLE: Emergency (Interim) License

HISTORY:

MOTIVATION: Shortage.

GRADE LEVELS AND/OR SUBJECT AREAS COVERED: All

WHO OPERATES: Education Standards and Practices Board

REQUIREMENTS TO ENTER PROGRAM:

The local school district requests issuance of the Emergency License, certifying that it is improbable that a regularly certified teacher can be employed, and stating its intent to offer the applicant a contract if the certificate is issued.

A bachelor's degree in area to be taught.

The applicant must have proficiency-- 4 year degree in the area to be taught.

PROGRAM DESCRIPTION:

For an individual to continue teaching under an Emergency License, the school district must show that it is unable to obtain a certified teacher for the position.

The individual must also continue college study, showing required progress toward completing the requirements for regular certification.

NUMBER OF CREDIT HOURS TO COMPLETE:

At least 8 semester hours or 12 quarter hours from a college approved teacher education program.

Additional college credit in area of study, leading to regular certification.

WHO EVALUATES: Education Standards and Practices Board Director.

LENGTH OF TIME: One year.

Approval of a renewal request depends on supply of and demand for the teacher, as evidenced by documented efforts by the school district to obtain a certified teacher for the position.

Renewal is also contingent on completion by the individual of at least 8 semester hours or 12 quarter hours of additional college credit in the area of study, leading to regular certification.

NORTH DAKOTA

Number of Teaching Licenses Issued

	2002-03	2001-02	2000-01	1999-00	1998-99	1997-98	1996-97	1995-96	1994-95	1993-94
Persons who completed an approved college teacher preparation program		* 669	* 645	723	731	790	677	902	943	980
Internship program										
Emergency		14	10	8	7	3	2	N/A	N/A	N/A
Temporary										
Alternative Route										

Number of Teachers Employed

	2002-03	2001-02	2000-01	1998-99	1997-98	1996-97	1995-96	1994-95	1993-94	1992-93
Total Teachers Employed in the State	* 8,830	* 8,845	* 8,886	8,007	8,430	8,402	8,270	8,268	8,186	8,766
Newly Hired Teachers in Each Year	* 306	* 273	* 285	250	232	217	193	245	206	266

* *Full-time equivalent (FTE).*

Education Standards and Practices Board
600 East Boulevard Ave.
Bismarck, ND 58505-0540
Attn: Janet Placek Welk, Exec. Dir.
Deb Jensen, Asst. Director
Phone: (701) 328-1659
Fax: (701) 328-2815
email: jwelk@state.nd.us

NORTH DAKOTA

Institutions of higher education that have developed alternative teacher preparation programs leading to a teaching license:

None

States with which the state has reciprocity of teacher licenses:

All

Institutions of higher education that have *any* teacher preparation programs leading to a license to teach.

Dickinson State College
Jamestown College
Mayville State College
Minot State College
North Dakota State University
Sitting Bull College/Sinte Gleske University
Trinity Bible Institute
University of Mary
University of North Dakota
Valley City State College

Contact information for persons interested in finding a teaching position in the state:

Note: Contact any college placement office.

OHIO

Class A

TITLE: Alternative Educator License

HISTORY: Rule for Alternative Educator, effective January 1, 2000.

GRADE LEVELS AND/OR SUBJECT AREAS COVERED: Secondary school (7-12) subjects. Intervention Specialist areas.

WHO OPERATES: Ohio Department of Education, Office of Certification Licensure and employing school/district.

REQUIREMENTS TO ENTER:

Prospective employing school district agrees to provide a structured mentoring program.

The candidate:

Holds a bachelor's degree from an accredited institution;

Has completed a major in a secondary teaching subject, OR evidence of five years of recent, related work experience in the teaching subject;

Has completed six semester hours of professional education coursework in the past five years with a GPA of 2.5, and from a college or university approved to prepare teachers, including:

1. Three semester hours in the developmental characteristics of the adolescent through young adult students, and
2. Three semester hours in teaching methods (this course must include field experience).;

Successful completion of the PRAXIS II examination for teacher licensure that measures content knowledge in the teaching subject.

PROGRAM DESCRIPTION:

The individual enters the classroom to teach full-time in the teaching subject for two years under the alternative educator license.

Must complete 12 additional semester hours of professional education coursework, with a GPA of 2.5 or above, prior to expiration of the alternative educator license, from a college or university approved to prepare teachers, in the principles and practices of teaching, student development and learning; pupil assessment procedures; curriculum development; classroom management; and teaching methodology.

Must successfully complete the Praxis II examination required for teacher licensure that measures professional knowledge.

The school district can then recommend licensure and the individual can be licensed as a two-year provisional teachers -- the initial teaching license issued to all beginning teachers.

After receiving the two-year provisional license, the educator must then meet the teacher licensure standards to transfer from a provisional to a professional license, and then to renew that license.

NUMBER OF CREDIT HOURS TO COMPLETE:

Up to two years to complete a total of 18 hours of professional education coursework, including six semester hours of pre-service and 12 semester hours of in-service course work.

LENGTH OF TIME: Two years, nonrenewable.

TITLE: Conditional Teaching Permit for Intervention Specialist (K-12)

HISTORY: Authorized in House Bill 196, enacted November 2001.

GRADE LEVELS AND/OR SUBJECT AREAS COVERED: Intervention Specialist areas.

WHO OPERATES: Ohio Department of Education, Office of Certification Licensure and employing school/district.

REQUIREMENTS TO ENTER:

Prospective employing school district agrees to provide a structured mentoring program.

The candidate:

Holds a bachelor's degree from an accredited institution.

Must pass the basic skills test prescribed by the State Board of Education.

Has completed 15 semester hours (or equivalent) in the principles and practices of teaching exceptional children, including such topics as child and adolescent development, diagnosis and assessment of children with disabilities, curriculum design and instruction, applied behavioral analysis, and methods of teaching students from culturally diverse backgrounds with the different learning styles.

PROGRAM DESCRIPTION:

The individual enters the classroom to teach full-time in the intervention specialist area for one year under the Conditional Teaching Permit.

Must complete an additional three semester hours in the content and methods of teaching reading during the year for which the Conditional Teaching Permit is issued.

Must complete the requirements for the Alternative Educator License for Intervention Specialist at the end of the year for which the Conditional Teaching Permit is issued.

NUMBER OF CREDIT HOURS TO COMPLETE:

One year to complete a total of 18 hours of professional education coursework, including 15 semester hours of pre-service and three semester hours of in-service coursework.

LENGTH OF TIME: One year, nonrenewable.

OTHER: The authorization for the One-Year Conditional Teaching Permit for Intervention Specialist is an emergency measure which expires November 2004.

TITLE: Conditional Teaching Permit for Adolescence to Young Adult (7-12)

HISTORY: Authorized in House Bill 196, enacted November 2001.

GRADE LEVELS AND/OR SUBJECT AREAS COVERED: Secondary (7-12) subject areas.

WHO OPERATES: Ohio Department of Education, Office of Certification Licensure and employing school/district.

REQUIREMENTS TO ENTER:

Prospective employing school district agrees to provide a structured mentoring program.

The candidate:

Holds a bachelor's degree from an accredited institution.

Must pass the basic skills test prescribed by the State Board of Education.

Has completed 15 semester hours (or equivalent) in the teaching subject area or subject area for which license is sought.

Has completed, within the previous five years, an additional six semester hours (or equivalent) of coursework, with a minimum GPA of 2.5, in one or more of the following areas: teaching content area, characteristics of student learning, diversity of learners, planning instruction, instructional strategies, learning environments, communication, assessment, and/or student support.

PROGRAM DESCRIPTION:

The individual enters the classroom to teach full-time for one year under the Conditional Teaching Permit.

Must complete an additional three semester hours in the teaching or content area during the year for which the Conditional Teaching Permit is issued.

Must complete the requirements for the Alternative Educator License at the end of the year for which the Conditional Teaching Permit is issued.

NUMBER OF CREDIT HOURS TO COMPLETE:

One year to evidence a total of 30 hours of coursework in the teaching or subject area, six semester hours of specified professional education coursework, and three semester hours of in-service coursework., including 15 semester hours of pre-service and three semester hours of in-service coursework.

LENGTH OF TIME: One year, nonrenewable.

OHIO

Class B

TITLE: Internship Certification Program

HISTORY: This program was mandated under an omnibus education reform bill, effective Oct. 1989. Standards were adopted in June 1990. The program became effective Fall 1990.

MOTIVATION:

GRADE LEVELS AND/OR SUBJECT AREAS COVERED: Secondary school subjects only.

WHO OPERATES: LEA jointly with IHE when Internship Certification Program has been approved by the Department of Education.

REQUIREMENTS TO ENTER:

The candidate may receive a contract from an approved district if he/she:

Holds a bachelor's degree;

Has completed a major in a high school teaching subject;

Has three years of related work experience in the subject;

Has been issued an Internship Certificate.

PROGRAM DESCRIPTION:

The candidate may receive an Internship Certificate if he or she successfully completes subject content portions of the Praxis II and completes 6 semester hours of pre-service course of study in the principles and practices of teaching.

The individual then:

Enters the classroom to do full-time teaching, is mentored, evaluated, and supervised by the school district and the college; low ratio of mentoring -- 1 to 5;

Must complete 12 additional semester hours in principles and practices of teaching within a two-year period while teaching full-time;

Must receive a satisfactory teaching evaluation and a satisfactory score on the professional knowledge portion of the Praxis II.

The school district can then recommend certification, and the individual can be certificated as a four-year Provisional Teacher -- the initial certificate issued to all beginning teachers.

NUMBER OF CREDIT HOURS TO COMPLETE:

Up to two years to complete a total of 18 hours of professional education coursework, including 6 semester hours of pre-service and 12 semester hours of in-service course work.

WHO EVALUATES: The LEA reports annually to the State Department of Education.

The State Department of Education reports to the state legislature every three years.

The State Department of Education conducts an on-site evaluation of the local school district every five years.

LENGTH OF TIME: One year, renewable one time.

OTHER: Currently no school districts are approved for the program.

OHIO

Number of Teaching Certificates Issued

	2000-01	1999-00	1998-99	1997-98	1993-94	1992-93	1991-92	1990-91	1989-90	1988-89
Persons who completed an approved college teacher preparation program	7,680	7,050	7,700	7,600	7,759	8,011	7,804	7,547	7,300	6,600
Emergency										
Alternative Route (2000-01)		31								
Internship Certification			0	0	0	1	0	0	0	0
Conditional License (2000-01)		3								

Number of Teachers Employed

	2000-01	1999-00	1998-99	1997-98	1993-94	1992-93	1991-92	1990-91	1989-90	1988-89
Total Teachers Employed in the State	112,545	112,563	111,500	107,500	112,370	110,921	111,900	110,411	113,711	100,829
Newly Hired Teachers in Each Year			9,500	8,500	5,845	5,800	N/A	4,231	4,068	4,133

Ohio Dept. of Education
Center for the Teaching Profession
Office of Certification/Licensure
25 S. Front St., Mail Stop 105
Columbus, OH 43215
Attn: Leonard Crawford
(614) 466-3593

OHIO

Institutions of higher education that have developed alternative teacher preparation programs leading to a teaching license:

States with which the state has reciprocity of teacher licenses:

NASDTEC Interstate Contract.

Institutions of higher education that have *any* teacher preparation programs leading to a license to teach.

Antioch College
Ashland University
Baldwin-Wallace College
Bluffton College
Bowling Green State University
Capital University
Case Western Reserve University
Cedarville College
Central State University
Cleveland State University
College of Mount St. Joseph
College of Wooster
Defiance College
Denison University
Franciscan University of Steubenville
Heidelberg College
Hiram College
John Carroll University
Kent State University
Lake Erie College
Lourdes College
Malone College
Marietta College
Miami University
Mount Union College
Mt. Vernon Nazarene College
Muskingum College
Notre Dame College
Oberlin College
Ohio Dominican College
Ohio Northern University
Ohio State University
Ohio University
Ohio Wesleyan University
Otterbein College
Shawnee State University
University of Akron
University of Cincinnati
University of Dayton
University of Findlay
University of Rio Grande
University of Toledo
Urbana University
Ursuline College
Walsh University
Wilmington College
Wittenberg University
Wright State University
Xavier University
Youngstown State University

Contact information for persons interested in finding a teaching position in the state:

For employment, contact: each school or school district.

For certification, contact:

Leonard Crawford, Administrator
Office of Certification/Licensure
25 S. Front St. Mail Stop 105
Columbus, OH 43215
Phone: (614) 466-3593

TITLE: Teacher Competency Review Panel

Beginning July 1, 1997, Oklahoma law created the Teacher Competency review Panel to make recommendations to the State Board of Education for the licensure and certification of people who have not graduated from an approved teacher education program in the state, or who have never held a standard teaching certificate in the state, or who are not currently certified to teach in another state.

According to the state regulation, "No person shall be certified to teach pursuant to the provisions of this section unless the person holds at least a baccalaureate degree from an accredited institution of higher education, has successfully completed the required competency tests, and has been assessed by and received a favorable recommendation from the Teacher Competency Review Panel. . . . The State Board of Education shall assess candidates seeking certification to teach through the recommendation of the Teacher Competency Review Panel fees for this service in an amount sufficient to fully fund the duties of the Teacher Competency Review Panel."

Applicants who do not receive a favorable recommendation from the panel may appeal to the State Board of Education.

NOTE: Attorney General Opinion Number 99-63, Sept. 23, 1999, determined that the requirement to be assessed by and receive a favorable recommendation from the Teacher Competency Review Panel includes applicants to the Alternative Certification program.

TITLE: Alternative Placement Program

HISTORY: Passed by the state legislature in 1991, this program replaced the Alternative Certification Program enacted in 1990.

MOTIVATION: To meet teacher shortages and expand the areas in which degreed, but non-certified, individuals possessing exceptional expertise can become certified.

GRADE LEVELS AND/OR SUBJECT AREAS COVERED:

Elementary-Secondary (grades PK-12); Secondary (grades 6-12); Career-Technology (6-12). Does not include early childhood education (PK-3) and elementary education (1-8).

WHO OPERATES: Operated under guidance from the State Board of Education through the Professional Standards Section of the State Department of Education. The Teacher Competency Review Panel was created by the state legislature in 1997.

REQUIREMENTS TO ENTER PROGRAM:

Pre-requisites: Prior to beginning work, an individual must meet the following conditions:

1. Hold a baccalaureate degree from an institution whose accreditation is recognized by the Oklahoma State Regents for Higher Education;

2. Have completed a major in a field that corresponds to an area of specialization for an elementary-secondary, secondary, or career-technology certificate;

3. Have passed the competency test in the subject area of specialization for which certification is sought and passed the general education test;

(Note: The professional education competency test may be taken after receiving a license, but would be required for a standard, five-year certificate)

4. Have provided documentation of at least two years of work experience which is related to the subject area of specialization if the person has only a baccalaureate degree

with no postbaccalaureate work in a related area. The State Board of Education may grant an exception to the requirements for licensure and certification and, upon demonstration by the individual of competency in the area of specialization, may grant a license or certificate to the individual.

5. The applicant must declare the intent to earn a Standard Certificate in not more than three years;

6. Have on file a plan for meeting standard certification requirements within three years; and

7. File appropriate application and fee with the Professional Standards Section of the State Department of Education.

PROGRAM DESCRIPTION:

In addition to meeting the prerequisites, the applicant must never have been denied admittance to a teacher education program approved by the Oklahoma State Regents for Higher Education, the North Central Association of Colleges and Schools, or the Oklahoma State Board of Education, nor have enrolled in and subsequently failed courses necessary to successfully meet the minimum requirements of such a program.

Qualified applicants must declare the intention to seek employment as a teacher at an accredited public school district in the state and have on file a plan for meeting certification requirements of the Alternative Placement Program.

Applicants who have no previous teaching experience must participate in the Resident Teacher Program with the same duties and responsibilities as other Resident Teacher program participants.

Participants will have three years in which to complete a block of up to 18 semester hours or 270 clock hours of professional education. The required hours may be reduced proportionately by either advanced degrees, work experience, or a combination of both. In no instance, however, will the required number of hours be reduced to less than 6 semester hours or 90 clock hours.

Participants will have three ears to pass the professional educational competency test.

The license is valid for one year, but can be renewed.

The program waives requirements of pre-student teaching field experiences, as well as student teaching.

NUMBER OF CREDIT HOURS TO COMPLETE:

A maximum of 18 semester hours or 270 clock hours of professional education courses are required for completion.

WHO EVALUATES: Evaluation of credentials presented in this program are conducted by the Professional Standards Section of the State Department of Education.

LENGTH OF TIME: Participants have a maximum of three years to complete the requirements for standard certification.

OKLAHOMA

Number of Teaching Licenses Issued

	2001-02	2000-01	1999-00	1998-99	1997-98	1996-97	1995-96	1994-95	1993-94	1992-93
Persons who completed an approved college teacher preparation program	1,929	1,569	2,968	3,306	3,604	3,674	3,623	3,690	3,410	N/A
Internship program	2,644	2,605	3,302	3,100	2,900	2,368	2,211	2,635	2,089	2,119
Emergency	52	49	123	342	281	272	209	296	310	387
Alternative Route *	599	255	533	661	595	468	342	413	241	** 54

Number of Teachers Employed

	2001-02	2000-01	1999-00	1998-99	1997-98	1996-97	1994-95	1993-94	1992-93	1991-92
Total Teachers Employed in the State	48,882	48,356	47,877	48,658	47,656	46,882	45,399	44,862	44,070	43,069
Newly Hired Teachers in Each Year***	N/A	N/A	N/A	N/A	N/A	N/A	N/A	N/A	N/A	N/A

** The "older" alternative route -- Emergency and Provisional Certificates. The Alternate Plan was passed by the Legislature in April, 1990 and was changed again in 1991and in 1992.*

*** As of Mar. 23, 1993.*

**** See internship program.*

Oklahoma Dept. of Education
Professional Standards Section
Teacher Education/Certification
2500 N. Lincoln Blvd., Room 211
Oklahoma City, OK 73105
Attn: Cindy Marose
Phone: (405) 521-3337
Fax: (405) 522-1520
e-mail: cindy_Marose@sde.state.ok.us

OKLAHOMA

Institutions of higher education that have developed alternative teacher preparation programs leading to a teaching license:

By legislative mandate, all 20 of Oklahoma's teacher preparation institutions must participate in the Oklahoma Alternative Placement Program.

States with which the state has reciprocity of teacher licenses:

NASDTEC Interstate Contract.

Out-of-State Applicant Certification ---

Applicants holding out-of-state certificates may either:

- Meet current Oklahoma certification requirements for standard certification; or
- Receive a Two-year certificate and have two years to fulfill the following requirements:

  Assessment and one year of successful employment in an Oklahoma school district.

States That Have Signed Certification Agreements for Oklahoma Teachers Going Out-of-State ---

Alabama
Arkansas
California
Colorado
Connecticut
Delaware
District of Columbia
Florida
Georgia
Guam
Hawaii
Idaho
Illinois
Indiana
Iowa
Kansas
Kentucky
Louisiana
Maine
Maryland
Massachusetts
Michigan
Mississippi
Missouri
Montana
Nebraska
Nevada
New Hampshire
New Mexico
New York
North Carolina
Ohio
Oregon
Pennsylvania
Rhode Island
South Carolina
South Dakota
Tennessee
Texas
Utah
Vermont
Virginia
Washington
West Virginia
Wisconsin

OKLAHOMA

Institutions of higher education that have *any* teacher preparation programs leading to a license to teach.

Bacone College
Cameron University
East Central University
Langston University
Mid-American Bible College
Northeastern State University
Northwestern Oklahoma State University
Oklahoma Baptist University
Oklahoma Christian University of Science/Arts
Oklahoma City University
Oklahoma Panhandle State University
Oklahoma State University
Oklahoma Wesleyan University
Oral Roberts University
St. Gregory's University
Southeastern Oklahoma State University
Southern Nazarene University
Southwestern Oklahoma State University
University of Central Oklahoma
University of Oklahoma
University of Science and Arts of Oklahoma
University of Tulsa

Contact information for persons interested in finding a teaching position in the state:

Note: Applicants should contact individual school districts.

TITLE: Restricted Transitional License

HISTORY: Adopted by the Teacher Standards and Practices Commission (TSPC) in 1999.

MOTIVATION: A Restricted Transitional Teaching License my be issued when there are insufficient applicants in an endorsement or in a region of the state. The license must be requested in a joint application from the candidate and the district desiring to hire the candidate.

SUBJECT AREAS COVERED: All

WHO OPERATES: The license is issued by TSPC at the request of a candidate and a school district, with the requirement that the candidate enroll in an approved teacher preparation program concurrently with employment. The institution providing the approved program and the district are both required to provide supervision of the candidate.

REQUIREMENTS TO ENTER:

At minimum the candidate must hold a bachelor's degree from a regionally accredited institution or the foreign equivalent.

There must be evidence of content expertise in the area for which the license is requested.

PROGRAM DESCRIPTION:

The Restricted Transitional Teaching License is valid for three years and is not renewable. During the life of the license the teacher must complete an approved teacher preparation program, including passing required basic skills and content tests, completion of two teacher work samples demonstrating the ability to foster student learning gains, and demonstration of all Initial Teaching License competencies as required in Oregon Administrative Rule 584-017-0100.

NO. OF CREDIT HOURS TO COMPLETE:

Varies depending on the enrolling institution.

WHO EVALUATES: Enrolling institution in cooperation with school district mentor.

LENGTH OF TIME: Three years maximum.

TITLE: Teaching Associate License

HISTORY: Adopted by the Teacher Standards and Practices Commission (TSPC) in 1999.

MOTIVATION: A Teaching Associate License is issued only to an experienced teaching assistant engaged in an intensive professional development program for teaching assistants approved by TSPC. The programs currently operating were developed specifically to recruit members of underrepresented ethnic and racial groups to the teaching profession. Both existing programs require the candidates to be bilingual.

SUBJECT AREAS COVERED:

All, but particularly encourage participation in preparation for the ESOL or ESOL/Bilingual license endorsement.

WHO OPERATES: The license is issued by TSPC at the request of a candidate, a school district, and an approved teacher preparation. The institution providing the approved program and the district are both required to provide supervision and intensive mentoring of the candidate.

REQUIREMENTS TO ENTER:

To be eligible for a Teaching Associate License, an applicant must satisfy the following requirements:

Be enrolled in a specified institutional program of undergraduate education and professional teacher preparation approved by TSPC and have completed 75% of the program required to qualify for assignment as a full-time intern.

Complete one year as a full-time intern in an approved program with the guidance of a mentor.

Obtain a passing score on a test of knowledge of US and Oregon civil rights laws at the conclusion of a course or workshop approved by TSPC.

Have three academic years of effectively full-time experience as a teaching assistant assigned primarily to direct instruction and related support.

Furnish fingerprints in the manner prescribed by TSPC.

PROGRAM DESCRIPTION:

The Teaching Associate License is valid for two years and is not renewable. During the life of the license the teacher must complete the approved teacher preparation program and complete all degree requirements, including passing required basic skills and content tests, completion of two teacher work samples demonstrating the ability to foster student learning gains, and demonstration of all Initial Teaching License competencies as required in Oregon Administrative Rule 584-017-0100.

NO. OF CREDIT HOURS TO COMPLETE:

Varies depending on the institutional program and prior college credits held by the candidate.

WHO EVALUATES: Enrolling institution in cooperation with school district mentor.

LENGTH OF TIME: Two years

TITLE: Limited Teaching License

HISTORY: Adopted by the Teacher Standards and Practices Commission (TSPC) in 1999.

MOTIVATION: The Limited Teaching License is issued for one or more highly specialized subjects of instruction for which TSPC does not issue a specific endorsement. An example would be dance.

SUBJECT AREAS COVERED:

Highly specialized subjects of instruction for which TSPC does not issue a specific endorsement. An example would be dance.

WHO OPERATES: Teacher Standards and Practices Commission.

REQUIREMENTS TO ENTER:

To be eligible for a Limited Teaching License the applicant must:

1. Have an accredited associates degree or its approved equivalent in objectively evaluated post-secondary education related to the intended subject of instruction.

2. Demonstrate knowledge of applicable civil rights laws.

3. Furnish fingerprints in the manner prescribed by TSPC.

4. Apply jointly with an employing school district.

5. Submit a job description and qualifications summarized on a resume.

The co-applicant district must:

1. Provide its particular need in relation to the co-applicant teacher's qualifications.

2. Agree to provide a mentor during the first year of the assignment.

3. Attest that circumstances prevent hiring a suitable teacher holding any other full-time license appropriate for the role to be filled.

PROGRAM DESCRIPTION:

During the life of the first Limited Teaching License the candidate must:

1. Obtain a passing score on the TSPC approved test of basic skills.

2. Obtain a passing score on a test of knowledge of US and Oregon civil rights laws at the conclusion of a course or workshop approved by TSPC.

NO. OF CREDIT HOURS TO COMPLETE: Not applicable.

WHO EVALUATES: Teacher Standards and Practices Commission

LENGTH OF TIME: The Limited Teaching License is valid for three years and is renewable under the conditions stated in "Program Description."

OREGON

Number of Teaching Licenses Issued

	2001-02	2000-01	1999-00	1998-99	1997-98	1996-97	1995-96	1994-95	1993-94	1992-93
Persons who completed an approved college teacher preparation program		1,579	1,500	1,490	1,342	N/A	1,388	1,355	2,835	1,360
Emergency *					742	911	300	235	165	127
Temporary *					1	2	113	231	142	226
Limited	29	30	73	10						
Transitional** (Reciprocal)	1,648	1,641	N/A	824	685	556	392			
Teacher Associate	2	0	7							
Restricted Transitional	271	291	N/A	N/A	0	0	0	0	0	0

* *License no longer in use*

** *Issued only to out-of-state applicants, replaces reciprocal*

Number of Teachers Employed

	2001-02	2000-01	1999-00	1998-99	1997-98	1995-96	1994-95	1993-94	1992-93	1991-92
Total Teachers Employed in the State	32,146	28,094	27,802	27,152	26,757	26,680	26,208	26,488	26,744	N/A
Newly Hired Teachers in Each Year	1,699	1,684	1,816	3,406	2,420	951	950	803	1,250	N/A

Oregon Teacher Standards/Practices
255 Capitol St., NE
Public Service Bldg., Suite 105
Salem, OR 97310-1332
Attn: Linda Samek
(503) 378-3757
e-mail: linda.samek@state.or.us

OREGON

Institutions of higher education that have developed alternative teacher preparation programs leading to a teaching license:

None

States with which the state has reciprocity of teacher licenses:

NASDTEC Interstate Contract.

Alabama
Arizona
Arkansas
California
Colorado
Connecticut
Delaware
District of Columbia
Florida
Georgia
Hawaii
Idaho
Illinois
Indiana
Kentucky
Louisiana
Maine
Maryland
Massachusetts
Michigan
Mississippi
Montana
Nevada
New Hampshire
New York
North Carolina
Ohio
Pennsylvania
Rhode Island
South Carolina
Tennessee
Texas
Utah
Vermont
Virginia
Washington
West Virginia

Note: Oregon issues 3-year Transitional Licenses to out-of-state-prepared and/or licensed educators in all U.S. states.

Institutions of higher education that have *any* teacher preparation programs leading to a license to teach.

- Concordia College
- Eastern Oregon University
- George Fox College
- Lewis and Clark College
- Linfield College
- Northwest Christian College
- Oregon State University
- Pacific University
- Portland State University
- Southern Oregon University
- University of Oregon
- University of Portland
- Warner Pacific College
- Western Baptist College
- Western Oregon University
- Willamette University

Contact information for persons interested in finding a teaching position in the state:

Confederation of Oregon School Administrators (COSA)
707 13th St. SE, Suite 100
Salem, OR 97301-4035
Phone: (503) 581-3141

Oregon Education Association (OEA)
1 Plaza SW, 6900 SW Haines Rd.
Tigard, OR 97223
Phone: (503) 684-3300

TITLE: **Alternative Candidate Certification**

HISTORY: Developed in Spring 1998 as a means of attracting highly-qualified individuals into teaching at the secondary level.

MOTIVATION: The use of this experimental program is to provide an opportunity for training and classroom experience for qualified individuals who may not meet the course requirements in educational methodology, but have the academic preparation, or experience in the workplace, in industry, or in specialized areas to be capable of imparting knowledge they have acquired to students in the classroom.

GRADE LEVELS AND/OR SUBJECT AREA(S) COVERED:

The program is limited to those instructional certificate areas that are grade 7-12 in scope and content area certificates that are K-12 in scope.

WHO OPERATES: The State Department of Education will recognize, for purposes of teacher certification, collaborative associations among education entities for the purpose of developing alternative teacher certification programs. These collaborative association shall be referred to as collaborative units.

REQUIREMENTS TO ENTER:

Any individual who meets the requirements of state law (relating to eligibility, minimum age, moral character, and good health) is eligible to pursue teacher certification through a Department-approved alternative teacher certification program.

The eligible applicant, prior to admission, must provide evidence of each of the following:

1. Having achieved a minimum undergraduate degree GPA of 3.0 in the subject area he/she intends to teach, or an advanced degree in the subject he/she intends to teach, or a minimum of 10 years of

exceptional service in a career compatible with the subject area he/she intends to teach in the public schools.

2. Having successfully completed 6 credit hours or its equivalent in college-level English.

3. Having successfully completed 6 credit hours or its equivalent in college-level mathematics.

4. Candidates must achieve satisfactory scores on the Praxis I, PreProfessional Skills tests in Reading, Writing, Mathematics, and Listening, and the appropriate Praxis II specialty area test; all K-12 candidates must also achieve a satisfactory score on the Elementary Education Content Knowledge test. Upon completion of the 15-month collaborative unit experience, the candidate must achieve a satisfactory score on the Praxis II Principles of Learning and Teaching 7-12.

5. Having successfully completed the two-week intensive seminar provided by the collaborative unit.

6. Having received an intern certificate upon the recommendation of the teacher preparation institution and other members of the collaborative unit. The certificate is valid for a period not to exceed 15 consecutive months and is not renewable.

PROGRAM DESCRIPTION:

The program envisions cooperation among the State Department of Education, a teacher preparation institution, a public school entity, an intermediate unit, another four-year degree-granting institution, a community or junior college, and an eligible candidate, to develop an individually-prescriptive educational plan to prepare the candidate for certification in his or her specialty. The training and experience must be supervised and mentored by a teacher preparation institution and the employing public school entity, in conjunction with any other participating education entities -- which shall comprise and be referred to as the collaborative unit.

The professional development team (consisting of at least one representative from each entity in the collaborative unit) will provide an educational program that consists of an initial intensive seminar, prior to the internship, with a requirement to develop a portfolio during the first semester of teaching (6 credit hours) and up to an additional

180 clock hours or 6 credit hours of instruction. The 180 clock hours of instruction may consist of any combination of credit hours, in-service credit, continuing education credits relative to the candidate's teaching area, or Department of Education-approved instructional clock hours designated by the collaborative unit.
The education program provided by the team will be limited to 15 consecutive months, to include the apprenticeship year in the school district, and will not exceed 180 clock hours or 6 credit hours of instruction, plus the intensive seminar with portfolio requirement.

The individually-prescribed educational plan should be related to the professional educational development of the candidate and include the following instructional program competencies:

1. Planning of instruction, based upon knowledge of subject matter, students, the community, and the Pennsylvania Academic Standards, which promote problem analysis, creativity, and decision-making skills.

2. Managing the instructional environment, to create a climate that promotes fairness, establishes rapport with students, communicates challenging learning expectations to each student, maintain consistent standards of classroom behavior, and makes the physical environment safe and conducive to learning.

3. Implementing, adapting, and assimilating effective instructional strategies, curriculum resources, and technologies, in collaboration with other educators.

4. Selecting, analyzing, and modifying instructional materials, to meet the learning needs and reading levels of diverse learners.

5. Monitoring student understanding of content through a variety of means, providing feedback to assist learning and adjusting instructional strategies.

6. Developing a knowledge of professional organizations, state and federal laws, regulations, and ethical practices.

7. Developing the ability to foster professional relationships with school colleagues to improve student learning.

8. Developing the ability to communicate effectively with parents/guardians, other agencies, and the community at large,. to support learning by all students.

NUMBER OF HOURS TO COMPLETE:

12 credit hours or no more than 360 clock hours.

Who Evaluates: Collaborative unit.

Length of Time: 15 consecutive months.

After July 1, 2000, all holders of a valid Pennsylvania certificate must meet the requirements of Act 48, Continuing Professional Development. These requirements are 6 college level credits or 180 hours of continuing education activities every five years in order to keep their certificate active.

TITLE: Teacher Intern Program

HISTORY: Since the 1960s at the graduate level; given greater emphasis since 1983 as a way of bringing additional competent individuals into teaching.

MOTIVATION: To attract minorities and mid-level executives near retirement; provide mathematics and science teachers for urban classrooms; and help long-term substitute teachers obtain certification.

GRADE LEVELS AND/OR SUBJECT AREAS COVERED:

Subject specialties vary from college to college. Although this program is more targeted to secondary-level teachers with specific subject matter specialization, it is not limited to secondary only.

WHO OPERATES: IHE

REQUIREMENTS TO ENTER PROGRAM:

A bachelor's degree related to the area of certification requested.

Acceptance by a preparing institution with an approved intern program.

Beginning September 1 2001, candidates must present a minimum of 2.6 GPA in their baccalaureate degree; a 2.8 GPA beginning September 1, 2002, a 3.0 GPA beginning September 1, 2003, and a 3.0 GPA thereafter.

Candidates must complete the program with at least the same GPA required for entrance.

Candidates must also have 6 credits of college level Mathematics and 6 credits of college level English Composition and Literature.

Candidates must achieve satisfactory scores on the praxis I, PreProfessional Skills tests in Reading, Writing, Mathematics and listening; and the appropriate specialty area test; all K-6 and K-12 candidates must also achieve a satisfactory score on the Elementary Education Content Knowledge test.

Upon completion of the Intern Program, the candidate must achieve a satisfactory score on the praxis II principles of Learning and Teaching test; K-6 for elementary and Early childhood; or Principles of Learning and Teaching 7-12 for all secondary certificate areas.

PROGRAM DESCRIPTION:

The applicant is accepted into an approved college intern certification program.

The college evaluates the individual's past education and experience and determines what additional coursework should be undertaken and when the individual is prepared to enter the classroom and teach.

When a school district offers the candidate a job, the college is notified and recommends that the Bureau of Teacher Certification and Preparation issue an Intern Certificate. The candidate must have passed the Praxis I tests, K-6 and K-12 candidates must have passed the Elementary Education Content Knowledge test and the praxis II specialty area test before receiving the Intern Certificate.

When coursework stipulated by the college has been completed and the individual has passed the Principles of Learning and Teaching – K-6 for Early Childhood and Elementary Education or the Principles of Learning and Teaching – 7-12, for Secondary content areas, the college can then recommend the intern candidate for a Level I certificate..

All beginning teachers must complete a first year induction program, regardless of whether they are graduates of a teacher education program or entered through an internship. During the induction program, the school district assigns each new teacher a mentor teacher trained by the district. However, in the case of someone with past teaching experience, this requirement may be modified.

After three years of successful teaching on a Level I certificate, completion of 24 semester hours of post-baccalaureate credit, and completion of the required induction program, the candidate can apply for conversion of a Level I to a Level II.

Specific requirements for college coursework which an intern must complete will vary from college to college. Some colleges have interns complete pre-school year training during the summer, before they enter the classroom.

NUMBER OF CREDIT HOURS TO COMPLETE: Varies from college to college.

WHO EVALUATES: The college determines when the intern is ready to enter the classroom and recommends to the state that he/she is ready to receive an Intern Certificate.

The college provides on-site supervision.

When all coursework and field experience are completed, the college recommends the intern to the state for issuance of an Instructional I Certificate.

The candidate is evaluated on-the-job by the school district and is supervised during the induction program by a mentor teacher.

LENGTH OF TIME: Varies, but the candidate must be continuously enrolled in the intern program.

Intern Certificate valid for three calendar years, non-renewable.

Instructional I Certificate is valid for 6 service years and requires three years of successful teaching and 24 semester hours of post-baccalaureate credit and the completion of an induction program in order to convert the certificate to an Instruction II certificate.

OTHER A listing of colleges and universities offering the Intern program and a handbook describing the program can be obtained from the address below.

PENNSYLVANIA

Number of Teaching Licenses Issued

	1999-00	1998-99	1997-98	1996-97	1995-96	1994-95	1993-94	1992-93	1991-92	1990-91	1989-90
Persons who completed an approved college teacher preparation program	10,204	11,423	11,377	11,782	11,088	10,999	10,255	10,406	N/A	N/A	N/A
Emergency	3,045	2,552	1,496	1,006	718	655	504	554	530	562	637
Alternative Route	296	308	231	197	310	201	259	351	321	178	265
Other											

Number of Teachers Employed

	1999-00	1998-99	1997-98	1996-97	1995-96	1994-95	1993-94	1992-93	1991-92	1990-91	1989-90
Total Teachers Employed in the State (includes full- and part-time)	115,673	109,691	109,156	107,610	106,028	104,081	102,405	101,984	101,540	101,345	105,415
Newly Hired Teachers in Each Year	7,437	3,152	5,159	3,207	3,095	2,906	4,795	2,475	2,326	2,220	3,957

Pennsylvania Dept. of Education
Bureau of Certification
333 Market Street
Harrisburg, PA 17108
Attn: Ronald Simanovich
Phone: (717) 783-9252
Fax: (717) 783-6736
e-mail: rsimanovic@state.pa.us

PENNSYLVANIA

Institutions of higher education that have developed alternative teacher preparation programs leading to a teaching license:

Intern Programs

- Alvernia College
- Arcadia University
- Bloomsburg University of Pennsylvania
- Cabrini College
- Carnegie Mellon University
- Cedar Crest College
- Chestnut Hill College
- Cheyney University of Pennsylvania
- De Sales University
- Drexel University
- Duquesne University
- East Stroudsburg Univ. of Pennsylvania
- Eastern College
- Geneva College
- Gwynedd-Mercy College
- Immaculata College
- Indiana University of Pennsylvania (English only)
- Kutztown University of Pennsylvania
- LaRoche College
- Lehigh University
- Lincoln University
- Lycoming College
- Mansfield University of Pennsylvania
- Marywood University
- Millersville University of Pennsylvania
- Moore College of Art and Design
- Pennsylvania College of Optometry
- Robert Morris College
- Saint Joseph's University
- Susquehanna University
- Temple University
- University of Pennsylvania
- University of Pittsburgh
- West Chester University of Pennsylvania
- Wilkes University
- Widener University
- Wilson College

States with which the state has reciprocity of teacher licenses:

NASDTEC Interstate Contract.

PENNSYLVANIA

Institutions of higher education that have *any* teacher preparation programs leading to a license to teach.

Albright College
Alvernia College
Beaver College
Bloomsburg University of Pennsylvania
Bryn Mawr College
Bucknell University
Cabrini College
California University of Pennsylvania
Carlow College
Carnegie-Mellon University
Cedar Crest College
Chatham College
Chestnut Hill College
Cheyney University of Pennsylvania
Clarion University of Pennsylvania
Clark Summitt Bible Baptist College
College Misericordia
Delaware Valley College
DeSales University
Dickinson College
Drexel University
Duquesne University
East Stroudsburg University of Pennsylvania
Eastern College
Edinboro University of Pennsylvania
Elizabethtown College
Gannon University
Geneva College
Gettysburg College
Grove City College
Gwynedd-Mercy College
Haverford College
Holy Family College
Johnstown Campus-Pittsburgh
Immaculata College
Indiana University of Pennsylvania
Juniata College
King's College
Kutztown University of Pennsylvania
LaRoche College
LaSalle College
Lancaster Bible College
Lebanon Valley College
Lehigh University
Lincoln University
Lock Haven State University
Lycoming College
Mansfield University of Pennsylvania
Marywood University
Mercyhurst College
Messiah College
Millersville University of Pennsylvania
Moore College of Art and Design
Moravian College
Muhlenberg College
Neumann College
Philadelphia College of Bible
Pennsylvania College of Optometry
Pennsylvania State University
Philadelphia College of Pharmacy and Science
Point Park College
Robert Morris College
Rosemont College
St. Bonaventure University (located in New York)
Saint Francis College
Saint Joseph's University
Saint Vincent College
Seton Hill College
Shippensburg University of Pennsylvania
Slippery Rock University of Pennsylvania
Susquehanna University
Swarthmore College
Temple University
Thiel College
University of Pennsylvania
University of Pittsburgh
University of Scranton
University of the Arts
Ursinus College
Villanova University
Washington & Jefferson College
Waynesburg College
West Chester University of Pennsylvania
Westminster College
Widener University
Wilkes College
Wilson College
York College

Contact information for persons interested in finding a teaching position in the state:

Note: Contact individual school districts.

Rhode Island is currently developing an alternative route to certification program. The program is aimed at the secondary and special subjects. An individual interested in becoming licensed to teach in Rhode Island should contact one of the following institutions offering approved teacher programs in the areas listed:

Brown University Dr. Lawrence Wakeford 401-863-2407

Areas: Biology, English, History, Social Studies, and Elementary Education

Providence College Dr. Lynn Ryan 401-865-2504

Areas: Administration, Biology, Chemistry, English, Foreign Language (French, Italian and Spanish), History, Math, School Counselor, Biology, Chemistry, Social Studies, Special Education and Elementary Education.

Rhode Island College Dr. John Bucci 401-456-8110

Areas: Administration, Art, Counselor, Early Childhood, Elementary Education, English, Foreign Language (French, Spanish), Health Education, History, Math, Music, Physical Education, Reading Specialist, School Psychologist, Science (Biology, Chemistry, General Science, and Physics), Social Studies, Special Education, Vocational Education, English as a Second Language Specialist, and Technology Education.

Johnson & Wales University Paul Hodges 401-456-4738

Areas: Administration, Business, Marketing and Food Service

Rhode Island School of Design Dr. Paul Sproll 401-454-6132

Area: Art Education

Roger Williams University Dr. Marie D. Basio 401-254-3019

Areas: Elementary Education, English, Biology, Chemistry, General Science, History, Social Studies, Dance, Foreign Language (French, German, Italian, Latin, Portugese, Spanish)

Salve Regina University Dr. Mary O'Brien 401-847-6650 X3111

Areas: Biology, Chemistry, Early Childhood, Elementary Education, English, Foreign Language (French, Spanish), History, Math, Special Education (Early Childhood and Elementary), Theatre.

University of Rhode Island Dr. Robert Felner 401-874-5930

Areas: Early Childhood, Elementary Education, English, Foreign Language (French, Latin, German, Italian, Russian and Spanish), Library Media, Math, Music, Physical Education, Reading Specialist, School Psychologist, Science (Biology, Chemistry, General Science and Physics), Social Studies/History, Speech Pathology and Audiology.

RHODE ISLAND

Number of Teaching Licenses Issued

	2000-01	1999-00	1998-99	1997-98	1996-97	1995-96	1994-95	1993-94	1992-93	1991-92
Persons who completed an approved college teacher preparation program	963	944	925	913	894	948	881	1,000	870	840
Internship program										
Emergency	269	116	183	151	87	80	60	140	162	83

Number of Teachers Employed

	2000-01	1999-00	1998-99	1997-98	1994-95	1993-94	1992-93	1991-92	1990-91	1989-90
Total Teachers Employed in the State	11,550	11,118	11,067	11,200	12,321	12,336	10.450	10,285	9,391	10,479
Newly Hired Teachers in Each Year	N/A	N/A	N/A	N/A	N/A	N/A	N/A	N/A	N/A	N/A

Rhode Island Dept. of Education
Office of Teacher Preparation,
Certification and Professional
Development
255 Westminster Street
Providence, RI 02903
Attn: Joseph Gaudiosi
(401) 277-4600 x2254
email: ride1512@ride.ri.net

RHODE ISLAND

Institutions of higher education that have developed alternative teacher preparation programs leading to a teaching license:

States with which the state has reciprocity of teacher licenses:

NASDTEC Interstate Contract. Rhode Island has signed reciprocity contracts with 45 states.

Institutions of higher education that have *any* teacher preparation programs leading to a license to teach.

Brown University
Johnson & Wales University
Providence College
Rhode Island College
Rhode Island School of Design
Roger Williams University
Salve Regina University
University of Rhode Island

Contact information for persons interested in finding a teaching position in the state:

Note: Contact individual school districts.

SOUTH CAROLINA — Class C

TITLE: Program of Alternative Certification for Educators

HISTORY: Established in 1984 by state law.

MOTIVATION: Shortage.

GRADE LEVELS AND/OR SUBJECT AREA(S) COVERED:

Areas of teacher shortage deemed critical by the State Board of Education. Areas are evaluated annually.

WHO OPERATES: State. Training sites located at Coastal Carolina University and within approved school districts..

REQUIREMENTS TO ENTER PROGRAM:

A bachelor's degree in an initial certification subject.

A passing score on the appropriate PRAXIS Specialty Area Examination(s).

Two years post-baccalaureate experience.

Employment by a public school district.

Successful completion of a pre-service institute to prepare the prospective teacher for the opening of school.

PROGRAM DESCRIPTION:

The individual completes:

A pre-service institute to prepare the prospective teacher for the opening of school (or in January). Training sessions throughout the first school year. Together, these should total 15 days.

An institute during the second summer of employment. Training sessions throughout the second school year. Together, these should total 12 days.

Over a three-year period, completion of three graduate-level professional education courses as prescribed in the teacher's professional development plan.

The individual must successfully complete no fewer than three years of full-time employment in an instructional role in a public school after issuance of the initial alternative certificate.

Participant must pass the Principals of Learning and Teaching exam prior to completion of the PACE program and issuance of the professional certificate.

All program expenses must be paid by the applicant.

NUMBER OF CREDIT HOURS TO COMPLETE:

Over a period of three years, completion of three graduate-level professional education courses as prescribed in the teacher's professional development plan.

WHO EVALUATES: Coastal Carolina University or district program provider in cooperation with employing school district evaluation team.

LENGTH OF TIME: The individual must complete the requirements for full certification within three years.

SOUTH CAROLINA

Number of Teaching Licenses Issued

	1999-00	1998-99	1997-98	1996-97	1995-96	1994-95	1993-94	1992-93	1991-92	1990-91
Persons who completed an approved college teacher preparation program	3,341	* 2,400	4,013	3,714	3,920	3,926	N/A	3,405	4,139	3,062
Emergency										
Alternative Route	434	191	139	77	68	65	N/A	42	32	48
Other --- Transcript Analysis			N/A	N/A	N/A	75	N/A	37	45	144

* *In-state.*

Number of Teachers Employed

	1998-99	1997-98	1992-93	1991-92	1990-91	1989-90	1988-89
Total Teachers Employed in the State	N/A	** 49,237	39,787	37,171	36,963	36,877	35,877
Newly Hired Teachers in Each Year	N/A	N/A	N/A	N/A	N/A	N/A	N/A

** *Includes administrators and counselors.*

South Carolina Dept. of Education
Teacher Education/Certification
1600 Gervais Street
Columbia, SC 29201
Sandra Rowe
(803) 734-2758

SOUTH CAROLINA

Institutions of higher education that have developed alternative teacher preparation programs leading to a teaching license:

Coastal Carolina University

States with which the state has reciprocity of teacher licenses:

NASDTEC Interstate Contract.

Institutions of higher education that have *any* teacher preparation programs leading to a license to teach.

Anderson College
Benedict College
Bob Jones University
Charleston Southern University
Citadel Military College
Claflin College
Clemson University
Coastal Carolina University
Coker College
College of Charleston
Columbia College
Columbia International University
Converse College
Erskine College
Francis Marion University
Furman University
Lander College
Limestone College
Morris College
Newberry College
North Greenville College
Presbyterian College
South Carolina State College
Southern Wesleyan University
University of South Carolina-Aiken
University of South Carolina-Columbia
University of South Carolina-Spartanburg
Winthrop University
Wofford College

Contact information for persons interested in finding a teaching position in the state:

Ms. Ann Byrd
South Carolina Teacher Recruitment Center
Winthrop University
Rock Hill, SC 29733
Phone: 1-800-541-7525

SOUTH DAKOTA

Class D

TITLE: Alternative Certification

HISTORY: Has existed as a pilot since 1985. It was formally enacted as a rule by the State Board of Education, effective July 1, 1991.

MOTIVATION: It is intended for a school district which is unable to fill a position with a properly certified teacher.

GRADE LEVELS AND/OR SUBJECT AREA(S) COVERED: Areas of need.

WHO OPERATES: State and IHE.

REQUIREMENTS TO ENTER PROGRAM:

An applicant:

Must have a bachelor's degree, with a major in a certifiable subject;

Has not had a student teaching experience; and

Must have an employing school district willing to cooperate in an alternative certification program.

PROGRAM DESCRIPTION:

When a prospective participant contacts the Office of Teacher Certification of the Department of Education and Cultural Affairs, he or she is directed to the colleges and universities which have approved programs in South Dakota.

The IHE will evaluate the applicant's transcript and draft an outline of courses in accordance with a professional development plan approved by the SEA. All courses must be taken through the participating IHE in no more than two years.

The individual must complete a teacher education program (professions development plan) according to schedule, and be supervised by the teacher education program. The IHE contact person is primarily responsible for supervising the candidate, although the LEA will provide pre-school orientation, as well as supervision and mentoring.

The alternative certification candidate teaches under a two-year provisional certificate while completing the professions development plan coursework requirements.

Recommendation for a five-year certificate will be made by the cooperating IHE, upon completion of the approved program for alternative certification and at least two years in the program.

NUMBER OF CREDIT HOURS TO COMPLETE:

Course requirements of a teacher education program.

WHO EVALUATES: IHE.

LENGTH OF TIME: Two years.

SOUTH DAKOTA

Number of Teaching Licenses Issued

	1999-00	1998-99	1997-98	1996-97	1995-96	1993-94	1992-93	1991-92	1990-91	1989-90
Persons who completed an approved college teacher preparation program	930	1,213	1,222	N/A	1,197	N/A	1,349	1,342	1,174	1,100
Emergency										
Temporary	0	0	N/A	N/A	N/A	N/A	N/A	27	120	55
Alternative Route	76	80	26	N/A	N/A	N/A	3	1	* 0	N/A
Other -- Associate Instructor **	0	0	N/A	N/A	N/A	N/A	N/A	N/A	400	N/A

Number of Teachers Employed

	1999-00	1998-99	1997-98	1996-97	1995-96	1994-95	1993-94	1992-93	1991-92	1990-91
Total Teachers Employed in the State	9,262	9,570	9,282	N/A	9.625	9,985	9,557	8,767	9,454	8,773
Newly Hired Teachers in Each Year	436	507	536	N/A	N/A	611	641	576	432	414

* *The program became officially available, by state board rule, effective July 1, 1991; 20 people have participated in a pilot since 1985.*

** *The state's One-Year Associate Instructor Program -- which has since been repealed -- offered a credential to persons who had completed a teacher education program, but had not been certified, or had completed less than one year of full-time teaching experience.*

South Dakota Dept. of Education and Cultural Affairs
Division of Elementary/Secondary Education
Kneip Building
Pierre, SD 57501
Attn: Dean Buchanan
Phone: (605) 773-4771
Fax: (605) 773-6139
email: dean.buchanan@state.sd.us

SOUTH DAKOTA

Institutions of higher education that have developed alternative teacher preparation programs leading to a teaching license:

States with which the state has reciprocity of teacher licenses:

Note: None. South Dakota is a signatory to the MOINKSA regional exchange agreement -- with Arkansas, Iowa, Kansas, Missouri, Nebraska, and Oklahoma.

Institutions of higher education that have *any* teacher preparation programs leading to a license to teach.

Augustana College
Black Hills State University
Dakota State University
Dakota Wesleyan University
Huron University
Mt. Marty College
Northern State University
Oglala Lakota College
Sinte Gleska College

South Dakota State University
University of Sioux Falls
University of South Dakota

Contact information for persons interested in finding a teaching position in the state:

Gerald Goering or Dean Buchanan
Director of Teacher Education & Certification
Kneip Building, 700 Governors Drive
Pierre, SD 57501-2291
Phone: (605) 773-4771

TITLE: Interim License Type E --
Alternative Licensure for persons not completing college programs

HISTORY: Approved by the State Board in May 2000.

MOTIVATION: To attract qualified individuals into the teaching field by offering a more flexible licensure route..

GRADE LEVELS AND/OR SUBJECT AREA(S) COVERED:

All initial areas except Elementary 1-8, Elementary K-8, and Middle Grades 5-8.

WHO OPERATES: State Department of Education

REQUIREMENTS TO ENTER:

Option 1

Bachelor's degree in teaching area from a regionally accredited institution.

Option 2

Bachelor's degree from a regionally accredited institution in any area.

Letter from college certification officer at approved institution verifying that the applicant has satisfied the subject area component of the approved teacher education program for the desired area endorsement.

Option 3

Bachelor's degree form a regionally accredited institution in any area and passing scores on the Praxis Specialty Test(s) required for the desired area(s) of endorsement.

PROGRAM DESCRIPTION:

The candidate must meet the subject matter requirements in one of the three was described in the previous section.

Then the applicant must receive an "Intent to employ" signature from a Local Education Agency (LEA).

Once the candidate is employed, he/she has three school years to (1) complete 24 semester hours of professional education coursework, (2) pass all required portions of the Praxis Exams (specialty tests and PLT) and (3) accrue at least two years of successful experience on the Interim E License.

Candidate submits documentation to the state verifying completion of these three things and requests a full Tennessee license.

NOTE: Candidates must meet university teacher education program admission requirements even though they are not formally being admitted.

NUMBER OF CREDIT HOURS TO COMPLETE: 24 semester hours of professional education coursework.

WHO EVALUATES: IHE, State Department of Education.

LENGTH OF TIME: One year. Renewal for two additional years if renewal requirements are met each year.

OTHER: The candidate must have met admission requirements to a teacher education program before the first renewal and obtain a program of study signed by a college certification officer outlining the professional education requirements lacking for full licensure not to exceed 24 semester hours. The candidate must complete at least six semester hours of coursework toward the program of study to renew the Interim E License each year.

TENNESSEE — Class D

TITLE: Interim License Type C --
Alternative Preparation for Licensure

HISTORY: Approved by the State Board in Nov. 1990. The University of Tennessee - Knoxville, the University of Tennessee - Chattanooga, and the University of Memphis offer this program.

MOTIVATION: Desire to attract extremely capable persons with maturity and a variety of work experiences to the teaching profession.

GRADE LEVELS AND/OR SUBJECT AREA(S) COVERED:

All licensure areas.

WHO OPERATES: IHE

REQUIREMENTS TO ENTER:

Bachelor's degree from an accredited institution in a teaching related field.

Screening by IHE and K-12 practitioners.

Testing requirements for admission to a teacher education program.

PROGRAM DESCRIPTION:

The LEA and the IHE collaboratively plan the employment. The candidate has the support of a mentor and participates in additional preparation activities.

Following successful completion of all education and test requirements, the candidate will be recommended for full licensure by the institution.

NUMBER OF CREDIT HOURS TO COMPLETE: Not applicable.

WHO EVALUATES: IHE, LEA.

LENGTH OF TIME: One year. May be reissued one time if requirements not completed within one year.

TITLE: Interim License Type D -- Alternative Preparation for Licensure

HISTORY: Approved by the State Board in 1990.

MOTIVATION: Desire to attract extremely capable persons with maturity and a variety of work experiences to the teaching profession.

GRADE LEVELS AND/OR SUBJECT AREA(S) COVERED:

All endorsement areas covered under internship teacher education programs.

WHO OPERATES: IHE

REQUIREMENTS TO ENTER:

Bachelor's degree from a regionally accredited institution of higher education.

Screening by IHE and K-12 practitioners.

Testing requirements for admission to a teacher education program.

PROGRAM DESCRIPTION:

The candidate teaches in a one-year internship, under a closely supervised mentoring program, and completes other credit specified by the IHE. Upon completion of program and test requirements, the candidate will be recommended for full licensure by the institution.

NUMBER OF CREDIT HOURS TO COMPLETE: Not applicable.

WHO EVALUATES: IHE, LEA.

LENGTH OF TIME: One year. May be reissued two times, but intern may teach using the license for the equivalent of no more than one school year.

TITLE: Interim License Type A

HISTORY: Legislation enacted in 1984.

GRADE LEVELS AND/OR SUBJECT AREA(S) COVERED:

Available in all endorsement areas except Elementary 1-8, Elementary K-8 and Middle grades 5-8.

WHO OPERATES: Office of Teacher Licensing in the Tennessee State Department of Education and IHEs.

REQUIREMENTS TO ENTER:

A bachelor's degree from an accredited college with an academic major in area of endorsement for which licensing is sought.

Applicants are eligible for an Interim A License in all areas except middle grades education, and elementary education.

The local district school superintendent must state the district's intent to employ and must provide a mentor teacher for the applicant during the first two years of teaching.

PROGRAM DESCRIPTION:

The individual must enter and complete an approved teacher preparation program in order to achieve full licensure.

NUMBER OF CREDIT HOURS TO COMPLETE:

Not applicable. To renew, an individual must complete 9 quarter hours or 6 semester hours of credit in areas of deficiency -- completed after license most recently issued/renewed. To satisfy this requirement the applicant for renewal must have been admitted to an approved teacher preparation program and his/her areas of deficiency must be identified on a program of studies prepared by the certification officer at the college or university.

The individual may not be issued a Type A license more than three times.

Upon completion of program and test requirements, a candidate may be issued a full teaching license.

WHO EVALUATES: LEA and IHE

LENGTH OF TIME: Valid for one calendar year -- until the following August 31.

OTHER: Thirty-nine Tennessee institutions of higher education (IHEs) offer approved post-baccalaureate programs which lead to initial licensure and a graduate degree in some instances. These programs range from twelve to fifteen months and include either a semester of student teaching or a year-long internship.

TITLE: Interim License Type B

HISTORY: Legislation enacted in 1984.

MOTIVATION:

GRADE LEVELS AND/OR SUBJECT AREA(S) COVERED:

Any endorsement area can be placed on the Interim B.

WHO OPERATES: State

REQUIREMENTS TO ENTER:

The local school district superintendent must state the district's intent to employ.

The individual must already meet all licensure requirements except completion of testing as determined by the State Department of Education.

PROGRAM DESCRIPTION:

While working under this credential, the individual must complete the required testing prior to being issued a full teaching license.

NUMBER OF CREDIT HOURS TO COMPLETE: Not applicable.

WHO EVALUATES: Not applicable.

LENGTH OF TIME: Valid for one calendar year -- until the following August 31.

Not to be issued more than two times, unless a one-year extension is requested by the school superintendent for persons with a handicapping condition.

TITLE: Permit to Teach

HISTORY:

MOTIVATION: A local school district has a documented need and a licensed educator cannot be found to fill a position.

GRADE LEVELS AND/OR SUBJECT AREA(S) COVERED: All, except School Counselor.

WHO OPERATES: State

REQUIREMENTS TO ENTER:

Bachelor's degree (except for occupational education).

The local school district must request and document its need.

PROGRAM DESCRIPTION:

A teacher working under this permit is not required to pursue additional training to qualify for a regular license.

NUMBER OF CREDIT HOURS TO COMPLETE: Not applicable.

WHO EVALUATES: LEA

LENGTH OF TIME: Valid for one year; renewable two times.

TENNESSEE

Number of Teaching Licenses Issued

	2000-01	1998-99	1997-98	1996-97	1995-96	1993-94	1992-93	1991-92	1990-91	1989-90
Persons who completed an approved college teacher preparation program	a/ 3,219	12,000	12,000	N/A	N/A	N/A	2,859	a/ 3,420	b/ 11,630	b/ 11,636
Emergency	1,603									
Alternative Route --										
Interim			-------	-------	--- 475	since	1984 ---	-------	-------	------
Licenses --										
Types A & B	1,327									
Type C c/	55									
Type E	196									

Number of Teachers Employed

	2000-01	1998-99	1997-98	1996-97	1995-96	1993-94	1992-93	1991-92	1990-91	1989-90
Total Teachers Employed in the State	67,379	44,000	58,000	57,000	47,670	N/A	43,693	43,640	43,051	43,330
Newly Hired Teachers in Each Year	N/A	4,600	N/A	2,441	N/A	d/ 2,714	N/A	d/ 2,881	10,000	N/A

a/ The number comparable to the totals for previous years is 12,091. The lower figure includes only individuals who completed programs at 39 teacher education institutions in the state.

b/ These totals include all new licenses and certificates issued, including career ladder, vocational trade shop, out-of-state, Interim Probationary License Types A and B, as well as persons who have completed an approved teacher education program.

c/ Approved by the State Board in Nov. 1990. Only three programs in operation.

d/ Persons who were not teaching in Tennessee during the previous year.

Tennessee Dept. of Education
Teacher Licensing
5th Floor, Andrew Johnson Tower
710 James Robertson Parkway
Nashville, TN 37243-0377
Attn: Vance Rugaard
(615) 532-4880

TENNESSEE

Institutions of higher education that have developed alternative teacher preparation programs leading to a teaching license:

States with which the state has reciprocity of teacher licenses:

NASDTEC Interstate Contract.

Institutions of higher education that have *any* teacher preparation programs leading to a license to teach.

Aquinas College
Austin Peay State University
Belmont University
Bethel College
Bryan College
Carson-Newman College
Christian Brothers College
Crichton College
Cumberland University
David Lipscomb University
East Tennessee State University
Fisk University
Free Will Baptist Bible College
Freed-Hardeman University
Johnson Bible College
King College
Lambuth College
Lane College
LeMoyne-Owen College
Lee College
Lincoln Memorial University
Maryville College
Martin Methodist College
Middle Tennessee State University
Milligan College
Peabody College of Vanderbilt University
Rhodes, Inc.
Southern Adventist University
Tennessee State University
Tennessee Technological University
Tennessee Wesleyan College
Trevecca Nazarene College
Tusculum College
Union University
University of Memphis
University of Tennessee-Chattanooga
University of Tennessee-Knoxville
University of Tennessee-Martin
University of the South

Contact information for persons interested in finding a teaching position in the state:

Note: N/A. No central placement service in Tennessee.

TEXAS

Class A

TITLE: Alternative Teacher Certification

HISTORY: First implemented in 1985 with single program in the Houston school district. The state currently has 52 programs, including 16 new progrrams in community colleges and 5 programs conducted by private entities.

MOTIVATION: Originally to alleviate shortages, but state legislation passed in 1989 eliminated that requirement.

GRADE LEVELS AND/OR SUBJECT AREA(S) COVERED:

The alternative preparation programs are approved to offer teacher preparation in all grade levels and content areas offered by the State of Texas. In addition, alternative preparation programs are currently available for administrators to include principal, superintendent, and educational diagnostician.

WHO OPERATES: Typically, each program involves a combination of three entities --- LEA, IHE, and regional education service center. Development of each certification area includes practitioners from the field. Recently, community colleges and private entities have created programs in partnership with LEAs.

REQUIREMENTS TO ENTER PROGRAM:

The individual must:

Hold a bachelor's degree.

Demonstrate acceptable college level skills in reading, oral and written communication, critical thinking, and mathematics as determined by the program.

Complete screening activities to determine appropriateness for the certification sought.

If seeking a Bilingual Education/English as a second language (ESL) certificate, must give evidence of oral and written language proficiency before being assigned to a bilingual education classroom.

PROGRAM DESCRIPTION:

All programs are jointly created through a collaborative process involving the local school districts, colleges, and education service center. Participants from these entities develop the curricula, based on the State's standards, that is necessary to prepare teachers for the target certificate. The curricula cover the same State standards that would be included in traditional undergraduate programs, as well as any unique local needs. Instruction is delivered by the partners most suited to the task, either in coursework or in contact hours, and includes a one-year internship.

During the one-year internship, the intern holds a one-year probationary certificate and receives close support and assistance on a regular basis from a certified mentor teacher who is teaching either in the same or in a related subject area.

Since the intern is on a probationary certificate, he or she receives the full financial benefits of a classroom teacher (i.e., salary and benefits)

Provisions are made for the intern to observe the teaching of the mentor teacher, and for the mentor teacher to observe the intern.

The intern must complete any training in teaching methods and classroom management prescribed by the state, either during the pre-assignment training or during the internship year.

The internship leads to a full teaching certificate, identical to that received by a graduate of a traditional undergraduate teacher preparation program.

NUMBER OF CREDIT HOURS TO COMPLETE:

Individual certificate programs require varying amounts of additional coursework to meet unique competency requirements of each certificate.

WHO EVALUATES: The school principal, ACP program supervisor or ACP director.

LENGTH OF TIME: Probationary certificate is valid for one year. It may be renewed for one additional year.

Number and Percentage of Initially Certified Teachers by Certification Route (1993-2002)

Route	1993		1994		1995		1996		1997	
	#	%	#	%	#	%	#	%	#	%
Traditional	9,523	56.8%	9,602	54.3%	9,446	52.3%	9,428	51.9%	8,960	50.9%
ACP	1,649	9.8%	2,186	12.4%	2,494	13.8%	2,610	14.4%	2,426	13.8%
Post-Bacc	1,933	11.5%	2,314	13.1%	2,719	15.1%	2,770	15.2%	2,615	14.8%
Experience	114	0.7%	185	1.0%	176	1.0%	210	1.2%	189	1.1%
Out-of-State	3,551	21.2%	3,404	19.2%	3,227	17.9%	3,147	17.3%	3,430	19.5%
IN-STATE*	**13,219**	**78.8%**	**14,287**	**80.8%**	**14,835**	**82.1%**	**15,018**	**82.7%**	**14,190**	**80.5%**
TOTAL*	**16,770**	**100%**	**17,691**	**100%**	**18,062**	**100%**	**18,165**	**100%**	**17,620**	**100%**

Route	1998		1999		2000		2001		2002	
	#	%	#	%	#	%	#	%	#	%
Traditional	9,102	49.2%	10,178	51.4%	8,143	53.0%	9,118	50.6%	9,290	45.0%
ACP	2,663	14.4%	2,660	13.4%	2,505	16.3%	3,528	19.6%	4,628	22.4%
Post-Bacc	2,630	14.2%	2,618	13.2%	920	6.0%	1,471	8.2%	3,408	16.5%
Experience	223	1.2%	341	1.7%	195	1.3%	261	1.4%	326	1.6%
Out-of-State	3,877	21.0%	4,004	20.2%	3,609	23.5%	3,632	20.2%	3,009	14.6%
IN-STATE*	**14,618**	**79.0%**	**15,797**	**79.8%**	**11,763**	**76.5%**	**14,378**	**79.8%**	**17,652**	**85.4%**
TOTAL*	**18,495**	**100%**	**19,801**	**100%**	**15,372**	**100%**	**18,010**	**100%**	**20,661**	**100%**

The increase in the number of individuals obtaining initial certification in 1999 is due in large part to individuals wanting to obtain a lifetime certificate. In 2000, all certificates were five-year certificates rather than lifetime certificates.

* Total exceeds the total number of teachers obtaining initial certification in other SBEC documents because some teachers were enrolled in more than one route. Thus, the total in this document is slightly greater (by no more than 50) than the actual number of teachers obtaining intial certification for each year. Totals also include teachers from unknown routes which are not displayed in the table.

Traditional = Individuals complete a traditional undergraduate preparation progam.

(ACP) Alternative = Individuals complete an alternative certification program. Individuals must hold a bachelor's degree before entering an ACP program. Alternative programs may include universities, region service centers, school districts, community colleges, or other approved entities.

Post-Baccalaureate = Individuals complete a post-baccalaureate program at a university. Individuals must already possess an undergraduate degree.

Experience-Based = Individuals with life experience in a subject area enroll in an educator preparation program. The program approves the life experiences of the individual and assigns courses to be completed by the individual. After completing the courses and teaching on an emergency permit for two years, the person can obtain her or his standard certificate. This route is for vocational education teachers only.

Out-of-State = Individuals apply for a one-year certificate during which time they must complete all Texas certification requirements. Applicants must either hold either a certificate from another state or have completed all requirements other than passing licensure tests in the home state.

DATA SOURCE: PEIMS, TEA
Initial Certification Files, SBEC

May 10, 2002

Ed Fuller, 2002
Director of Research
SBEC

TEXAS

Number of Full-Time Equivalent Teachers Employed

	2002	2001	2000	1999	1998	1997	1996
Total Teachers Employed in the State	288,986	280,108	272,534	264,997	258,438	251,372	243,867
Newly Hired Initially Certified Teachers in Each Year *	N/A	5,299	6,858	6,631	6,530	6,808	6,475

* *Numbers represent only those teachers who obtained certification in the year before employment and had never been a classroom teacher before obtaining full certification. By definition, this eliminates all alternatively certified teachers and teachers holding emergency permits.*

State Board for Educator Certification
4616 W. Howard Lane, Suite 120
Austin, TX 78728
Attn: Dr. William Wale
Dr. Ed Fuller
(512) 238-3200

Number of Certificates Issued by Route to Certification for the Initial Certification Class of 2002

	University Traditional	Alternative Program	Post-Bacc.	Experience-Based	Out-of-State	**Total Certificates**
Self-Contained	5,795	1,874	1,325		3,660	**12,654**
Elementary Early Childhood Educ.	1,103		93			**1,196**
Early Childhood Education	240		6		1,227	**1,473**
English	1,485	178	496		605	**2,764**
English Language Arts	27	14	24		83	**148**
Journalism	6	10	16		9	**41**
Reading	2,045	27	239		80	**2,391**
Speech Communications	88	33	72		47	**240**
Mathematics	1,160	197	311		538	**2,206**
Science - Composite	49	137	57		141	**384**
Biology	238	143	252		173	**806**
Chemistry	20	26	42		65	**153**
Earth Science	57	5	21		24	**107**
Life-Earth Science	112	22	33		211	**378**
Physical Science	24	16	13		31	**84**
Physics	4	11	8		25	**48**
Geography	30	5	9		45	**89**
Government	38	3	42		67	**150**
History	614	45	294		188	**1,141**
Economics	2	4	9		29	**44**
Social Studies - Composite	147	70	89		623	**929**
Sociology	6	1	6		19	**32**
Psychology	19		22		30	**71**

Number of certificates exceeds the number of individuals obtaining initial certification since individuals obtain ,ultiple certificates.

Number of Certificates Issued by Route to Certification for the Initial Certification Class of 2002

	University Traditional	Alternative Program	Post-Bacc.	Experience-Based	Out-of-State	**Total Certificates**
Bilingual Chinese		1		132		**133**
Bilingual Spanish	624	714	146		44	**1,528**
Bilingual/ESL					3	**3**
English as a Second Language	81	136	2		126	**345**
Art	185	37	84	13	155	**474**
Dance	27	1	10		1	**39**
Music	412	28	48		521	**1,009**
Theatre Arts	62	25	32		32	**151**
Spanish	254	54	92		158	**558**
French	8	5	11		45	**69**
German	5	5	3		23	**36**
Latin	3	4	3		4	**14**
Russian					3	**3**
Physical Education	859	58	225		703	**1,845**
Health Education	169	5	47		155	**376**
Computer Information Systems	19	13	26		17	**75**
Technology Applications		21				**21**
Generic Special Education	585	1,309	179		543	**2,616**
Early Child Ed - Handicapped Child	4		1		28	**33**
Seriously Emotion Disturb/Autistic	2				23	**25**
Severely/Profoundly Handicapped	1				13	**14**
Occupational Orientation	1					**1**
Visually Handicapped	2				6	**8**
Hearing Impaired	20		9		40	**69**

Number of certificates exceeds the number of individuals obtaining initial certification since individuals obtain ,ultiple certificates.

Number of Certificates Issued by Route to Certification for the Initial Certification Class of 2002

	University Traditional	Alternative Program	Post-Bacc.	Experience-Based	Out-of-State	Total Certificates
Learning Resources	12				13	**25**
Learning Resources Specialist					15	**15**
Agriculture - Production	103		18		20	**141**
Agriculture - Ornamental Horticult		1		19	11	**31**
Business - Administration	30	15	29		32	**106**
Business - Basic	20	44	42		41	**147**
Business - Composite	7	24	12		36	**79**
Business - Secretarial	2		6		2	**10**
Health Science Technology	4			48		**52**
Home Economics Education	27	7	22		63	**119**
Industrial Technology	11	17	5		19	**52**
Trades and Industry - Coop				3	1	**4**
Trades and Industry - Pre-Emp Lab	1			118	6	**125**
Marketing Education	1	1			16	**18**
Office Education	4				5	**9**
Information Processing Tech I	20				37	**57**
Information Processing Tech II	2				1	**3**
Total	**16,886**	**5,346**	**4,531**	**333**	**11,193**	**38,289**

Number of certificates exceeds the number of individuals obtaining initial certification since individuals obtain ,ultiple certificates.

TEXAS

Institutions of higher education that have developed alternative teacher preparation programs leading to a teaching license:

Huston-Tillotson College
Lamar University
Prairie View A&M University
Tarleton State University
University of North Texas
Schreiner College
Texas A & M University-College Station
University of Texas at Brownsville
University of Texas at El Paso
University of Texas Pan American-Edinburg
West Texas A&M University
Texas A & M University-Commerce

Community Colleges that have developed alternative teacher preparation programs leading to a teaching license:

Collin County Community College District
Laredo Community College
Lamar State College-Orange
Weatherford College
Kingwood College
Cy-Fair College
Galveston County Alternative Teacher Certification
Houston Community College System
Lamar State College-Port Arthur
North Harris College
San Jacinto College North
Brookhaven College
Blinn College
Alamo Community College District
Tyler Junior College
McLennan Community College

Private entities that have developed alternative teacher preparation programs leading to a teaching license:

Education Career Alternatives Program (ECAP)

Alternative Certification for Teachers-Rio Grande Valley (act-rgv)

Alternative-South Texas Educator Program (A-STEP)

IteAChtexas.com

Western Governors University

States with which the state has reciprocity of teacher licenses:

Note: Texas has no formal reciprocity agreements with any other state. Texas recognizes all states' certified teachers in areas in which Texas recognizes teachers' certificates. Texas is a member of the NASDTEC Interstate Contract, through which about 35 states now recognize Texas certification.

TEXAS

Institutions of higher education that have a teacher preparation programs leading to a license to teach.

Abilene Christian University
Angelo State University
Austin College
Arlington Baptist College
Baylor University
Concordia Lutheran College
Dallas Baptist University
East Texas Baptist University
Hardin-Simmons University
Houston Baptist University
Howard Payne University
Huston-Tillotson College
Jarvis Christian College
Lamar University
Letourneau University
Lubbock Christian University
McMurry University
Midwestern State University
Our Lady of the Lake University
Paul Quinn College
Prairie View A&M University
Rice University
St. Edwards University
St. Mary's University
Sam Houston State University
Schreiner College
Southwest Texas State University
Southwestern Adventist College
Southwestern Assemblies of God College
Southwestern University
Stephen F. Austin State University
Sul Ross State University-Alpine
Sul Ross State University-Uvalde
Southwestern University
Tarleton State University
Texas A&M International University
Texas A&M University-College Station
Texas A&M University-Commerce
Texas A&M University-Corpus Christi

Texas A&M University-Kingsville
Texas A&M University-Texarkana
Texas Christian University
Texas College
Texas Lutheran College
Texas Southern University
Texas Tech University
Texas Wesleyan University
Texas Woman's University
Trinity University
University of Central Texas
University of Dallas
University of Houston
University of Houston-Clear Lake
University of Houston-Downtown
University of Houston-Victoria
University of Mary Hardin-Baylor
University of North Texas
University of St. Thomas
University of Texas at Arlington
University of Texas at Austin
University of Texas at Brownsville
University of Texas at Dallas
University of Texas at El Paso
University of Texas at San Antonio
University of Texas at Tyler
University of Texas-Pan American
University of Texas of the Permian Basin
University of Incarnate Word
Wayland Baptist University
West Texas A&M University
Wiley College

TEXAS

Independent School Districts (ISDs) that have teacher preparation programs leading to a certificate to teach:

Dallas ISD
TMATE-Fort Worth ISD
Houston ISD
Pasadena ISD

Regional Education Service Centers (ESCs) that have teacher/administrator preparation programs leading to a certificate to teach/administrate:

ESC Region I
ESC Region II
ESC Region III
ESC Region IV
ESC Region VI
ESC Region VII
ESC Region IX
ESC Region X
ESC Region XI
ESC Region XII
ESC Region XIII
ESC Region XIV
ESC Region XVIII
ESC Region XIX
ESC Region XX

Additional information about ACP programs in Texas is available on the SBEC Web site at: www.sbec.state.tx.us or by contacting:

Dr. William Wale
State Board for Educator Certification
4616 W. Howard Lane, Suite 120
Austin, TX 78728
Phone: (512) 238-3200

Or

SBEC Information and Support Center

1-888-863-5880

TITLE: Alternative Routes to Licensure (ARL)

HISTORY: In April 2002, the Utah State Board of Education adopted Administrative Rule 277-503, which governs alternative routes to licensure and endorsements.

MOTIVATION: To increase the number of eligible, qualified, and prepared teachers through non-traditional paths to licensure.

GRADE LEVELS AND/OR SUBJECT AREA(S) COVERED:

Early childhood, elementary, and secondary teaching.

WHO OPERATES: Utah State Office of Education (USOE).

REQUIREMENTS TO ENTER:

There are two eligibility requirements for the program:

1. To hold a minimum of a bachelor's degree in an area similar to subjects taught in schools; and

2. To be employed by a Utah school district or an accredited Utah school.

PROGRAM DESCRIPTION:

The program is a cooperative effort between USOE and Utah school districts. USOE is responsible for: administration of the program; evaluation of the candidates' course requirements; developing curriculum; tracking candidates' progress toward licensure; and recommending the candidates for licensure. Districts are responsible for assigning trained mentors and conducting observations of classroom performance skills and dispositions.

Program participants are required to show competency in four areas: content knowledge, pedagogical knowledge, classroom performance skills and dispositions. Content knowledge is required coursework established by USOE curriculum specialists, A streamlined curriculum of pedagogical knowledge was established by USOE, in partnership with Weber State University College of Education. University courses, district professional development classes, or achieving a passing score on state-approved content tests can fill program requirements.

Program participants are required to show competency in four areas: content knowledge, pedagogical knowledge, classroom performance skills and dispositions. Content knowledge is required coursework established by USOE curriculum specialists, A streamlined curriculum of pedagogical knowledge was established by USOE, in partnership with Weber State University College of Education. University courses, district professional development classes, or achieving a passing score on state-approved content tests can fill program requirements.

Participants' transcripts are evaluated by the ARL Advisor, and a Professional Growth Plan is developed. Once the requirements of the Plan are completed, the candidate is recommended for licensure.

NUMBER OF CREDIT HOURS TO COMPLETE:

The number varies with each candidate, but the core curriculum is 15 semester hours.

WHO EVALUATES: The ARL Advisor and the principal.

LENGTH OF TIME: Four years.

TITLE: LAUNCH

HISTORY: Initiated through a Title II grant under the Elementary and Secondary Education Act (ESEA), awarded to the Granite School District in 2001.

MOTIVATION: To provide an alternative program that would train teachers for the Granite School District.

GRADE LEVELS AND/OR SUBJECT AREA(S) COVERED: All

WHO OPERATES: Granite School District.

REQUIREMENTS TO ENTER:

Candidates must:

Hold a bachelor's degree;

Obtain employment in a local school district; and

Successfully complete a background clearance check.

PROGRAM DESCRIPTION:

The program is a partnership with the University of Utah Department of Education.

Candidates must complete a teacher preparation program of 21 semester hours in three semesters. They teach, while attending classes at night.

NUMBER OF CREDIT HOURS TO COMPLETE:

The number varies with each candidate, but the core curriculum is 21 semester hours.

WHO EVALUATES: The principal evaluates the participants.

LENGTH OF TIME: Pedagogical coursework is completed in three semesters, Content requirements could take additional semesters.

TITLE: Northern Utah Alternative Routes to Licensure (NUARL)

HISTORY: NURAL was initiated through a Title II grant under the Elementary and Secondary Education Act (ESEA), awarded in 2002 to a partnership of the Utah Office of Education, Weber State University, and six school districts in Northern Utah: Box Elder; Davis; North Summit; Morgan; Ogden; and Weber.

MOTIVATION: To provide a streamlined alternative program that would train, support, and retain teachers in high-need areas.

GRADE LEVELS AND/OR SUBJECT AREA(S) COVERED:

Needs assessments studies identified math, science, fine arts, English as a second language, technology, and elementary teaching as areas with teacher shortages. Another needs assessment was to be conducted in January 2003.

WHO OPERATES: Utah Office of Education (USOE).

REQUIREMENTS TO ENTER:

Candidates must:

Hold a bachelor's degree in one of the high-need areas; and

Successfully complete a background clearance check.

PROGRAM DESCRIPTION:

The program has four distinct parts: recruitment, preparation, internship, and professional support.

Target pools for recruitment of candidates include: substitutes; classroom aides; foreign-credentialed educators; new university graduates; and career changers.

Twenty-five (25) individuals will be accepted into the program and will attend a streamlined curriculum, consisting of: instruction; assessment and technology; classroom management and child development; teaching the exceptional student; multicultural and bilingual society; and reading and writing in the content area. Some participants will need additional content coursework. Tuition scholarships will be provided.

Participants will be placed in high-need schools as interns and will teach for one year.

Professional support includes: working with a trained mentor for three (3) years; classroom observations; developing a portfolio; and achieving a passing score on the Praxis I Principles of Learning and Teaching exam.

Participants must agree to teach for three (3) years in the high-need area or repay the tuition scholarship.

NUMBER OF CREDIT HOURS TO COMPLETE:

The number varies with each candidate, but the core curriculum is 15 semester hours. Additional hours are required through a strong mentor/professional support program.

WHO EVALUATES: The principal evaluates the participants. Numerous levels of program evaluation are in place.

LENGTH OF TIME: Each cohort is three years. There are three cohorts. The grant is funded for five years.

UTAH — Class B

TITLE: Applied Technology Education / Alternative Preparation Program

HISTORY: Applied Technology Education was previously called Vocational-Technical Education. Initiated in 1985, with revisions in 2001. Additional revisions are scheduled for 2003.

MOTIVATION: To provide an avenue for individuals with experience in trade and industry to teach Applied Technology subjects in secondary schools.

GRADE LEVELS AND/OR SUBJECT AREA(S) COVERED:

Secondary schools. Agriculture, business, marketing, trade, industry, technology, home economics, or health occupations.

WHO OPERATES: Utah Office of Education (USOE).

REQUIREMENTS TO ENTER:

Verification of six (6) years of occupational experience in one of the required subjects, or four (4) years of postsecondary education and training in the content area, or passing a state-approved competency examination in the respective field.

PROGRAM DESCRIPTION:

Teachers holding a Level 1 license (valid for three years) with a concentration in Applied Technology Education/Alternative Preparation Program are limited to:

Teaching only those courses found on the current list of program endorsements.

Teaching only those courses related to an occupational work experience.

Teachers holding a Level 1 license with an endorsement in teaching the handicapped are restricted to teaching in workshop centers for the handicapped and must have 18 months of work experience in business or industry related to the teaching assignment.

Teachers holding a Level 2 license (valid for five years) must meet the following requirements:

Completion of 12 semester hours of professional development experiences. (Professional development experiences must have prior approval of the State Applied Technology Specialist.)

Coursework must be in the following areas:

Principles, philosophy, organization, and coordination of Applied Technology Education;

Curriculum development and methods of teaching Applied Technology Education;

Classes/workshops sponsored by USOE.

NUMBER OF CREDIT HOURS TO COMPLETE: 12-15; varies with program.

WHO EVALUATES: USOE Applied Technology Specialists.

LENGTH OF TIME: 2-3 years.

OTHER: The Applied Technology Education/Alternative Preparation Program is currently being redesigned to align with requirements for a Secondary Teaching license. The number of required hours will be increased to 15 and participants will be required to work with a trained mentor.

TITLE: Troops to Teachers

HISTORY: Ronald M. Stanfield, Coordinator, Educator Licensing, is the Utah representative.

MOTIVATION: To relieve overall teacher shortages and to improve teacher quality by attracting mature, highly-experienced personnel to the classroom.

GRADE LEVELS AND/OR SUBJECT AREA(S) COVERED: All subjects.

WHO OPERATES: Utah State Office of Education (USOE).

REQUIREMENTS TO ENTER:

Candidates must be:

Retired military personnel;

OR

Department of Defense civilian employees seeking a career change;

AND

Successfully complete a background clearance check.

PROGRAM DESCRIPTION:

The program has a referral and placement assistance program for candidates.

NUMBER OF CREDIT HOURS TO COMPLETE:

Varies with each candidate; core program is 15 semester hours.

WHO EVALUATES: The Alternative Routes to Licensure Advisor and the principal.

LENGTH OF TIME: 1-2 years.

UTAH — Class G

TITLE: Letter of Authorization

HISTORY: Initiated in 1971; revised in 1998. Will be revised in 2003 to meet reporting requirements under the federal No Child Left Behind (NCLB) Act of 2002.

MOTIVATION: Shortage; a fully licensed person cannot be found.

GRADE LEVELS AND/OR SUBJECT AREAS COVERED: All

WHO OPERATES: State

REQUIREMENTS TO ENTER PROGRAM:

After the supply of qualified, licensed teachers has been exhausted, a local school district may apply for a Letter of Authorization from the State School Board to employ a particular person to fill a specified position on a temporary basis. The Candidate agrees to complete the requirements for licensure within a four year period.

A bachelor's degree.

PROGRAM DESCRIPTION:

Authorization to teach will be granted on a temporary basis. Individuals provide an acceptable recommendation from the local school district and a deficiency statement from a State Office of Education Curriculum Specialist or an educator preparation institution indicating how the requirements for licensing will be met. Approval is granted by the State Board of Education.

NUMBER OF CREDIT HOURS TO COMPLETE:

WHO EVALUATES: Educator Preparation, Institution or USOE Curriculum Specialist.

LENGTH OF TIME: Issued on a year-by-year basis.

The completion of the requirements may not extend beyond four years.

TITLE: Eminence or Special Qualification Authorization

HISTORY: Initiated about 1975; revised in 1989. Will be revised in 2003 to meet reporting requirements under the federal No Child Left Behind (NCLB) Act of 2002 for teachers teaching in core academic subject areas.

MOTIVATION: To employ an individual who has not been through a traditional teacher education program, but who is recognized as an expert in his/her field or is otherwise well-qualified for a particular assignment. Example: an actor or actress, artist, musician, scientist or other person who has achieved prominence or outstanding qualification, but who could not qualify for a teaching license.

GRADE LEVELS AND/OR SUBJECT AREA(S) COVERED:

Areas of recognized expertise.

1. Eminence is defined as "Distinguished superiority as compared with others in rank, status, character, and attainment or superior knowledge and skill in comparison with the generally accepted standards and achievements in the area in which authorization is sought."

2. Special Qualification is defined as "Outstanding background in a subject field or area but not to the degree of eminence."

WHO OPERATES: State

REQUIREMENTS TO ENTER:

Any person who has achieved eminence or outstanding qualification in a field taught in the public schools of Utah.

PROGRAM DESCRIPTION:

The authorization is issued for a limited assignment and responsibility in a specified field. The individual is limited to teaching two periods per day.

NUMBER OF CREDIT HOURS TO COMPLETE: Not applicable.

LENGTH OF TIME: One year; renewable for one-year periods.

UTAH

Number of Teaching Licenses Issued

	2001-02	2000-01	1999-00	1998-99	1997-98	1996-97	1995-96	1994-95	1993-94	1992-93
Persons who completed an approved college teacher preparation program	2,330	2,268	2,697	2,793	2,734	2,550	2,551	2,348	N/A	N/A
Emergency	96									
Temporary (includes Letters of Authorization)	998	1,121	* 1,308 (406)	* 2,082 (635)	* 1,000 (635)	N/A	N/A	N/A	N/A	N/A
Alternative Route	15	6	5	7	16	29	35	9	75	N/A
Applied Technology - Alternative Preparation Route	105	98	103	85						

* *These totals included new graduates who had not completed the licensing paperwork, but were in the process. The actual numbers of those who had not completed a teacher preparation program or completed the appropriate coursework to be endorsed in the subject area of their assignment are shown in parenthesis.*

Number of Teachers Employed

	2001-02	2000-01	1999-00	1998-99	1997-98	1996-97	1995-96	1994-95	1993-94	1992-93
Total Teachers Employed in the State	24,663	24,567	26,260	25,740	21,114	22,582	N/A	N/A	N/A	19,883
Newly Hired Teachers in Each Year	1,949	1,410	1,934	1,937	N/A	N/A	N/A	N/A	N/A	2,035

Utah State Office of Education
Division of Teacher Certification
250 East Fifth South
Salt Lake City, UT 84111
Attn: Ronald Stanfield/Diane De Man
Phone (801) 538-7741
Fax (801) 538-7973
email: rstanfie@usoe.k12.ut.us

UTAH

Institutions of higher education that have developed alternative teacher preparation programs leading to a teaching license:

None.

States with which the state has reciprocity of teacher licenses:

ICA.

Institutions of higher education that have *any* teacher preparation programs leading to a license to teach.

Brigham Young University
Dixie State College
Southern Utah University
University of Phoenix
University of Utah
Utah State University
Utah Valley State College
Weber State University
Westminster College

Contact information for persons interested in finding a teaching position in the state:

Visit the Web site at: http://www.usoe.k12.ut.us/cert
Click on job vacancies

TITLE: License by Evaluation

HISTORY: Regulations issued in 1971.

MOTIVATION:

GRADE LEVELS AND/OR SUBJECT AREA(S) COVERED: Not specified.

WHO OPERATES: State

REQUIREMENTS TO ENTER:

A bachelor's degree.

Competence, preparation, and experience in the subject to be taught.

PROGRAM DESCRIPTION:

The individual may be licensed by the Standards Board for Professional Educators through an evaluation process.

The Standards Board shall recommend individuals for evaluation based on evidence of competence, preparation, and experience in the field for which a license is being sought.

The evaluation is conducted by a peer review panel, with members including a faculty member from a college (for example, to evaluate a person to teach science, this panel member might be a college science professor) and licensed teachers (who have experience in that same specialty).

The panel may recommend that the individual be licensed without reservation or that he/she be licensed only after completing additional specified coursework.

NUMBER OF CREDIT HOURS TO COMPLETE: Coursework may be required.

WHO EVALUATES: Professional Standards Board.

LENGTH OF TIME: Not applicable, unless additional coursework is required.

VERMONT — Class F

TITLE: Waiver

HISTORY: In operation since 1982.

MOTIVATION: Shortage

GRADE LEVELS AND/OR SUBJECT AREA(S) COVERED: Not specified.

WHO OPERATES: State

REQUIREMENTS TO ENTER:

The local school district must advertise for a certified teacher during the summer. If none can be found by fall, the school district selects the best available candidate and requests a waiver for him/her from the state.

PROGRAM DESCRIPTION:

The state may approve or disapprove the waiver, and the state professional standards board -- which has a teacher majority -- must officially ratify the waiver.

The state expects the local school district to provide the teacher with supervision.

A large number of teachers serving under waivers take courses toward regular certification.

NUMBER OF CREDIT HOURS TO COMPLETE:

None, unless the individual seeks certification.

WHO EVALUATES: LEA

VERMONT — Class G

TITLE: Transcript Analysis

HISTORY: In operation since about 1964.

MOTIVATION:

GRADE LEVELS AND/OR SUBJECT AREA(S) COVERED: Not specified.

WHO OPERATES: State

REQUIREMENTS TO ENTER:

Must hold a valid Vermont license.

PROGRAM DESCRIPTION:

The individual's transcripts are analyzed for additional endorsement purposes.

The state will specify certain courses the individual must complete in order to qualify for certification.

NUMBER OF CREDIT HOURS TO COMPLETE: Varies for applicants.

WHO EVALUATES: Professional Standards Board.

LENGTH OF TIME: Varies according to coursework required.

OTHER: Transcript analysis is used only for additional endorsement purposes OR for areas of licensure in which there are no preparation programs.

VERMONT

Number of Teaching Licenses Issued

	1994-95	1993-94	1992-93	1991-92	1990-91	1989-90	1988-89
Persons who completed an approved college teacher preparation program	~500	N/A	N/A	~600	560	550	487
Internship program							
Emergency							
Temporary							
Alternative Route	~50	N/A	N/A	~20	~20	~20	~20
Other ---							
Transcript Analysis	~200	N/A	N/A	~25	~25	~25	~25
Waiver *	34	N/A	N/A	31	70	73	64

Number of Teachers Employed

	1994-95	1993-94	1992-93	1991-92	1990-91	1989-90	1988-89
Total Teachers Employed in the State	6,700	N/A	N/A	~ 6,500	~6,500	~6,500	6,700
Newly Hired Teachers in Each Year	N/A	N/A	N/A	N/A	N/A	N/A	N/A

* *Includes those who were already certified and were given waivers to allow them to teach a limited number of hours in a second subject.*

Vermont Dept. of Education
Educational Resources Unit
State Dept. of Education
Montpelier, VT 05602
Attn: Patricia Pallas
(802) 828-2445

VERMONT

Institutions of higher education that have developed alternative teacher preparation programs leading to a teaching license:

None.

States with which the state has reciprocity of teacher licenses:

NASDTEC Interstate Contract. A graduate of a state-approved teacher preparation program, whether or not a Vermont resident, is entitled to an initial Vermont license. This license may used to obtain an initial license/certificate in states that are participants, along with Vermont, in the NASDTEC Interstate Contract.

Only graduates of approved programs are transferable. Recent graduates with minors leading to a Vermont license qualify for interstate certification/licensure only if they have completed a State Department of Education approved program.

Non-residents who are qualified educators are welcome in the state, but licenses are issued to non-residents only when they have been engaged to serve in Vermont or become residents of Vermont, whichever occurs first.

Institutions of higher education that have *any* teacher preparation programs leading to a license to teach.

Castleton State College
Champlain College
College of St. Joseph
Goddard College
Green Mountain College
Johnson State College
Lyndon State College
Middlebury College
Norwich University
St. Michael's College
School for International Training
Trinity College
University of Vermont
Vermont College of Norwich University

Contact information for persons interested in finding a teaching position in the state:

Note: .The state does not have a placement service.

TITLE: Alternate Route to Licensure

HISTORY: The implementation of the licensure regulations for Virginia school divisions became effective on July 1, 1998. After that effective date, local school division personnel interested in adding a teaching area will be required to complete the newly-approved regulations. However, institutions of higher education with approved teacher preparation programs will be required to implement the regulations for individuals entering their programs by the fall of 2000.

MOTIVATION: To make an alternate route available to individuals employed by an educational agency in Virginia who seek teaching endorsements in grades PreK-12.

GRADE LEVELS AND/OR SUBJECT AREA(S) COVERED: PreK-12.

WHO OPERATES: IHE, LEA, and State.

REQUIREMENTS TO ENTER:

An individual who is employed by a Virginia school division or non-public school can be issued a three-year, non-renewable Provisional License upon the request of the Virginia employing educational agency if the individual:

1. Holds a baccalaureate degree from a regionally-accredited institution; and

2. Satisfies one or more specific endorsement areas (teaching areas).

PROGRAM DESCRIPTION:

The following requirements must be satisfied in order to become eligible for the five-year renewable license:

1. Professional Teacher's Assessment.

2. Professional Studies Requirements: Professional studies

coursework specified below from a regionally-accredited four-year institution or an alternative program for licensure may be submitted by the employing educational agency for review and approval by the Superintendent of Public Instruction, Virginia Department of Education.

Early/primary education, elementary education, and middle education -- 18 semester hours

Special education -- 18 semester hours

Adult education, PreK-12 endorsements, and secondary grades 6-12 endorsements -- 15 semester hours

3. One year of successful, full-time teaching experience in the endorsement area in an accredited public or non-public school. A fully-licensed experienced teacher must be available in the school building to assist the beginning teacher employed through the alternative route.

NO. OF CREDIT HOURS TO COMPLETE:

15 to 18 semester hours of professional education coursework and specific endorsement area course requirements.

WHO EVALUATES: State.

LENGTH OF TIME: Non-renewable Provisional License issued for three years; renewable license issued for five years.

TITLE: Career Switcher Alternative Route to Licensure Pilot Programs for Career Professions

HISTORY: Created in response to Senate Joint Resolution 384 and the 1999 Appropriation Act (Item 127D and 129Q). A pilot for military personnel was conducted in summer 2000. Four pilots were conducted in summer 2001 to prepare individuals in other professions to become teachers. In March 2002, six program providers were established.

MOTIVATION: Provide an alternative pathway into teaching for individuals who have not completed a teacher preparation curriculum but had considerable life experiences, career achievements and an academic background that was relevant for teaching in pre-K through grade 12.

GRADE LEVELS AND/OR SUBJECT AREA(S) COVERED:

All teaching areas, except special education.

WHO OPERATES: State and program providers.

REQUIREMENTS TO ENTER:

Complete application process.

Earned bachelor's degree.

Meet teaching area requirements or equivalent

Satisfy Virginia's cut scores on Praxis I (reading, writing, and mathematics) and Praxis II (subject area content).

Five years of full-time employment in a profession.

PROGRAM DESCRIPTION:

Individuals must complete Praxis I; Praxis II; and preparation in curriculum and instruction, including educational technology, reading instruction, and other specified course content relating to the Standards of Learning, differentiation of instruction, classroom/behavior management, human growth and development. These requirements must be completed by one of the following options:

1.) completion of professional coursework at a college or university, not to exceed 15 semester hours in curriculum and instruction content focusing on the areas outlined above: or

2.) completion of a program developed by the program provider integrating the curriculum and instruction content above and designed to be completed within one year.

NO. OF CREDIT HOURS TO COMPLETE:

180 clock hours of instruction. At least 160 of the 180 hours will be in an intensive induction program. In addition, 20 hours of the 160 hours will include field experiences..

WHO EVALUATES: State.

LENGTH OF TIME: One year.

TITLE: Special Education Conditional License

HISTORY: Available with the implementation of the Licensure Regulations for School Personnel on July 1, 1998.

MOTIVATION: To provide an alternative route to individuals employed by an educational agency in Virginia who seek a special education endorsement in grades PreK-12, to help meet shortages in this critical field.

GRADE LEVELS AND/OR SUBJECT AREA(S) COVERED:

Special education only.

WHO OPERATES: State.

REQUIREMENTS TO ENTER:

A candidate must:

Be employed by an accredited Virginia public or nonpublic school.

Hold a bachelor's degree from a regionally accredited four-year college or university.

Have an assigned mentor, fully endorsed in special education.

Have a planned program of study in the assigned endorsement area and have completed a minimum of six semester hours in the core competencies of students with disabilities and the legal aspects associated with students with disabilities.

VIRGINIA

Class G

PROGRAM DESCRIPTION:

Working with support from the mentor, the candidate must complete the planned program of study in the assigned endorsement area.

NO. OF CREDIT HOURS TO COMPLETE:

WHO EVALUATES: State.

LENGTH OF TIME:

TITLE: Provisional Licensure

HISTORY: Available since 1982.

MOTIVATION: Issued to an individual who has not yet met all professional studies, specific endorsement area course requirements, and/or the professional teacher's assessment prescribed by the Board of Education.

GRADE LEVELS AND/OR SUBJECT AREA(S) COVERED: K-12.

WHO OPERATES: State.

REQUIREMENTS TO ENTER:

A bachelor's degree from an accredited institution.

The individual must satisfy one or more specific endorsement area requirements.

Beginning teachers in Virginia are required to satisfy the professional teacher's assessment prescribed by the Board of Education, unless exempted by prior teaching experience (a minimum of two years of full-time, successful teaching experience in an accredited public or non-public school at the K-12 level, outside the state of Virginia).

The Provisional License is a three-year, non-renewable license available to individuals who are employed by a Virginia educational agency and are:

a. Entering the teaching field through the alternative route to licensure upon recommendation of the employing educational agency;

b. Failing to meet an allowable portion of general, professional, or specific endorsement requirements;

c. Seeking the Technical Professional License; or

d. Eligible for licensure but need to complete successfully the professional teacher's assessment prescribed by the Board of Education.

VIRGINIA

Class G

PROGRAM DESCRIPTION:

The individual must satisfy all professional studies education requirements, specific endorsement area requirements, and the professional teacher's assessment prescribed by the Board of Education during the three-year period of validity.

An applicant for licensure shall have completed a minimum of 18 semester hours of professional studies coursework, with the distribution of semester hour requirements as follows:

1. Human growth and development (birth through adolescence) -- 3 semester hours.
2. Curriculum and instructional procedures -- 6 semester hours.
3. Foundations of education -- 3 semester hours.
4. Language Acquisition and Reading -- 6 semester hours.

NO. OF CREDIT HOURS TO COMPLETE:

A minimum of 18 semester hours of professional education coursework and specific endorsement area course requirements.

WHO EVALUATES: State.

LENGTH OF TIME: Provisional License issued for three years.

VIRGINIA

Number of Teaching Licenses Issued

	1999-00	1998-99	1997-98	1995-96	1994-95	1993-94	1992-93	1991-92	1990-91	1989-90
Persons who completed an approved college teacher preparation program	***	**	N/A	4,249	3,939	3,731	N/A	* 1,800+	* 1,800+	1,698
Internship program										
Emergency		0								
Alternative Route	2,746	1,980	N/A	N/A	458	390	N/A	N/A	* 750	650
Other -- Out of State		N/A	N/A	N/A	N/A	N/A	N/A	* 6,700	6,500	N/A

Number of Teachers Employed

	2001-02	2000-01	1999-00	1997-98	1994-95	1993-94	1992-93	1991-92	1990-91	1989-90
Total Teachers Employed in the State	88,609	88,600	88,000	80,949	73,000	* 73,000	N/A	* 73,000	73,000	67,433
Newly Hired Teachers in Each Year	N/A	N/A	N/A	N/A	6,800	N/A	N/A	* 3,000	2,800	2,714

* *Note: These are approximate numbers.*

** *Virginia issued 11,859 initial licenses between July 1, 1998 and June 30, 1999.*

*** *3,822 to graduates of teacher education programs in institutions of higher education in Virginia; 3,698 to graduates of teacher education programs in institutions of higher education from other states.*

Virginia Dept. of Education
Division of Teacher Education and Licensure
P.O. Box 2120
Richmond, VA 23218-2120
Attn: Paul F. Joseph
(804) 371-2472
e-mail: pjoseph@mail.vak12ed.edu or
pjoseph@pen.k12.va.us

VIRGINIA

Institutions of higher education that have developed alternative teacher preparation programs leading to a teaching license:

Virginia Wesleyan University
Old Dominion University

Note: Other Virginia institutions with approved teacher preparation programs offer other alternative programs to licensure.

States with which the state has reciprocity of teacher licenses:

NASDTEC Interstate Contract.

Institutions of higher education that have *any* teacher preparation programs leading to a license to teach.

Averett College
Bluefield College
Bridgewater College
Christopher Newport College
Clinch Valley College
College of William and Mary
Eastern Mennonite College
Emory and Henry College
Ferrum College
George Mason University
Hampton University
Hollins College
James Madison University
Liberty University
Longwood College
Lynchburg College
Mary Baldwin College
Mary Washington College
Marymount University
Norfolk State University
Old Dominion University
Radford University
Randolph-Macon College
Randolph-Macon Woman's College
Regent University
Roanoke University
Saint Paul's College
Shenandoah University
Sweet Briar College
University of Richmond
University of Virginia
Virginia Commonwealth University
Virginia Intermont College
Virginia Polytechnical Institute and State University (Virginia Tech)
Virginia State University
Virginia Union University
Virginia Wesleyan College

Contact information for persons interested in finding a teaching position in the state:

Contact local Virginia school districts. Contact information can be found on the Department of Education Web site at: http://www.pen.k12.va.us.

TITLE: Alternative Routes One, Two, and Three under Partnership Grants Program

HISTORY: Legislation creating this program was signed into law on May 3, 2001. The law expires June 30, 2005.

MOTIVATION: The program permits creation of three different alternative routes, "aimed at recruiting candidates to teaching in subject matter shortage areas and areas with shortages due to geographic location," and allows recruitment of future teachers from "a great untapped resource" – individuals who are already employed as "classified instructional staff in public schools." Funds from the state legislature and a Transition to Teaching Grant from the U.S. Department of Education will provide stipends for both interns and mentors and tuition assistance for interns in the form of loan forgiveness.

GRADE LEVELS AND/OR SUBJECT AREA(S) COVERED: K-12 all areas

WHO OPERATES: Washington Professional Educator Standards Board.

REQUIREMENTS TO ENTER:

Route One programs shall enroll currently employed classified instructional employees of schools in Washington state, who have transferable associate's degrees and are seeking residency teacher certification with endorsements in special education, bilingual education, or English as a Second Language (ESL).

Entry requirements:

District or building validation of qualifications, including three years of successful student interaction and leadership as a classified instructional employee;

Successful completion of the statewide basic skills exam, when available; and

Meeting age, good moral character, and personal fitness requirements for teachers.

Route Two programs shall enroll currently employed classified staff with baccalaureate degrees seeking residency teacher certification in subject matter shortage areas and areas with shortages due to geographic location.

Entry requirements:

District or building validation of qualifications, including three years of successful student interaction and leadership as a classified instructional employee;

A baccalaureate degree from a regionally accredited institution of higher education. The individual's grade point average may be considered as a selection factor;

Successful completion of the content test, once the state content test is available

Meeting age, good moral character, and personal fitness requirements for teachers; and

Successful completion of the statewide basic skills exam, when available.

Route Three programs shall enroll individuals with baccalaureate degrees, who are not employed in the district at the time of application, or who hold emergency substitute certificates.

Priority in selection shall be given to individuals seeking residency teacher certification in subject matter shortage areas or areas with shortages due to geographic location.

Districts may include additional candidates in nonshortage areas if the candidates are seeking endorsement with a secondary grade level designation. The districts shall disclose to candidates in nonshortage subject areas available information on the demand in those subject areas.

Entry requirements:

Five years' experience in the work force;

A baccalaureate degree from a regionally accredited institution of higher education. The individual's grade point average may be considered as a selection factor;

Successful completion of the content test, once the state content test is available;

External validation of qualifications, including demonstrated successful experience with students or children, such as references letters and letters of support from previous employers;

Meeting the age, good moral character, and personal fitness requirements for teachers; and

Successful completion of the statewide basic skills exam, when available.

PROGRAM DESCRIPTION:

Route One -- Candidates complete both their baccalaureate degrees and requirements for residency certification in two years or less, including a mentored internship to be completed in the final year

Route Two -- Candidates must complete a mentored internship complemented by flexibly scheduled training and coursework offered at a local site, such as a school or educational service district, or online or via video-conference over the K-20 network, in collaboration with the partnership program's higher education partner.

Route Three -- Cohorts of candidates shall attend an intensive summer teacher academy, followed by a full year employed by a district in a mentored internship, followed, if necessary, by a second summer teacher academy.

Alternative Route Conditional Scholarships --

Scholarships are limited to classified staff enrolled in **Route One** and **Route Two**.

To receive scholarships, candidates shall be accepted and maintain enrollment in alternative certification routes through the partnership grant program. Candidates must continue to make satisfactory progress toward completion of the program and receipt of a residency teaching certificate.

Conditional scholarships are loans that are forgiven, in whole or in part, in exchange for service as a certified teacher employed in Washington state K-12 public schools;

The state shall forgive one year of loan obligation for every two years a recipient teaches in a public school;

Recipients who fail to continue a course of study leading to residency teacher certification or cease to teach in public schools in their endorsement area are required to repay the remaining loan principal with interest;

The amount of each scholarship is the annual cost of tuition for the alternative route certification program in which the recipient is enrolled, not to exceed $4,000.

NUMBER OF CREDIT HOURS: Varies, depending on prior credits applicable and the subject area in which candidate is being certified.

LENGTH OF TIME: Varies, depending on the program and the IHE.

WHO EVALUATES: IHE and LEA.

TITLE: Troops to Teachers Program

HISTORY: The Department of Defense Troops to Teachers (TTT) Program was officially established on Jan. 19, 1994, and is managed by the federal Defense Activity for Non-Traditional Education Support (DANTES).

MOTIVATION: This program was established to help relieve teacher shortages, provide positive role models in the nation's public schools, and to assist military and civilian personnel impacted by military reductions to enter a new career in public education.

GRADE LEVELS AND/OR SUBJECT AREA(S) COVERED: K-12 all areas

WHO OPERATES: The Office of Superintendent of Public Instruction, IHE, LEA, and DANTES cooperatively work together to provide resources and a plan for the TTT applicant.
Washington state contact person for this program:
Dr. George Willett
Phone: (800) 743-2357

REQUIREMENTS TO ENTER:

Bachelor's degree with 45 quarter hours in an endorsement area or an associate degree to be accepted into the TTT program which leads to certification.

PROGRAM DESCRIPTION:

DANTES and the local TTT office assist interested individuals in locating a certification program, and/or securing a position as a teacher (or teacher's aide if there is only an associate's degree).

NUMBER OF CREDIT HOURS:
Varies, depending on prior credits applicable and the subject area in which candidate is being certified.

LENGTH OF TIME: Varies, depending on the program and the IHE.

WHO EVALUATES: DANTES, IHE, and LEA.

TITLE: Conditional Certificate

HISTORY: Instituted in 1989; changed in 1990 and 1998.

MOTIVATION: Shortage. No person with regular certification in the field is available as verified by the local school district or educational service district superintendent or the applicant has unusual distinction.

GRADE LEVELS AND/OR SUBJECT AREA(S) COVERED:

Persons highly qualified and experienced in fields of knowledge to be taught in the common or non-public schools.

WHO OPERATES: State; employing school district or educational service district superintendent.

REQUIREMENTS TO ENTER:

Conditional certificates are issued to individuals who are screened by the local school district or educational service district superintendents, who verify that these conditions have been met:

1. The applicant is highly qualified and experienced in the subject matter to be taught and has unusual distinction or exceptional talent;

2. No person with regular teacher certification in the endorsement area is available or that circumstances warrant consideration of issuance of a conditional certificate;

3. Conditional certificates are issued to persons in the following categories only if no person with regular certification is available:

    Traffic safety instructor

    Intramural/interscholastic activities instructor (coach)

    Licensed registered nurse provided the district will be responsible for orienting and preparing individuals for their assignment

    Applicant who has completed a baccalaureate degree level school speech pathologist or audiologist certification preparation program, who was eligible for certification at the time of the program completion and who has served in the role for three of the last seven years.

PROGRAM DESCRIPTION:

The educational service district or local district superintendent or administrator of an approved private school will verify that the following criteria have been met when requesting the conditional certificate:

The individual is competent for the assignment and is being certified for that specific assignment only;

The individual will be delegated primary responsibility for planning, conducting, and evaluating instructional activities with the assistance of the district and will not be serving in a paraprofessional role which would not require certification;

The individual will complete a minimum of 60 clock hours of pedagogy and child/adolescent development within the first 60 working days.

LENGTH OF TIME: Valid for two years, and only for the activity specified. The certificate may be reissued upon completion of 60 clock hours (6 quarter hours) of coursework.

OTHER: The State of Washington also issues EMERGENCY CERTIFICATES. Emergency certification for specific positions may be issued upon the recommendation of local school district and educational service district superintendents to persons who hold the appropriate degree and have substantially completed a program of preparation in accordance with Washington requirements for certification: Provided, that a qualified person who holds regular certification is not available or that the position is essential and circumstances warrant consideration of issuance of an emergency certificate.

WASHINGTON

Class H

Number of Teaching Licenses Issued

	1998-99	1997-98	1996-97	1995-96	1994-95	1993-94	1991-92	1990-91	1989-90	1988-89
Persons who completed an approved college teacher preparation program	3,598	3,323	3,590	2,972	2,910	3,273	2,519	2,433	2,544	2,596
Emergency	* 455	424	215	241	281	268	136	19	6	38
Conditional	86	231	178	177	243	276				
Alternative Route --										
Internship Program	0	0	0	1	17	0	8			
Instructional Specialist	0	3	3	2	4	0	2			
Other	15	29	14	15	17	19	N/A	412	383	414

Number of Teachers Employed

	1996-97	1995-96	1994-95	1993-94	1992-93	1991-92	1990-91	1989-90	1988-89
Total Teachers Employed in the State	49,996	48,573	48,063	45,456	45,874	44,360	41,767	40,271	38,827
Newly Hired Teachers in Each Year	1,667	1,292	1,579	1,727	1,833	1,617	1,497	1,481	439

* *The statistics' printout is 455 emergency certificates. This includes teachers, administrators, and substitute teachers. The actual number of teacher certificates is about 40.*

Professional Educator Standards Board
Old Capitol Bldg.
P.O. Box 47236
Olympia, WA 98504-7200
Attn: Jennifer Wallace
(360) 725-6275
email: jwallace@ospi.wednet.edu

Institutions of higher education that have developed alternative teacher preparation programs leading to a teaching license:

Seattle Pacific University
Pacific Lutheran University
City University

States with which the state has reciprocity of teacher licenses:

NASDTEC Interstate Contract.

Institutions of higher education that have *any* teacher preparation programs leading to a license to teach.

Antioch University-Seattle
Central Washington University
City University
Eastern Washington University
Evergreen State College
Gonzaga University
Heritage College
Northwest College of the Assemblies of God
Pacific Lutheran University
Pacific Oaks College Northwest
St. Martin's College
Seattle Pacific University
Seattle University
University of Puget Sound
University of Washington-Seattle
University of Washington – Tacoma
University of Washington - Bothell
Walla Walla College
Washington State University
Western Washington University
Whitman College
Whitworth College

Contact information for persons interested in finding a teaching position in the state:

Note: Interested persons should contact individual school district personnel officers. A directory with names and addresses may be purchased for $13.00 each from:

Barbara Krohn & Associates
835 Securities Bldg.
Seattle, WA 98101-1162
Phone: (206) 622-3538

WEST VIRGINIA

Class A

TITLE: Alternative Program for the Education of Teachers (APET)

HISTORY: Mandated by legislature to be in place by July 1, 1991. Program has never been used.

MOTIVATION:

GRADE LEVELS AND/OR SUBJECT AREA(S) COVERED:

As approved by the West Virginia Board of Education.

WHO OPERATES: A school, school district, consortium of schools, regional education service agency, or IHE.

REQUIREMENTS TO ENTER:

The candidate must:

have at least a bachelor's degree in a subject taught and in a teaching specialization approved by the State Board for APET;

not have previously completed a state approved teacher preparation program;

have a passing score on basic skills test and subject matter test, or have completed three years of successful teaching experience within the last seven years in the area for which licensure is being sought;

be a U.S. citizen at least 18 years of age; and

have an overall grade point average (GPA) of 2.5 (effective July 1, 1994).

An individual meeting these requirements may apply to the State Department of Education for a letter of eligibility to seek employment in a school included in an approved alternative program.

Once employed, application must be made to the State Department of Education for an APET Certificate, which must be on file in the employing county office within three months of employment.

A school, school district, consortium of schools, regional education service agency, or IHE must submit a plan to the State Department of Education. A plan submitted by any of these entities other than an IHE must provide evidence of having sought sponsorship with one or more IHEs approved by the State Board for offering teacher preparation.

State Board approval is valid for three years; an additional three years may be sought and must include a written report on the program's delivery and effectiveness. The State Board may terminate an APET before its approval period expires, if conditions no longer exist to support a viable APET.

PROGRAM DESCRIPTION:

An APET shall consist of three required phases:

Phase I -- A full-time seminar/practicum of 20 to 30 days before the alternative program teacher has full responsibility for a classroom. The seminar/practicum shall:

a) provide formal instruction in the essential areas for professional study, emphasizing student assessment, development and learning, curriculum, classroom management, and the use of educational computers and other technology;

b) introduce basic teaching skills, through supervised teaching experiences with students;

c) integrate the seminar and practicum components; and

d) include an orientation to the policies, organization, and curriculum of the employing district.

Phase II shall consist of:

a) a period of intensive on-the-job supervision, beginning the first day on which the alternative program teacher assumes full responsibility for a classroom and continuing for a period of at least two weeks;

b) during the initial teaching period, the alternative program teacher shall be visited and critiqued no less than one time per week by members of a professional support team, and shall be observed and formally evaluated at the end of five weeks and 10 weeks by the appropriately certified members of the team;

c) formal instruction shall continue in the essentials for professional study;

d) at the end of the 10 week period, the alternative program teacher shall receive a formal written progress report from the chairperson of the support team.

Phase III -- An additional period of continued supervision and evaluation, of no less than 20 weeks. During this period, the alternative program teacher shall be visited and critiqued at least twice per month, and observed formally and evaluated at least twice. No more than two months shall pass without a formal evaluation. Formal instruction shall continue in the essential areas for professional study.

Opportunities shall be provided for the alternative program teacher to observe the teaching of experienced colleagues.

Training and supervision shall be provided by a professional support team, comprised of a school principal, experienced classroom teacher, IHE education faculty member, and a curriculum supervisor. Districts or schools which do not employ a curriculum supervisor or have been unable to establish a relationship with an IHE shall provide for comparable expertise on the team. The school principal or the teacher education chair, in

the case of an IHE-sponsored program, shall serve as chairperson of the team.

Following completion of the alternative program, the chairperson of the support team will prepare a comprehensive evaluation report on the candidate, including a recommendation for issuance of the professional certificate or re-entry to an APET or disapproval of future participation in the program. Disapproval may be appealed to the Certification Appeals Board.

NUMBER OF CREDIT HOURS TO COMPLETE:

Approximately 200 hours of formal instruction.

WHO EVALUATES: Chairperson of support team.

LENGTH OF TIME: The APET Certificate expires on June 30 of the school year in which it is issued. It may be reissued one time, upon verification by the county superintendent that the candidate is continuing employment and participation in APET.

WEST VIRGINIA — Class F

TITLE: "Permit for Full-Time Teaching" (an emergency license)

HISTORY: Since the 1960s or early 1970s.

MOTIVATION: Shortage

GRADE LEVELS AND/OR SUBJECT AREA(S) COVERED:

All teaching and student support services specializations, principal, supervisor of instruction or vocational administrator.

WHO OPERATES: IHE

REQUIREMENTS TO ENTER:

A bachelor's degree in any subject.

A master's degree for educational leadership endorsements (principal, supervisor of instruction or vocational administrator).

25 % of the approved program or 6 semester hours, whichever is greater.

An overall grade point average of 2.5 (effective July 1, 1994).

PROGRAM DESCRIPTION:

The individual is given five years to complete a traditional approved college teacher education program; requirements of programs vary from college to college.

The state does not require student teaching as a part of approved programs. It requires "performance assessment," which most colleges interpret as being the equivalent of student teaching. Some colleges instead use on-the-job assessment to meet this requirement, but other colleges will not permit it.

NUMBER OF CREDIT HOURS TO COMPLETE:

As required to complete an approved teacher education program.

WHO EVALUATES: IHE

LENGTH OF TIME: One year permit, renewable to five years.

WEST VIRGINIA

Number of Teaching Licenses Issued

	1997-98	1996-97	1995-96	1994-95	1993-94	1992-93	1991-92	1990-91	1989-90	1988-89
Persons who completed an approved college teacher preparation program	a/ 1,267	a/ 1,659	1,928		1,770	N/A	1,929	1,913	N/A	1,499
Internship program	a/ 404	a/ 385	b/ 373							
Emergency (Permits)	a/ 616	661	799		951	888	c/ 569	927	596	1,365
Temporary -- Alternative Certification Program	0	0	0	0	0	0	0	1		
Alternative Route	d/	d/	d/	N/A	0	N/A	0	N/A		

Number of Teachers Employed

	1998-99	1997-98	1996-97	1995-96	1994-95	1993-94	1992-93	1991-92	1990-91	1989-90	1988-89
Total Teachers Employed in the State	a / 24,533	20,819	20,823	20,817	21,013	22,010	22,222	21,179	21,807	21,653	22,177
Newly Hired Teachers in Each Year	e/ 415.15	e/ 229	e/ 294	e/ 201	204.5	209.25	e/ 183.7	585	1,005	2,168	1,400

a/ These figures include original teaching, student support services, and administrative certificates issued.

b/ Includes Temporary Certificates and Internship Licenses.

c/ As of May 30, 1993.

d/ No alternative programs have been submitted for approval.

e/ This figure represents only those newly employed teachers with no previous experience

West Virginia Dept. of Education
Capitol Complex
Building #6, Rm. 337
Charlestown, WV 25305-0330
Attn: Barbara Brazeau
(304) 558-7010
(800) 982-2378

WEST VIRGINIA

Institutions of higher education that have developed alternative teacher preparation programs leading to a teaching license:

States with which the state has reciprocity of teacher licenses:

NASDTEC Interstate Contract.

Institutions of higher education that have *any* teacher preparation programs leading to a license to teach.

Alderson-Broaddus College
Bethany College
Bluefield State College
Concord College
Davis & Elkins College
Fairmont State College
Glenville State College
Marshall University Graduate College **
Ohio Valley College
Salem Teikyo College
Shepherd College
University of Charleston
West Liberty State College
West Virginia Univ. Institute of Technology *
West Virginia State College
West Virginia University
West Virginia University-Parkersburg
West Virginia Wesleyan College
Wheeling Jesuit College

* *Vocational/technical program only*
** *West Virginia Graduate College and Marshall University merged in July 1997.*

Contact information for persons interested in finding a teaching position in the state:

Note: "The West Virginia Department of Education doesn't serve as a clearinghouse. Contacts should be made directly to the county(ies) where the individual is interested in teaching."

TITLE: Alternative Programs Leading to Initial Educator Licensing

HISTORY: Under new rules promulgated in 2000, the state superintendent could approve alternative programs that lead to initial educator licensing, beginning in 2001. Some pilot programs are underway.

MOTIVATION: In order to address shortages and provide accelerated, performance-based programs to non-traditional students, new rules were promulgated, which allow colleges and universities, agencies, school districts, and others to develop alternative programs.

These programs are required to have students demonstrate proficiency in Wisconsin's teaching standards, in order to be recommended for the Initial Educator License.

GRADE LEVELS AND/OR SUBJECT AREA(S) COVERED:

Depends on the individual program.

WHO OPERATES: Not limited.

REQUIREMENTS TO ENTER:

Defined by the individual program.

PROGRAM DESCRIPTION:

Varies from program to program.

Programs submitted for approval must include the following:

Components to assure program completers are proficient in the Wisconsin standards:

1. Need, Mission Philosophy of Program

2. Goals and Objectives

3. Resources Statement

4. Instructional Design

5. Student Admission Criteria

6. Student Assessment and Program Completion Requirements

7. Program Evaluation Plan

NUMBER OF CREDIT HOURS TO COMPLETE:

Dependent on a candidate's background and the individual program.

WHO EVALUATES: Program provider.

LENGTH OF TIME: Dependent on individual program.

OTHER: A partial list of the programs is available online on the Web site at: http://www.dpi.state.wi.us/dlsis/fel/altern.html.

TITLE: Experimental and Innovative Teacher Education Programs

HISTORY: Began as a pilot in 1991.

MOTIVATION: To provide colleges and universities with approved teacher education programs opportunities to apply for approval of pilot programs. Programs submitted must be substantially different from existing traditional programs to qualify for approval as an experimental or innovative program.

GRADE LEVELS AND/OR SUBJECT AREA(S) COVERED: Not specified.

WHO OPERATES: IHEs which have approved teacher education programs.

REQUIREMENTS TO ENTER:

IHEs may apply to the state for approval to pilot models of alternative preparation programs, containing a heavy evaluation component.

An IHE must provide evidence of a screening process for admitting candidates to the program, a plan for formative evaluation during the period the candidate is in the program, and a summative evaluation prior to exiting the program -- the institutional endorsement for a teaching license. There must also be a plan for an evaluation of the pilot program itself.

IHE proposals must contain program goals and specific objectives which define the intent and expectations of the program's outcomes, as well as specific objectives to be obtained by individuals enrolled in the experimental or innovative program.

Proposals must also: verify how the program will meet state standards for minimum competencies in teacher preparation; include a listing of standards for which waivers are being sought and a rationale for each exception; provide documentation of admission criteria, faculty qualifications, and institutional support, including budget data, syllabi or detailed descriptions of any courses expressly developed for the program; provide documentation of recruitment processes; and show evidence of a direct relationship between the program's structure and its goals and objectives.

PROGRAM DESCRIPTION:

May vary with each program.

NUMBER OF CREDIT HOURS TO COMPLETE: May vary with each program.

WHO EVALUATES: IHE responsible for evaluation of candidates and evaluation of its pilot program.

LENGTH OF TIME: May vary with each program.

OTHER: A state official said this program should allow IHEs to develop a variety of models -- with evaluations of each.. Then, the state can weigh the results in deciding whether to adopt any of the models.

TITLE: Permits

MOTIVATION: Shortage; a licensed person is not available

GRADE LEVELS AND/OR SUBJECT AREA(S) COVERED: Not specified.

WHO OPERATES: Not specified.

REQUIREMENTS TO ENTER:

The individual meets minimum statutory requirements but does not meet the minimum code requirements for teaching.

The district administrator or designated official of the school system shall request a permit in writing with full explanation and justification of the need. The request shall state that a licensed person is not available.

PROGRAM DESCRIPTION:

The permit is recognized as a substandard license issued to an unqualified person and expires on June 30 or earlier in the school year of issuance.

NUMBER OF CREDIT HOURS TO COMPLETE:

Renewal of a permit may be granted under circumstances which include the satisfactory completion by the applicant of a minimum of 6 semester credits in an approved program of teacher education between the date of issuance and the date of renewal.

WHO EVALUATES: The state superintendent may issue or deny a permit.

The district administrator shall request a renewal of a permit.

LENGTH OF TIME: One year or fraction thereof; renewable.

OTHER:

LICENSE BASED UPON EXPERIENCE: a regular license may be issued to an applicant who presents evidence of having completed an approved program from another state, except student teaching, if the applicant verifies eligibility for acceptance into student teaching from the institution, meets all applicable requirements of this chapter, except student teaching, and verifies three or more years of successful teaching experience in the subject and grade level of preparation.

LICENSE BASED ON EQUIVALENCY. a regular license may be issued to an applicant who has not completed an approved program, if the applicant has obtained a statement from a college or university offering an approved program that the applicant has completed the equivalent of an approved program, and if the applicant meets all of the requirements of this chapter for the license, except completion of an approved program.

WISCONSIN

Number of Teaching Licenses Issued

	2000-01	1999-00	1998-99	1997-98	1996-97	1995-96	1994-95	1993-94	1992-93	1991-
Persons who completed an approved college teacher preparation program in WI	4,313	4,445	4,724	4,807	4,929	5,281	5,001	5,024	5,654	5,64
Internship program	475	568	800	425	512	415	366	320	N/A	18
Emergency Licenses (Permits & Specials)	2,579	2,500	2,112	1,855	1,615	1,871	1,777	1,095	2,032	1,99
Temporary	N/A	N/A	N/A	N/A	0	0	N/A	N/A	N/A	N/
Alternative Route			N/A	19	0	0	N/A	0	0	

Number of Teachers Employed

	1998-99	1997-98*	1996-97	1995-96	1994-95	1993-94	1992-93	1991-92	1990-91	1989-
Total Teachers Employed in the State in PublicSchools	* 59,923	59,016	54,714	54,891	55,892	51,011	52,282	52,276.7	50,983	49,32
Newly Hired Teachers in Each Year in Public Schools	** 2,747	N/A	2,164	2,210	3,802	2,877	3,167	2,503	1,484	1,01

* *Headcount not FTE.*

** *Includes newly hired with and without experience*

Wisconsin Dept. of Public Instruction
Bureau of Teacher Education
Licensing and Placement
P.O. Box 7841
Madison, WI 53707-7841
Attn: Peter Burke
(608) 266-1027

WISCONSIN

Institutions of higher education that have developed alternative teacher preparation programs leading to a teaching license:

Alverno College
Cardinal Stritch University
Lakeland College
University of Wisconsin-Madison
University of Wisconsin-Milwaukee
University of Wisconsin-Oshkosh
University of Wisconsin-Parkside

Contact information for persons interested in finding a teaching position in the state:

Laurie Derse
Department of Public Instruction
125 S. Webster, P.O. Box 7841
Madison, WI 53707
Phone: (608) 266-1028

States with which the state has reciprocity of teacher licenses:

None.

Institutions of higher education that have *any* teacher preparation programs leading to a license to teach.

Alverno College
Beloit College
Cardinal Stritch University
Carroll College
Carthage College
Concordia University
Edgewood College
Lakeland College
Lawrence University
Maranatha Baptist Bible College
Marian College of Fond du Lac
Marquette University
Mount Mary College
Northland College
Ripon College
St. Norbert College
Silver Lake College
Viterbo University
University of Wisconsin-Eau Claire
University of Wisconsin-Green Bay
University of Wisconsin-LaCrosse
University of Wisconsin-Madison
University of Wisconsin-Milwaukee
University of Wisconsin-Oshkosh
University of Wisconsin-Parkside
University of Wisconsin-Platteville
University of Wisconsin-River Falls
University of Wisconsin-Stevens Point
University of Wisconsin-Stout
University of Wisconsin-Superior
University of Wisconsin-Whitewater
Viterbo College
Wisconsin Lutheran College

Contact information for persons interested in finding a teaching position in the state:

Note: "The Wisconsin Department of Education doesn't serve as a clearinghouse. Contacts should be made directly to the districts where the individual is interested in teaching."

There is a JOBS Bulletin posted on the Department of Public Instruction home page: http://badger.state.wi.us/agencies/dpi/tcert

TITLE: Portfolio Certification

MOTIVATION: Recognition of an individual's knowledge and competencies gained through a variety of life experiences.

GRADE LEVELS AND/OR SUBJECT AREA (S) COVERED:

The portfolio can be used either to receive a standard teaching certificate or to add an endorsement area to a current Wyoming teaching certificate. All areas of endorsement are accepted.

WHO OPERATES: Professional Teaching Standards Board.

REQUIREMENTS TO ENTER:

A bachelor's degree from an NCATE or regionally accredited college or university.

PROGRAM DESCRIPTION:

The portfolio certification method allows the Professional Teaching Standards Board to certify teachers based upon professional, educational and life experiences. A portfolio is a collection of documented evidence that shows the applicant's lifetime of activities and verifies how these activities meet Wyoming certification standards. The portfolio certification process is an alternative way to obtain a standard teaching certificate or to add an endorsement area to a current Wyoming teaching certificate.

NUMBER OF CREDIT HOURS TO COMPLETE: N/A

WHO EVALUATES: A two-four member team evaluates portfolios and makes a recommendation to the Professional Teaching Standards Board.

LENGTH OF TIME: Standard five-year certificate.

WYOMING

Class F

TITLE: Temporary Employment Permit

MOTIVATION: Shortage of qualified/certified teachers.

New Development: Wyoming's Professional Teaching Standards Board became a partner with the federally-funded Troops to Teachers Program in June 2002.

GRADE LEVELS AND/OR SUBJECT AREA (S) COVERED: All

WHO OPERATES: Professional Teaching Standards Board.

REQUIREMENTS TO ENTER:

A bachelor's degree from an NCATE or regionally accredited college or university.

Extensive training and/or experience related to the discipline to be taught.

The Temporary Permit is requested by the local school district.

PROGRAM DESCRIPTION:

The state requires that the school district develop a plan including in-service training, monitoring, and supervision by certified personnel.

The permit holder must submit a plan on how he or she will receive full certification by three years.

NUMBER OF CREDIT HOURS TO COMPLETE:

The permit holder must show yearly progress toward meeting full certification.

WHO EVALUATES: Professional Teaching Standards Board.

LENGTH OF TIME: Current school year only; non-renewable, unless by action of the Professional Teaching Standards Board.

WYOMING

Number of Teaching Licenses Issued

	2000-01	1999-00	1998-99	1997-98	1996-97	1995-96	1994-95	1993-94	1992-93
Persons who completed an approved college teacher preparation program	1,000		745	711	N/A	N/A	* 3,083	3,103	* 3,841
Internship program	N/A	N/A	N/A	N/A	N/A	N/A	N/A	4	5
Emergency	171	107	70	N/A	N/A	N/A	N/A	0	0
Temporary	14	13	7	4	5	2	1	0	1
Alternative Route	10	20	11	6	N/A	N/A	N/A	N/A	N/A

Number of Teachers Employed

	2000-01	1999-2000	1998-99	1997-98	1996-97	1995-96	1994-95	1993-94	1992-93
Total Teachers Employed in the State		8,307	8,285** (6,645***)	6,673	7,295	7,201	N/A	N/A	6,581
Newly Hired Teachers in Each Year	378	N/A	N/A	~200	N/A	N/A	N/A	200	~200

* *Total number of teachers certified or renewed.*

** *Professional Staff*

*** *Instructional Staff*

Wyoming Professional Teaching
Standards Board
2300 Capitol Ave.
Hathaway Building, 2nd Floor
Cheyenne, WY 82002-0190
Attn: Linda Stowers
(307) 777-6261
email: lstowe@missc.state.wy.us

WYOMING

Institutions of higher education that have developed alternative teacher preparation programs leading to a teaching license:

The University of Wyoming has developed a teacher preparation program for individuals who have earned a liberal arts degree. Generally, the program takes three semesters to complete.

States with which the state has reciprocity of teacher licenses:

NASDTEC Interstate Contract.

Alabama
Alaska
Arizona
Colorado
District of Columbia
Georgia
Hawaii
Idaho
Indiana
Iowa
Kansas
Kentucky
Louisiana
Maryland
Massachusetts
Minnesota
Missouri
Montana
Nevada
New Hampshire
New Jersey
New Mexico
North Carolina
North Dakota
Ohio
Pennsylvania
Rhode Island
South Carolina
South Dakota
Tennessee
Utah
Vermont
Wisconsin

Institutions of higher education that have *any* teacher preparation programs leading to a license to teach.

University of Wyoming and Regis University

Contact information for persons interested in finding a teaching position in the state:

University of Wyoming
Career Services
College of Education
P.O. Box 3374
Laramie, WY 82071
(307) 766-2019

Also, visit the Professional Teaching Standards Board Web site at: http://www.K12.wy.us.